LOOKING FOR ASHLEY

LOOKING FOR ASHLEY

Re-reading What the Smith Case
Reveals about the Governance of Girls,
Mothers and Families in Canada

Rebecca Jaremko Bromwich

D1508411

DEMETER

DEMETER PRESS

Funded by the Government of Canada
Financé par la gouvernement du Canada

Demeter Press
140 Holland Street West
P. O. Box 13022
Bradford, ON L3Z 2Y5
Tel: (905) 775-9089
Email: info@demeterpress.org
Website: www.demeterpress.org

Demeter Press logo based on the sculpture "Demeter" by Maria-Luise Bodirsky <www.keramik-atelier.bodirsky.de>

Cover art: Rebecca Jaremko Bromwich, "Looking for Ashley," 2014, acrylic on canvas, 16 x 20 inches.

Printed and Bound in Canada

Library and Archives Canada Cataloguing in Publication

Bromwich, Rebecca, author
        Looking for Ashley : re-reading what the Smith case reveals about the governance of girls, mothers and families in Canada / by Rebecca Jaremko Bromwich.

Includes bibliographical references.
ISBN 978-1-926452-69-2 (paperback)

        1. Smith, Ashley, 1988-2007--Death. 2. Women prisoners--Canada--Death--Case studies. 3. Mentally ill prisoners--Canada--Death--Case studies. 4. Teenage girls--Canada--Death--Case studies. 5. Suicide--Canada--Case studies. 6. Prisons--Canada--Case studies. I. Title.

HV9507.B76 2015   365'.60820971   C2015-906710-3

I dedicate this book to the ghosts who were with me as I wrote it.

First, to my much missed friend Deb Shelly because, and she would smile to read this, friendship is magic. She was my longtime colleague in the law, friend in life, and partner in what she called "intellectual fierceness." Had she not passed away while I was writing the dissertation that became this book, Deb would have made good on her offer to read it. She would have understood it and no doubt had some excellent criticisms of it.

I also dedicate this to Mary Jo Frug and Ardeth Wood, feminist academics I wish I had met and whose work is missed by the world. Also, I dedicate this to the adolescent girl I once was, whose ghostly presence was with me throughout this work.

And, of course, finally, and most importantly, I dedicate this book to Ashley Smith.

Table of Contents

Acknowledgements   xi

List of Acronyms   xv

L. THE PROJECT

    Telling Stories   1

    Defining the Project   3

    Commonly Accepted Facts of the Smith Case   5

    Overview   8

2. FOUNDATIONS OF THE PROJECT: THE PROJECT
IN CONVERSATION

    Literature Review   12

    The Smith Case and Similar Recent Cases   12

    Girls' Studies   17

    Governmentality, Security, Risk and the

        "Criminalized Girl"   20

    Policy Scholarship   29

    Feminist Legal Studies   32

Theories and Methods: This Case Study 34

Power and Representation in Discourse 37

Governmentality: Risk, Security, and Necropolitics 41

Agency 51

Feminist Theory 55

Methods 58

Research Design 62

Notes and Limitations 63

3. INMATE SMITH: NECROPOLITICAL SUCCESS

Introduction 67

Three Configurations 70

What is Lost 102

The Inquests 104

Inmate Smith and Macro-Power 108

4. CHILD ASHLEY: RECUPERATION

Introduction 117

Trajectory: Sites, Emergence, and Fluorishing 119

Ashley the Improper and Risky Girl 117

Ashley the Game-Playing Child 123

Recuperation: Ashley the Normal Child 128

Troubling the "Normal Child" 133

Discursive Work – Fitting Ashley Smith In 138

Obesity and Social Exclusion – "One Size Does
  Not Fit All" 147

Child Ashley and the Logic of Exclusion 152

5. PATIENT SMITH — FROM PROBLEM INMATE TO MENTAL PATIENT: PATHOLOGIZATION, ASSIMILATION, DOMESTICATION

Introduction   158

Nuisance   163

Inmate – Patient   167

Patient Smith: A Sympathetic Victim   179

6. CONCLUSION: MULTIPLE AGENCIES

Summary: Producing Ashleys   200

Looking for Ashley's Agencies:

Alternative Imaginings   210

The Locked Room   220

Denouement   223

Bibliography   229

Acknowledgements

Writing is a conversation with life.
—Julia Cameron, *The Artist's Way*

While this book is dedicated to ghosts, acknowledgements should also go to the living. One simply does not complete major projects alone. I would be unconscionably remiss if I did not offer thanks to Dr. Andrea O'Reilly for believing in this work, to my Ph.D. examiners Rebecca Johnson and Augustine Park, committee members Lara Karaian and Doris Buss and especially to my extraordinary dissertation supervisor Sheryl Hamilton for brilliance, patience, and sage guidance. I want to thank also Maeve McMahon and many others at the Faculty of the Department of Law and Legal Studies at Carleton University for their wonderful support and collegiality.

Also, I want to acknowledge my family. It would have been impossible to do any of this writing without the partnership of Matt, my steady, visionary travelling companion and partner in crime, or my parents, Beverley Smith and Gordon Jaremko, who fought — and still fight — for me in all the ways they can, my brilliant motley crew of siblings, and my wild, beautiful children for whom I want change to come and who teach me so much every day. A shout out should go to my colleagues, supporters, and friends. To Deborah Mervitz, who is brave. Also to Kerri Froc, a better "thesis boot camp" collaborator than I could have ever hoped for, Gordana Eldjupovic, a strong mentor, Tamra

Thomson who knows the power of legality is in its details, to my colleague Sarah Mackenzie for her kindness and support, and generally to my lawyer peeps who keep me company at the Canadian Bar Association, and who make the practice of law into art. Also to Nick Bala, Mark Weisberg, Maria Sowden, Rev. Andrew Johnston, and fitness trainers Tina, Lisa and Lia, who each with their own modalities of care helped me to sustain the (not insignificant) energy and effort necessary to start, re-start and then finish a Ph.D. dissertation, and turn it into a book, while working as a lawyer and mothering four kids.

Finally, I think it is important politically and pedagogically to direct an anonymous nod to all the folks who said I wouldn't finish high school and couldn't write a Ph.D. dissertation. In addition to those who supported and believed in me, it is also those who did not that I have to thank for revitalizing my rebellious spirit and inciting anger I could alchemize into this work. Thinking of all of those who are not as well-supported, well-resourced, and lucky as me, I feel I should mention you. May this work be taken as evidence that many people can do what they have been told they are not capable of doing, and what the statistical odds are ostensibly against them doing, and may it encourage others to speak, read, and write.

> This is what you shall do: Love the earth and sun and the animals, despise riches, give alms to everyone that asks, stand up for the stupid and crazy, devote your income and labor to others, hate tyrants, argue not concerning God, have patience and indulgence toward the people, take off your hat to nothing known or unknown or to any man or number of men, go freely with powerful uneducated persons and with the young and with the mothers of families, read these leaves in the open air every season of every year of your life, re-examine all you have been told at school or church or in any book, dismiss whatever insults your own soul, and your very flesh shall be a great poem.
>
> — Walt Whitman, Preface to *Leaves of Grass*, 1855

* * All comments made herein are my own and do not represent the views of any organization with which I am or have been affiliated.

List of Acronyms

ADHD	Attention Deficit Hyperactive Disorder
BPD	Borderline Personality Disorder
CAEFS	Canadian Association of Elizabeth Fry Societies
CBC	Canadian Broadcasting Corporation
CCRA	Corrections and Conditional Release Act
CDA	Critical Discourse Analysis
FASD	Fetal Alcohol Spectrum Disorder
CSC	Corrections Canada
GVI	Grand Valley Institution
JDA	Juvenile Delinquents Act
MHA	Mental Health Act (Ontario)
NB	New Brunswick
NBYC	New Brunswick Youth Centre
RCMP	Royal Canadian Mounted Police
SITREPS	CSC Situation Reports, circulated throughout its administration
SMM	Situation Management Model for Woman Offenders
WRAP	Restraint device used by CSC to entirely immobilize inmates

| YCJA | *Youth Criminal Justice Act* |
| YP | Young Person (subject to processes of youth criminal justice regime) |

We still have Ashleys, we still have Ashleys being treated in the same tortuous, horrendous ways that Ashley was treated.
—Coralee Smith, mother of Ashley Smith[1]

There's really no such thing as the "voiceless." There are only the deliberately silenced, or the preferably unheard.
—Arundhati Roy[2]

[E]yes that fix you in a formulated phrase/ when I am pinned and wriggling on your wall/ then how should I begin?
—T. S. Eliot[3]

And you, what are you looking for? ... I had the dream again. I was looking for something. I was at school, running through the hallways, my heart pounding, tearing up and down the stairs, looking for it: "I can't find the meaning; have you seen it?" I asked a group of people by the lockers outside my homeroom, who stared at me blankly. Woke up in a cold sweat.
—Rebecca Jaremko, Journal, March 10, 1993

One must be careful of books, and what is inside them, for words have the power to change us.
—Cassandra Clare, *The Infernal Devices*[4]

[1]"Teen Ashley Smith Inquest Begins Today" MSN News,14 Jan. 2013.
[2]Speech on accepting the Sydney Peace Prize, 2004.
[3]"The Love Song of J. Alfred Prufrock" 1920.
[4]Margaret McElderry Books, 2013. Print.

1. The Project

TELLING STORIES

Once upon a time, many years ago, I bought a typewriter. It became one of very few things I owned. I also owned a field hockey stick because I played on my high school team. That, my clothes, my winter coat and my journals, were about all I had put on or stuffed into plastic garbage bags and carried off. I hadn't remembered to take a toothbrush but by then I had bought one. It was winter in Calgary, −30 Celsius, cold enough to take your breath away, so cold there was no point in crying because tears would just freeze on my face. I had ridden the C-Train to Value Village, about an hour's trip each way, and walked several blocks through blowing dry prairie snow carrying that small black ancient typewriter back to the train. It cost all of my money: $15. I bought it and then I stole food.

I had a plan. I bought a typewriter so I could tell my story. I wanted to tell a story about my interactions with health, child welfare, education, family and criminal legal systems and how angry I was about them, how disappointed I was in everyone. In a dark rented basement room, hunched over that typewriter with my field hockey stick near me for protection against any possible intruders, clothes folded on the floor as I had no hangers, at sixteen I promised to write. I clacked away, hammering out the first pages that I promised myself would be a transformative story about what it was like to be limited, restrained and oppressed as an adolescent girl in Canada. It was slow going. The "a" stuck.

1

Every time I typed an "a" I had to pull the key back up.

There are a lot of years between the writing of this book and that promise. I have tried to fulfill it in a number of ways. I became a lawyer to large extent to remedy what I experienced and perceived as injustice. I did criminal defense work and represented young mothers in child protection and domestic violence proceedings. Now, I do law reform work, attempting to make changes to the formal discourses of legislative and regulatory provisions. When I did my LL.M., I was actively involved (in a very junior capacity) in advocacy accepted in the crafting of Canada's *Youth Criminal Justice Act* (YCJA) in 2001. I have a lot for which to be very grateful. I have a lot to be happy about. Many of the legislative changes I sought to include in the YCJA have been made. Now, ironically, I am, to a very large extent, someone else: not an adolescent girl but the lawyer mother of three girls (and a boy) soon to enter adolescence. I can't really write the story I wanted to tell. I have the pages I wrote, somewhere. I don't know what became of that typewriter. We all use computers now.

I am worried in light of recent cases and in particular the case of an adolescent girl who died in prison named Ashley Smith, that the law reform work in which I have been engaged is not getting to the heart of the problems I experienced. Feminist theorists have contended that hegemonic discourses in late modern liberal discourse define and socialize adolescent young women as something less than we are: they move us from an experience of ourselves as agents to a relegation in a particular space defined by our relationships with men. I wonder how contemporary discursive figurations of the girl, how we talk about adolescent young women, continue to affect the agencies of variously situated adolescent young women in their experiences with criminal and quasi-criminal legality. Restlessly, I wonder how the conditions of possibility for young people in Canada could be transformed; I feel a sense of growing urgency as time passes; how might changes be effected before my own children enter adolescence?

Maybe I shouldn't be quite so literal in remembering my plan. Maybe the central question for me to consider is my longing, the longing that led me with my last few dollars to go to Value Village on the C-Train and walk those long cold blocks carrying the black typewriter back, enjoying seeing in my breath like smoke over it — a confirmation of my existence — my hands burning from the cold despite the gloves over them. More than anything else maybe what I felt was a desire to speak, to talk back, to have a role in authoring my own story, not just on paper but to actively, agentically, find and make meanings in, be actively involved in constructing and narrating my own life.

DEFINING THE PROJECT

We now ask you to speak for Ashley.
—Dr. John Carlisle, Coroner for Ontario,
Charge to the Jury in the Inquest of Ashley Smith,
December 2, 2013

Maya Angelou, in *I Know Why the Caged Bird Sings*, wrote that "there is no greater agony than bearing an untold story inside you." (Angelou) Probably because, many years ago, when an adolescent girl, I was in a great deal of trouble with various systems, I was not surprised to learn that it was as a result of minor disciplinary infractions that she was found to have committed while in prison that Ashley Smith accumulated hundreds of criminal charges. However, what struck me about Ashley Smith's case is one fact in particular: shortly before her 2007 death at age 19 in solitary confinement in Grand Valley Prison, guards took away her access to paper and a pen.[1] Because she was divested of her ability to otherwise tell her story, I wondered whether it could be that Ashley Smith subsequently used self-harm, at least sometimes and partially, *meaningfully*, either communicatively, or as political resistance, or both. I wonder what Ashley Smith's own story about her case might have been had she been accorded an opportunity to tell it, and what she might have contributed to authoring in dialogue with other systems, agents and forces in constructing her life had she been able to live it.

The very first of the recommendations of jury in the verdict in the Inquest into the death of Ashley Smith is that her death should be reviewed by Corrections Canada management and staff and used as a "case study."[2] However, not a lot of energy has been expended on asking, not assuming, of what "type" Ashley Smith is a "case." Further, it doesn't seem that the question of what Ashley might have wanted, let alone wanted to say was particularly bothersome, or even thinkable, for experts engaged in writing, arguing, commenting or otherwise speaking of Ashley Smith as her inquest progressed. Also given very little consideration are ways in which being a particular type of "girl" might have been relevant to how she was governed, disciplined and punished. In a variety of interlinked social sites, figurations of Ashley Smith have become symbols and representations used to suit various agendas. Almost without exception, she is pathologized while various forms of expertise retrench their power and individuals working in the justice and correctional systems are condemned.

There is very little attention paid in explanations of Ashley's case to constructions of the girl and to gender. This study looks critically at why and how is there is such a dearth of interest in to what extent and in what ways it mattered that Ashley Smith was a specifically embodied as a particular female adolescent in corrections custody. Also missing from arguments in, policy analyses of, as well as media narratives about her case is an accounting for Ashley Smith's agency. This study looks at how, and posits analyses as to why, she is not being portrayed as a meaning-maker. This critical discourse analysis looks at why and how it is that very few texts say much, if anything, about what meanings Ashley Smith was agentically engaged in making through her actions.

This book studies figurations of Ashley Smith as girl as technologies of power that emerge in three discursive sites: formal legal documents, docudramas and print media texts. In this book, I conduct a critical discourse analysis that unpacks what stories were told about Ashley, what stories are still being told about her and how these stories engage discourses of the girl. I look critically at how Ashley Smith's case is constructed, what Ashley Smith is a "case" of, and at what alternative imaginings of Ashley Smith's case are possible. I cannot reasonably or realistically offer a book that tells "the" "true" story of Ashley Smith. Were I to try to tell Ashley's story, I would just create another representation of her that would be problematic in many of the ways existing representations are problematic. Ashley Smith's internal self will be forever unknown and unknowable. Rather, what I can know and examine and what readers can understand better through this project is a reading, a history, a genealogy of her representation within her case. I look at when and how certain representations of Ashley Smith are constructed and certain figurations emerge while others, which are supportable and plausible, do not. Each figure of Ashley Smith analyzed in this book enacts power in discourse and is deployed in the construction of the Smith case as a *case of a* particular sort of social problem. Multiple stories are told about Ashley Smith. I seek to critically examine these tellings.

COMMONLY ACCEPTED FACTS OF THE SMITH CASE

In this book, I work from an understanding of the Smith case as a unit of inquiry in the social sciences that constitutes an enactment of governmental power. I am relying on the definition of "caseness" advanced by Lauren Berlant. (2007) "Caseness" is a state in which the singular is both individual and marked as an exemplar: "the case can incite an opening, an altered way of feeling things out, of falling out of line." (Berlant, 666) The Ashley Smith case is a site where discourses and forms of expertise intersect, collide and otherwise meet. In this case, power is negotiated at a variety of levels: between agents in spaces designated as correctional facilities, between discourses, and, at the macro level, between interlocking systems of power. In the discursive formations generated by the texts that comprise the Smith case, a variety of representations of Ashley Smith overlap, oppose one another, smash together, and compete for dominance. Imaginings of Ashley Smith can be analyzed as producing certain figures of Ashley Smith. These figures construct the "caseness" of Ashley Smith: they set her out as an example of a particular type and, in so doing, they define social problems, call for particular treatment, militate for particular remedies and thereby do governmental work.

Below, without claiming these "facts" to be "true," I summarize a standard narrative of what have come to be the commonly accepted and widely understood facts of the Smith case. In the rest of this book, I look closely at the assumptions and truth claims in this widely accepted narrative, paying close attention to the assumptions on which the claims are based and to the sources to which the truth claims are attributed.[3]

Ashley Smith was a middle class, Canadian white girl who died from self-strangulation in prison on October 19, 2007 at age 19. She died while several prison guards watched and videotaped her last moments, not intervening for 45 minutes as she lay dying then dead. Ashley Smith was born January 29, 1988, in New Brunswick. She was adopted when she was five days old. It is widely accepted that she had a normal childhood in Moncton, New Brunswick.

However, immediately upon passing into adolescence, Ashley started to get into trouble with various authorities and questions began to be raised about her mental health. She was tall and over-weight. At age 13 or 14, her parents report that they saw distinct behavioural changes in her. By age 15, she had been before juvenile court 14 times for various minor offences such as trespassing and causing a disturbance. In March 2002, Smith was assessed by a psychologist who found no evidence of mental illness. However, her behavioural problems continued and she was suspended from school numerous times in the fall of 2002. In March 2003, after a series of court appearances, Ashley was admitted to a mental health centre for assessment. She was diagnosed with various mental conditions, including "ADHD, learning disorder, borderline personality disorder and narcissistic personality traits." Ashley was discharged early from the Centre for unruly and disruptive behaviour.

Ashley Smith was first incarcerated as a "youth" at age fifteen in 2003. Smith was initially sent to "custody" for a single offence: throwing apples at a postal carrier. There is no indication that anyone was injured by the apples, but the target was an agent of the state, so the apple throwing incident was taken very seriously. Ashley had been in trouble for minor things before, like disobeying teachers and stealing a CD. Her initial sentence for throwing the apples was to a period of one month in custody. However, she ended up in solitary confinement for what corrections officers determined to be disruptive behaviour on her part on her first day in custody. While the original sentence was a short one, as a result of the accumulation of hundreds of further convictions against her arising from disciplinary incidents that took place while she was in youth prison, she remained in custody.

In January 2006, Ashley Smith turned 18. On the same day, a motion was made under the YCJA by the Crown to transfer her to an adult facility. Ashley retained a lawyer to fight the transfer, but was unsuccessful. On October 5, Ashley was transferred to adult prison. Ashley spent most of her time there in segregation. While there, she was also subjected to repeat cavity and strip searches, tasered and pepper-sprayed. After being transferred to adult custody, Ashley was transferred a total of 17 times between eight institutions over a period of eleven months. She was under the care of a series of psychiatrists, several of whom prescribed psychtropic drugs for her. She was sometimes given these drugs by force. Smith was also periodically given an opportunity to speak with a series of psychologists, but only through the food slot in her cell. It is widely understood that Ashley Smith had very serious issues with mental illness that were never properly assessed and went untreated.

Although she was initially sentenced to one month in prison, Ashley was involved in more than 800 reported "incidents" while in custody. She was also charged for new offences as a result of situations that arose while she was in "open custody" foster homes. Corrections officers also documented at least 150 attempts by Ashley to physically harm herself, some of which were treated as disciplinary infractions. She was never released. She was held in prison on a series of accumulating charges for four years. For long periods of her time in solitary confinement, Smith was not given soap, deodorant, adequate sanitary supplies, clean underwear and was prohibited from having writing material or paper.

While in adult prison, she died by self-induced strangulation while being videotaped by guards who stood outside her cell and watched.

In 2011, Ashley Smith's family filed a "wrongful death" lawsuit against Corrections Canada for $11 million. The suit was settled confidentially in May of 2011 for an undisclosed amount. The warden of the prison where she died was fired.

Ashley Smith's death has been the subject of two inquests, or investigations, by the coroner in Ontario. The first was complex and involved many legal challenges as well as a change of coroner before it finally ended as a mistrial in September 2011. A new inquest into Ashley Smith's death began in September 2012 and concluded in December 2013 with a surprise verdict of homicide.

In response to this homicide verdict, government actors and social reformers have been looking at how the mentally ill, and in particular mentally ill women, can be better addressed by the prison system and at how to limit use of solitary confinement in prisons. The Correctional Service of Canada (CSC) released a report in December of 2014 that essentially claimed it had already addressed the concerns raised by the recommendations of the Smith inquest. In this report, CSC rejected the recommendation that they place limits on the use of solitary confinement and rejected the further inquest recommendation that their management be independently overseen. The Ashley Smith case remains unresolved in that a homicide verdict has been entered but no one and nothing in particular have been officially blamed or held accountable for her death.

OVERVIEW

This book explores governmental work done by figures of Ashley Smith as a "case" of three types: an inmate, a child and a patient. It analyzes how configurations of power relations are maintained, retrenched or challenged by these figures. It critically evaluates what is gained, and what is lost, in discursive processes through which Ashley Smith is turned into an exemplar of different social problems. In Chapter 2, I review literatures in existing academic works with which this research is in conversation. I explicate the theoretical foundations of the project, the methodology employed in the research and the specific methods and research design used. Then, I move on to my analysis. In Chapter 3, I look at discursive figures of Ashley Smith that foreground her status as a carceral subject or "inmate." In Chapter 4, I look at figures of Ashley Smith that give pre-eminence to her status as a "child." The last analytical chapter concerns what have come to be the commonly accepted discursive figures of Ashley Smith: these representations foreground her mental health as the most significant aspect of her beingness and treat her as a "patient." In the final chapter, I then present my conclusions. I summarize the research and my analysis and make the following set of claims.

In this book, I demonstrate how dominant constructions of Ashley Smith — as inmate, child and mentally ill person ("patient") — allow for certain understandings of her case while they make opaque, unimaginable and unthinkable others. My central claims are:

- The death of Ashley Smith can be understood as a predictable outcome of intersecting logics of risk and security in necropolitical[4] governmental processes that continue to affect adolescent young women in particular, and more broadly endanger us all;
- In none of the dominant constructions of Ashley in the Smith case is her agency adequately made legible: in none of these constructions does her voice get heard nor does her expressive, creative or political agency get taken seriously.
- The illegibility of Ashley Smith's agencies in the Smith case functions as a technology of governance that serves to maintain the invisibility of, and even further obscure, the agencies and voices of adolescent young women from the formal discourses of law while supporting racist, classist, unequal valuations of which mothers are "good" and count;
- Reform activism has been implicated in the necropolitical processes that successfully effected Ashley Smith's social, juridical and biological deaths; and
- Discursive processes that transform Ashley Smith into a mental patient once she becomes recuperatively represented as a "good" girl raise serious questions about the statistical discrepancy between the putative criminal offending rates of adolescent girls and boys.

Dominant narratives of Smith, which all deny her agency, are operating on other young women, and even on older women, particularly mothers. Widely held assumptions about Ashley Smith's family in general and mother in particular, are working to bolster classist, settle colonial normativities. Ashley Smith's unthinkability as a subject within the category girl sets the stage for her necropolitical exclusion. The social, juridical and biological deaths of Ashley Smith begin with girlhood, and more specifically with discourses of the girl that make an agentic, disobedient, willful girl an unthinkable subject but can imagine a girl martyr. Once her agency is finally extinguished, it is as a passive, deceased subject that Ashley Smith becomes thinkable within the category of girl. And, once she is thinkable as a girl, her socially dead status is repudiated, but at the cost of her existence as a meaning-making, world-creating agent. Activists have participated in configuring Ashley Smith in ways that fit her into accepted discourses of who can be a noble victim. These configurations reinforce narrow, profoundly racist and classist, confines to categories, confirming the monstrosity of those who cannot easily fit within available categories of girlhood, and sustaining the illegibility of adolescent girls' agencies. I posit that the pathologizing of adolescent girls' resistances as mental illness may follow almost inevitably from widely accepted cultural constructions of the feminine and of mental illness. This suggests that behavioural differences relating to resistance and criminality between adolescents may well be significantly less predictable or regular along binary gender lines than has been assumed. I contend that statistical differences between boys' and girls' criminal offending rates may reflect not that they *are* different but that they are governed differently. In other words, it matters very much that Ashley Smith is a girl.

ENDNOTES

---

[1]This is reported in various sources, including testimony at her inquest by Kim Pate, who, on behalf of the Elizabeth Fry Society, had to take a dictation of Ashley Smith's grievance about her treatment. On September 24, 2007, Ashley was permitted nothing in her cell except her gown: see e.g. "Ashley Smith Looked Hopeless and Dejected, Inquest Hears" *Toronto Star* (October 15, 2013). This disciplinary confiscation of Ashley's writing implements is nowhere denied and is also documented in the 2008 Report of the New Brunswick Ombudsman.

[2]*Smith (Re)*, 2013 CanLII 92762 (ON O CCO) *Inquest Touching the Death of Ashley Smith*, December 2013, Recommendation #1.

[3]See generally, Vincent and Zlomistic "Excerpt: The Life and Death of Ashley Smith" *The Toronto Star* (15 December 2013); CBC Timeline: The Life and Death of Ashley Smith" CBC: *The Fifth Estate* http://www.cbc.ca/fifth/blog/the-life-and-death-of-ashley-smith. Unusually, Wikipedia provides precisely what I mean to summarize in this section, that being the widely accepted (but not necessarily plausible, supportable, evidence-based or verifiable) story of Ashley Smith: http://en.wikipedia.org/wiki/Ashley_Smith_inquest.

[4]As will be discussed later in this book, I am referring to the concept of "necropolitics" as developed by Mbembe and Agamben, as a relationship between sovereign power and control over life and death. See Agamben, Giorgio. *Homo sacer: Sovereign Power and Bare Life*. Trans. Daniel Heller-Roazen: Stanford: Stanford University Press, 1998. Print.

2. Foundations of the Project

The Project in Conversation

LITERATURE REVIEW

I devised and conducted this research, and wrote this book, in conversation with writing from a variety of academic fields and knowledge communities. By building on these existing works, I was able to define a discursive space where asking different critical questions about Ashley Smith's case is possible. In conducting this research I have considered: academic writing about Smith and similar recent cases; critical theorizations of "girls" as particular representations; research about social constructions of the child, adolescent girls and gender; scholarship about criminal and quasi-criminal regimes affecting adolescent young women; and, feminist legal theory.

THE SMITH CASE AND SIMILAR RECENT CASES

The research undertaken for this book was designed to address gaps in academic writing about the Ashley Smith case. Criminologist Jennifer Kilty has very recently provided insightful analysis of how the medicalization of woman prisoners as an intervention strategy is demonstrated in Ashley Smith's death. Her very useful research, unlike mine, however, is about Smith's death, not about the "case" as an exercise in public sense-making. This work is complementary to, and supportive of, my general points. (Kilty, 2015) However, legal scholarship about the Smith case has, to this point, not engaged closely with certain assumed truths in its established facts.

For example, Jena McGill's analysis of the case assumes, without reference to any data, that Ashley Smith was an aboriginal woman, and this reading of Smith as aboriginal is integral to her analysis of the case as an instance of Canada's maltreatment of First Nations populations. (McGill) Rather than simply being incorrect about Smith's aboriginal heritage, the reading of her as a First Nations individual in McGill's paper underscores the problematic slipperiness of Ashley Smith's racialization. Similarly, Bingham and Sutton in 2012 presented an analysis of the Smith case as an instance of Canada's failure to properly address the needs of the mentally ill in the correctional context. (Bingham and Sutton) Like McGill's, this analysis rests on problematic assumptions about Ashley Smith. The key assumption unexamined in this work is that Smith had a stable mental illness that pre-existed her time in prison and caused her problems there.

Jessica Ring (2014) has published a more useful critical analysis of media portrayals of mental illness in the Smith case. Ring's paper concludes with a suggestion that alternative imaginings of Smith's conduct as evidence of something other than stable mental illness would be useful, identifying a gap in existing research that cries out for this in-depth critical research. Similarly, an Op/Ed piece by Dawn Moore offered a contextualized critique of the CSC response to the inquest recommendations (Moore, December, 2014). Moore linked the Smith case to general, systematic problems in CSC, going beyond solitary confinement and mental health beds, to the governing logics that subject women and aboriginal people to higher levels of scrutiny. This opinion piece suggests the usefulness of a study that looks at the bureaucratic and discursive logics active in the construction of the Smith case.

In addition to these analyses, non-legal critical scholarship about analogous recent spectacular cases is useful. There is a growing body of writing about Smith's case in medical and psychological fields. However, much academic writing about Ashley Smith relates to research conducted before the inquest decision was rendered and, in consequence, does not address the entire duration of the legal and governmental case. Advocates for women prisoners, including those representing the Elizabeth Fry Society, have cited Smith's case as a demonstration of the inadequacy of applying "gender-neutral legislation" to women. (Pate) This writing is helpful in drawing attention to the implicit maleness of the law but does not look at intersections of age and gender by presenting a specific analysis of the treatment of *girls*.[1]

While there will no doubt be more critical scholarship produced about the Smith case, the circumstances of Smith's case do not lend themselves to traditional legal scholarship. They present little data to study: as far as the common law doctrine of *stare decisis* is concerned, her case is invisible and largely irrelevant. Many of the myriad little decisions affecting her that took place outside of the public space of a courtroom will not be scrutinized under formal legal analysis. There will never be caselaw that can be studied doctrinally that documents or explains the cumulative combination of hundreds of little decisions that together led to Smith's death. Nor will there ever be a public judgment in the tort lawsuit for her wrongful death. That was settled, reportedly for millions of dollars. The settlement is sealed. The family had sued for $11 million; the amount of the settlement is not disclosed (Seglins). Now that the inquest is completed, there is a decision in the inquest in her case that legal scholars may study. However, since inquest decisions do not bind courts to act, and make recommendations only, if the decision does advance legal doctrine, it will be in respect of what sorts of questions can be asked at an inquest, an issue that is quite tangential to the particularities of Ashley Smith's embodiment and death. Also, this inquest decision was made by a jury selecting from a checklist of recommendations, which means there are no written reasons for the decision or a narrative of judicially accepted facts to unpack. In any case, the inquest is about what happened only in the last few months of her time in (adult) custody, with a focus on the last days. It is therefore likely that analysis of Ashley Smith's case using traditional legal research methodology is not going to ask important questions or reveal significant dimensions of her situation.

In non-legal academic literature in the social sciences, there is currently little analysis where Smith's case is concerned. However, this gap is clearly going to be transitory. Scholars from a wide range of fields are looking at the case. I am unlikely to be alone in thinking that her case is one that governmentality analysis is well situated to fill. Her case has been studied in at least one master's thesis in concert with other cases about women in Canadian prisons as an instance for how recommendations for reform to those prisons identified decades ago by the Arbour Commission were never implemented. (Ferrari) Further, criminologist Hannah-Moffat, who testified at Ashley Smith's inquest in October 2013, is virtually certain to produce academic writing either directly about, or relevant to the case. Certainly, a number of works already published by Hannah-Moffatt are relevant to the analysis of risk and security logics as they operate in Canadian carceral institutions. (Hannah-Moffatt, 2011) Writing by Maeve McMahon is also relevant.

Academic literature about analogous spectacular cases concerning adolescent female accuseds has been highly relevant to this project. Works of this kind include academic writing about the death of BC teen Reena Virk and prosecution of Kelly Ellard for it.[2] Writing about the prosecution and sentencing of Melissa Todorovic[3] and the prosecution, sentencing and parole proceedings in relation to Jasmine Richardson is also relevant.[4] Smith's case is different from these other high profile criminal cases dealing with adolescent female accuseds. Typically, spectacular "bad girl" cases are framed as "sexy." Ashley's case is not. Salacious media narratives in these other cases paint a dominant picture of a villainous girl who is "mean" and "nasty." There are other "nasty girls" constructed in other contexts, but these notable Canadian cases are constructed in media sites as fantastic tales of hypersexual nasty girl super villains.

By saying that Smith's case is not sexy by typical spectacular "nasty girl" case standards, I do not mean to imply that sexuality is not relevant to its theorization. As will be discussed later in this book, Smith's sexuality is conspicuously absent from the texts that make up the case. It is erased.

How feminist and critical thinkers have intervened in the case of Reena Virk is salient. Sociologists have used a feminist anti-racist critical framework to explore perspectives left out of mainstream media and policy discourse about Virk's case. (Ravija and Batacharya) Ravija and Batacharya unpack how portrayals of Virk's murder erase race and social class. (Jiwani; Ravija, Mithili, Batacharya) Also useful is a critical exploration of what features of the accused Kelly Ellard's embodiment and social location made her into a "saveable" white girl.

According to available quantitative studies, paradigmatic spectacular "bad girl" cases tend to be statistically unusual cases. The usual pop culture fodder in relation to adolescent female offending tends to statistically unusual subject matter. This makes Ashley Smith's case even more important to study. Smith's case is anomalous because it breaks with this frame, and in so doing belies the contention made in mainstream policy writing that media coverage is always simplistically exploitative. Rather than simplistically preying on her case as salacious, media writers have constructed Smith's case as a social problem calling out for some sort of response, and their profit has been made in the public attention raised by making those calls. The mainstream media broke the story about Ashley's death and was instrumental in calling for an inquiry, the inquest, a CSC response to the inquest, and changes to correctional practices.

I reviewed expert literature in medicine and psychology that characterizes the Smith case as a tragic instance where matters better dealt with in the mental health system were dealt with in the criminal justice system. (MacDonald; Kilty) This literature is consistent with contentions made by psychiatrists and psychologists testifying in Smith's inquest that what Ashley needed was better access to mental health care. This literature accepts as a condition of possibility that there is a choice between *either* mental health "care" for individuals *or* punishment in the correctional system. It presents strong criticisms of the treatment of Smith by Corrections and is self-interested in expanding the hegemony of psychological expert discourses over social apparatuses of governmentality by demanding more mental health beds. These analyses are remarkably unreflexive and uncritical of the treatment mental health patients receive in psychiatric care, which is a striking, considering (as will be discussed) that many cavity searches, forced injections, beatings and other instances of mistreatment that Ashley received were authorized by mental health legislation or happened while she was in psychiatric care. My governmentality analysis will contribute a different understanding of governance by the mental health, child welfare and correctional systems as systems that, rather than being alternatives to one another, interlock and mutually constitute both the offender and the responses to her.

I also looked at scholarship that contends Smith's behaviours match characteristic effects of solitary confinement. Psychologists and psychiatrists are unreflexive about the rationality that leads prisoners to be held in solitary confinement (Grassian and Freidman) but they are putting forth a developing consensus that the experience of prolonged solitary confinement causes behaviours for which Smith was being punished by means of solitary confinement. (Zlomistic, 2012) Some psychologists, as well as the Canadian Civil Liberties Association,[5] are saying that she was caught up in a cycle of being further punished for exhibiting symptoms resulting from her punishment. This contention grounds social activism.

GIRLS' STUDIES

Especially because primary texts (reports, decisions, official CSC documents) in Ashley Smith's case, like the policy literature discussed below, treat the categories of "woman" and "girl" as static, homogenous and largely self-evident, considering research and writing that critically interrogates and troubles the category of girl has been important to my research. Critical writing with foundations in non-essentialist and intersectional theoretical frameworks about social constructions of ideal and non-ideal types of girl contributed a foundation for understanding in what ways Smith might have been unable to conform to, unwilling to accede to, invisible to, or unthinkable within, these ideal types.

While I am focused on the girl subject, writing that critically interrogates social constructions of the child and of childhood for all subjects regardless of gender has also been relevant to my work. I found useful writing from the field of childhood studies that historicizes and situates in broader processes of colonialism, social class and race the constructions of childhood and capacity. (Kehily; Platt) These texts explore ways in which the social identities of "child," "juvenile," and "delinquent" exist as always already gendered, raced and classed. Further, while it is not specifically about children, Frankenburg's (2004) work towards elucidating the dimensions of the discursively empty social category of "whiteness" as it intersects with femininity is useful in helping unpack how the social category of "child" is raced.

As a field of critical studies, girls' studies starts from cultural studies and critical theoretical foundations and troubles the category of girl. This scholarship can be used to trouble the monolithic category of girl and get beneath the girl/boy binary, complicating oversimplistic assumptions that typically characterize policy discourse as it relates to youth criminal justice. While it is neither monolithic nor unitary, taken as a whole, girls' studies literature looks at how social power relations and knowledge about girls have shaped what "girl" means as an idea, discourse and cultural figure. It also investigates sites of production of discourse, and in particular performativity and social construction in respect of childhood, adolescence and gender. It looks at deployment of the idea of "adolescent girl" as related to concepts of masculinity, femininity, womanhood, manhood and childhood as well as in relation to other discourses, including legal, mental health, educational, capitalism and colonialism. (Crowly and Kitchin) Scholars explore prevalent interlocking constructions of girl and of goodness or moral virtue, specifically in respect of dominant western discourses of ideal femininity, hetero-normative sexuality and the ways in which adolescent young women's agency is constrained by constructions of sexual morality.

Girls' studies has developed as a field in academic literature since the 1990s. Eline Lipkin defines the field as made up of inquiries into how girls are shaped by popular culture and "how the stamp of girl is impressed upon them."(Lipkin, viii) Anita Harris describes the field as a body of "feminist work about and with young women" (xix) that seeks to explore issues relating to young women "standing at the corner of feminism and neoliberalism." (xviii) It seeks to inquire into dimensions of girls' power, cultures and identities in the twenty-first century. In addition to focusing on the "girl," this writing is also thematically unified by a sense that feminist research should take seriously a number of constructs and practices formerly dismissed as commonplace, unimportant and trivial.

Critical writing in the field seeks to unpack assumed monolithic categories of childhood and of girl as distinct from woman. Writing in the field of girls studies links young women's agency and choices with popular expectations about young femininity, and in particular consider construction of girls' identities at intersections of racialization, class and gender. (Harris; Jiwani, Steenbergen and Mitchell; Walkerdine)

Analyses of gender as discourse and performance are developed in this field as they pertain specifically to girls. (Butler, 1986) I found useful writing that critically analyzes how women and girls actively perform actions and discipline, even surgically alter, their bodies, to conform to what a "good" girl should do and be. Girls' studies scholarship links technologies of the self with governance, looking at how gender takes socially mandatory work to perform and achieve. This work provides a starting point for a critique of the assumed pre-existing mental infirmity of Ashley Smith. For instance, sociologist Christie Barron looks at how figures of the bad/nasty/risky girl are constructed not just through legal discourse, but also through expert discourse. (Barron)

Girls studies explores how constructs of the girl are socially located. The identity of girl has excluded some people entirely while it has been forcibly imposed upon others; girls have intersectional identities. Studies show how particular figurations of the girl emerge at particular historical times in specific locations and are enmeshed in broader social and political processes like colonialism and racism. Critical analyses of historical figurations of the girl enrich an understanding of how the social category is raced, classed and exclusionary. For instance, ways race and social class were written in to girls' virtue are made clear in Strange and Loo's analysis of the entanglement of white nation building in Canada's nineteenth century with technologies of the self, especially moral regulation, for white girls. (Strange and Loo)

I also build on the strand in girls' studies writing about the missing discourses of girls' agencies, including sexual agency, to theorize Smith's subjectivity. This scholarship contributes to analyses of how girls exercise agencies in contexts of oppressive constraints, both in their lived realities and online. (Bailey and Steeves) Girls studies supports an intersectional understanding that the Canadian public knows (and cares) about the conditions of Smith incarceration precisely *because* of her putative race and social class. This understanding helps address questions of why media have raised questions about Smith's death in texts that configure her as a victim when the assumed paradigmatic media portrayal of adolescent female offending is more salacious and less activist.

While not falling exclusively within the field of girls' studies, feminist critiques of discourses of mental health in respect of how these discourses affect women and girls was also helpful to my work. I drew on feminist critiques of mental health discourses, and the borderline personality disorder diagnosis. (Proctor; Bosworth; Ussher; Chesler; Wirth-Cauchon; Ring) Relatedly, writing that theorizes representations of adolescent girls' mental illness has informed has informed the analysis in this book of how the diagnosed mental illness of Ashley Smith intersects with discourses of the madwoman circulating in popular culture. (Edwards; Leverenz; Showalter)

GOVERNMENTALITY, SECURITY, RISK AND THE "CRIMINALIZED GIRL"

Historically, women and girls were understudied by criminologists, and girls' particular circumstances were neglected in policy discourse. However, feminist researchers have, since the middle of the twentieth century, developed literature about adolescent girls, gender and youth criminal justice law. An important early text in this vein is Adelberg and Currie's (1987) aptly titled book, *Too Few to Count: Canadian Women in Conflict with the Law*. A variety of different kinds of scholarship about adolescent girls, gender and youth criminal justice law has since developed.

"Expert" writing now constructs empirical data sets and derives from them theorizations about criminalized adolescent girls. These quantitative studies of adolescent girls are both useful and problematic. Statistics paint a different picture of the criminalized girl from that stereotypically constructed in media sites. Academic and policy experts use numbers to paint a shadowy picture of a 14 to 15 year old, the dominant trait of whom is victimization. She is most likely racialized, probably aboriginal, and impoverished with serious and complex challenges in her family circumstances. She has likely survived abuse — in particular sexual abuse — and has a history of involvement with the child "protection" system, which was probably the milieu (in the form of some sort of group home or foster care facility) where she was charged. A figure of the criminalized girl emerges that emphasizes the context of her victimhood by varied social circumstances, including violence.

Investigations of differences between male and female offending behaviour and constructions of statistical data sets about these differences provide context for this study. Doob and Sprott (2009) as well as Jane Worrall (2004) present analyses of recent statistics from the U.S. and Canada about offending and incarceration rates. They statistically debunk the common assumption that adolescent young women are changing and becoming more violent. Empirical studies of rates of charging, sentencing and incarceration of adolescent girls also compare situations before and after legal regimes changed. Doob, Sprott and Worrall's work provides insight into the ways that law reform *can* influence material conditions in the juridical field when laws changed. After the *Youth Criminal Justice Act* SC 2002 c 1. came into force, their research indicates that disproportionate incarceration of girls for "administration of justice offences" (such as failure to appear in court) was significantly reduced. (Doob and Sprott)

With some relatively recent exceptions, much of the literature about the criminalization of girls is in large part problematic for two reasons. First, it generally assumes the existence of a monolithic category of "girl" without considering how it is constituted. Second, it defines the category "girl" in binary opposition to the category "boy" as "not-boy," which provides little insight into analysis about what "girl" might actually mean and who those labeled girls might be. However, with the caveat that these statistics are problematic because they are invariably produced in comparison to the "normal" adolescent offender, the boy, and this binary prevents full exploration of the conditions of diversely situated girls from being undertaken, they do provide context for this research.

Statistical data sets consistently show that those identified as adolescent girls are less likely to offend than are boys, and that, when they do offend, they commit far less serious crimes on the whole than boys do. Their offending rates peak at earlier ages. (Bala; Sprott and Doob) They tend to be criminalized for different kinds of offences; girls are generally charged for non-violent offences or as accessories to crimes where male accuseds are ringleaders. In addition to characteristically doing different things, girls reflected in offending statistics are differently situated than boys. The girls tend much more strongly to hail from economically and socially marginal populations.(Sprott and Doob) In addition to marginality, victimization by violence, including but not limited to, sexual violence is a common characteristic of adolescent young women who become criminalized: statistically, the single biggest predictor of female offending behaviour is abuse of the girl and especially child sexual abuse. While these studies are limited in historical depth because of inattention to girls and women in previous research, available numbers consistently show that girls' patterns of behaviour have not changed over the past several decades but are rather now being documented differently. For example, abolition of, or reduction in the use of, status offences, is leading police to charge girls for offences for which no charges would have historically been laid, which is skewing offending rate statistics. (Feld)

Empirical research consistently shows although they may be less quickly dealt with formally for minor infractions, once formally charged, girls receive harsher treatment in youth criminal justice systems than do boys. This matches a discrepancy in Canadian statistics in which girls self-report committing minor, non-violent crimes at rates more comparable to the rates at which boys self-report minor crimes than their relative charge rates would suggest. (Savoie) Certainly feminist criminologists and feminist legal studies scholars, have found this to be the case historically in jurisdictions as varied as Australia, the United States, the United Kingdom and Canada. (Smart; Naffine; Daly and Maher) More recent symbolic interactionist research looks at ways in which girls and boys are subjected to different forms and degrees of social control. (Heimer) The harsh redress women have faced for crimes under Canadian criminal law has been well explored, particularly by Renke in the context of Canada's "dangerous offender" designation and how it has been used differently in relation to women than men. (Renke)

One area of unresolved debate in this research concerns to what extent changes in formal laws determine or even affect the way girls are treated in the criminal justice system. Criminologists Smart and Smart, writing in 1978, advocated that researchers shift their focus away from the doctrinal law of legislation and judgments. They argued that "the limited effectiveness of recent legislation serves to reveal the extent to which the primary sources of women's oppression are outside or even beyond judicial influence." (Smart and Smart, 1978, 1) However, Doob and Sprott (2009) use statistics to argue that recent legislative changes have mattered a great deal. Their work documents how, after the abolition of status offences, administration of justice offences that demarcate resistance to authority came to be disproportionately laid against girls as compared to boys.

Statistical pictures of the criminalized girl contribute one lens on adolescent girls' experiences with the criminal and quasi-criminal justice systems in Canada. This lens, as noted, is imperfect because it is inherently limited by what it tests *for* (differences from boys) and also always mediated by how categories of offenders are defined, crimes are defined, and by reporting rates. Rates of reported crime do not fully describe criminal offending behavior, and rates of reported victimization almost certainly under-represent actual experiences. Also, while statistical records are kept in the United States and some other jurisdictions that demographically situate persons charged and incarcerated on the basis of race, in Canada no statistical data is kept about the race of adolescents accused, convicted or sentenced in the criminal and quasi-criminal systems except for documentation of aboriginal status. Further, when the factual similarities between detentions by child protection systems, mental health treatment and criminal sentences are considered, it is problematic that statistics document the criminal justice system separately from detentions in facilities run nominally under these other forms of governance. Relatedly, empirical expert quantitative analyses of offending by girls relative to boys rarely if ever unpack the complexity of the diversity of embodied circumstances that are experienced by girls. Finally, as noted, quantitative studies almost never trouble the category of "girl," which is a particularly obvious limitation because the ages of who constitutes a "girl" and a woman are different under the legislative regimes of every country as well as having changed over time from the operation of the *Juvenile Delinquents Act* (JDA)[6] to the *Young Offenders Act*

(YOA)[7] in Canada.

Quantitative research confirms that gender is relevant to the way that adolescents enter, experience, and are treated in, the juridical field. As discussed, this discourse has its gaps and limits. Other than showing she is *not* a typical boy, these numbers do little else to fill in the features of the criminalized girl. She remains a shadowy figure because she is not analyzed for her own sake but comparatively.

Research that makes the conditions of victimization by violence experienced by girls visible is important background to my project. (Batacharya; Jiwani; Chesney-Lind; McMahon) Meda Chesney-Lind's (2006) work helps unpack how the social circumstances of adolescent girls are made invisible in criminal proceedings involving them. Chesney-Lind (2008) has also explored ways in which relational aggression and "bullying" are far from the most significant problems adolescent young women face.

As noted, in reaction to popular discourses perceived to vilify girls, feminist academic writing tends to deliberately empha-size girls' roles as victims. In doing so, it often problematically neglects the ways in which girls actively participate in living their lives. Besides depicting her as an extremely marginal and victimized "not-boy," discourses of the criminalized girl do not devote attention to the varied experiences and agencies of those girls. Statistical documentation of charge rates and social circum-stances of girls entering the criminal and quasi-criminal systems provides only indirect evidence of girls' behaviour. Analysis of the way girls' cases are processed provides a lens into how they are treated by the system and provides a basis to compare and contrast their treatment from one another and from the treatment received by variously situated boys. Writing that seeks to analyze and theorize the multiple dimensions of girls' identities and how differently situated girls receive different treatment is crucial to an intersectional analysis that appreciates the complexity and instability of identity.

Qualitative research explores in detail how historical criminal and quasi-criminal governance enforces gender performativity and sexualizes both punishment and criminality. Intersectional anal-yses of the differential treatment of adolescents by criminal and quasi-criminal systems crucially contribute depth to my analysis.

While early feminist criminological literature was limited in that it treated girls as a unified social category, there has developed significant literature that contains intersectional analysis about which adolescent young women get constructed as dangerous and for what reasons. "Squaws," "dirty girls," "incorrigible girls," "sexually immoral girls," "modern girls," "nasty black girls," "masculinized girls," "risky girls," "impure girls," and "witches" all take shape on these analyses as figurations of the girl as demonized other.

Faith and Jiwani (2006) look at how race and racism affect how adolescent girls get treated by the criminal legal system, be they victims or accuseds. Ann Worrall's (2000) theorization of changing constructions of the "female juvenile delinquent" critically analyzes who, and what behaviours, are criminalized when adolescent young women are concerned. Wendy Mesley (2012) and others inquire into the over-representation of, and marginalization within discourses of, the criminal and quasi-criminal systems of aboriginal women and girls. They provide an intersectional understanding of the different ways in which diversely situated adolescent girls have been constructed as dangerous.

Behaviours for which adolescent young women are criminally sanctioned have been different depending upon their social location. However, across these differences, there are similarities in what behavior has warranted laying of criminal charges against a girl. Acts by girls that have been met with charges in response have usually been either acts of sexual agency not considered criminal for adults or, more recently, offences where girls challenge or flout authority, under the YOA, including administrative offences. Sexual agency and perceived persistent resistance to authority seem to be the usual grounds for particularly harsh sanctions against girls. Carolyn Strange and Tina Loo (1997) contribute an understanding of how regulation of adolescent girls' sexuality, reproduction and gender performance by criminal and quasi-criminal systems in Canada was enmeshed with broader, racist and colonial historical projects of white nation building, and Mariana Valverde (1991) similarly looks at criminal and quasi criminal control over adolescent girls as a historically situated aspect of moral regulation crucial to the white settlement and domestication of the West.

The notion of female delinquency as well as the consequences governance frameworks imposed for it were historically sexualized. (Backhouse; Myers; Sangster) These works describe cases taking place in past regimes of criminal law where adolescent girls were incarcerated, punished, beaten and sexually violated in a series of acts strikingly similar to those undergone by Ashley Smith.

Criminal and quasi-criminal law were used historically as means of enforcing disciplines of gender performativity. (Chesney-Lind; Myers; Naffine) Female compliance to authority, subordination to males, domesticity and the channeling of sexual and reproductive labour into accepted roles were all practices in which various quasi criminal and criminal regimes in many jurisdictions have been engaged. Lara Karaian (2012) theorizes sexual expression and the rise of criminal sanction and censorship for de-authorizing some adolescent girls' sexual agencies and others' sexual exploitability, as is discussed in more detail later in this chapter.

Feminist critical writing also explores how, for girls, there has historically been no bright line between restrictions constructed and justified in discourses of protection, medical treatment and mental health, and punishment by means of criminal sanctions. Expert discourse continues to construct the dangerousness of girls. (Barron and Lacombe) Karen Busby (2003) has explored connections between punishment and protection of adolescent girls with reference to "protective confinement" statutes now being used across Canada to effectively incarcerate adolescent girls suspected of involvement with sex work. The Vancouver-based NGO "Justice For Girls" has also critiqued this protective confinement regime. (Dean) Historical and persisting links between criminalization, medicalization, protective custody and mental health treatment for adolescent girls trouble the assumption ubiquitous in reports about Ashley Smith's case that the mental health system is separate, apart, alternative, and preferable to the criminal justice and corrections context.

I also looked at theorizations about the criminality of adolescent girls. One of the influential "expert" texts that sought to theorize female criminality was Freida Adler's (1975) *Sisters in Crime: The Rise of the New Female Criminal*. Adler hypothesized that feminism would lead to a "masculinization" of girls, who would become comparably violent to boys and men. While this hypothesis is not supported by the empirical data discussed above, in contemporary popular culture, it is generally accepted. The discursive figuration of the changed, more masculine, nasty girl, was circulating before Adler's work was published. Attribution of the idea of the "liberation hypothesis" to Adler or to journalist Patricia Pearson's book *When She Was Bad* (1997) is problematic. As Barron and Lacombe point out, "the dominant idea throughout most of the twentieth century was that females who offend are rejecting their feminine role and are emulating their male counterpart." (56) Anti-essentialist feminist theorists have critically unpacked how misconduct, offending and unruliness by girls is seen in mainstream discourses of femininity as *unnatural*. Popular culture naturalizes, tacitly condones and even romanticizes offending by boys: getting into trouble is understood as a rite of passage in achieving masculinity. (Messerschmidt) Conversely, criminal offending by adolescent girls is seen as unnatural and treated extremely seriously. (Smart; Daly; Naffine)

Many theoretical understandings of adolescent girls contend that systems have been resistant to criminalizing those who fit into available identities of the normative or "nice" girl. There is research statistically showing an apparent lenience to girls under juvenile justice law, or at least a reluctance to deal with certain girls in the public sphere. (Worrall) This is reinforced by the discrepancy between girls' rates of self-reporting criminal behavior in comparison with that of boys and charge rates for girls that seem artificially low. (Savoie) However, as Naffine found, as soon as a determination is made that a particular girl does not fit into normative figurations of the good girl, she is treated harshly indeed. (Naffine)

Despite this research, girls remain marginal to mainstream policy discourse. Criminologists have long pointed out that adolescent girls are not given serious consideration in mainstream law reform. (Geller) Mainstream policy writing's engagement with feminist critical literature appears to have reached an apex at the turn of the twenty-first century in Canada. Then, it appears feminist writers had lively engagement with policy scholars about reforms to youth criminal justice law, (Boyle) even if that discussion was peripheral in policy debates. As is discussed below, however, by the time of the Nunn report (2006) and the amendments to youth criminal justice law it precipitated, the consequences of law reform to adolescent girls were sidelined in, if not totally absent from, policy discussion.

Scholarship that theorizes the social construction of deviance (Goode and Ben-Yahuda) also provided me useful background to consider in the analysis performed in this book. Others have applied critical analysis to contemporary multi-media contexts. (McRobbie and Thornton) Some of this theorization centres around the adolescent young offender, who is expressly or implicitly male. (Newburn and Messerschmidt) theorize relationships between discourses of masculinity and adolescent male offending behaviour. Adolescent offending, including especially "roughness" and "toughness," is critically unpacked as socially condoned as part of the achievement of masculinities. Mark Totten (2003) has applied analysis of discourses of masculinity to study how violence against girls by marginal adolescent boys can form part of their assertion of masculinity. This literature critically deconstructs discourses of masculinity and provides analysis of gender performativity, achievement of gendered identities and coercive maintenance of gender in a binary two-gender system.

Policy writing about adolescent offenders tends to draw on and reproduce a figuration of a saveable white boy. It is generally sympathetic to the economic and social circumstances of male adolescent offenders and explores relationships among young men in "gangs." Stanley Cohen and Stuart Hall's groundbreaking work on "moral panic" is based on studies of male youth gangs in the UK. The functioning of adolescent sexual offenders as "monstrous others" in the context of a moral panic model has been studied. (Douard) Some of the writing that develops the moral panic theorization of adolescent offending is polarized. It characterizes adolescents as "misguided children" in the face of an assumed or perceived onslaught. (Schissel) Schissel theorizes the adolescent offender as other, particularly in light of changing racial demographics in Canada. As Bala (2013) has documented, a rise in anti-youth sentiment has corresponded to aging white populations and increased proportions of ethnically diverse and racialized adolescents.

POLICY SCHOLARSHIP

My prior LL.M. studies, and work as a lawyer, familiarized me with policy writing about the youth criminal justice regime in Canada. There are gaps in widely held understandings about the relationships between adolescent young women and governmentality in this literature where girls are concerned that I intend this project to fill. Policy scholarship about adolescent girls in Canada includes promotional and apologetic literature about the current regime from official sources (like the Federal Department of Justice), academic textbooks and articles that explain the legislation and formal, reported legal decisions under it. It is targeted for an audience of people working in the justice and correctional systems as well as adolescents themselves. It also contains writing that criticizes the current legislative regime. There is significant overlap between who writes this policy literature and who contributed to the crafting of the YCJA. Legal scholar Nicholas Bala and criminologist Sanjeev Anand (2012) have produced encyclopedic work that explicates formal details of the legal and policy regime set out under the YCJA. They offer gentle critiques of the current regime and are influential within it.

In general, feminism has a ghostly existence in this literature as the work tends to assume an egalitarian, enlightened post-feminist present tense where inequalities faced by girls existed in a less evolved past. This literature does not deny discrimination and oppression against girls took place in the past but treats this injustice as irrelevant to, and certainly not produced by, current conditions. It assumes a postfeminist present tense where gender equality has been realized. It assumes the formal legal and discursive separation of punishment from "child saving" has a concrete reality.

Canadian academics writing about youth justice policy tend to describe the treatment of adolescents by the criminal and quasi-criminal systems in a grand narrative of historical progress. (Doob; Bala; Anand; Davis-Barron) Grounding their thinking in rights discourse, they are critical of the way adolescents were not differentiated from adults under the law until the 19th century. Indeed, it is in expert discourses, and especially developmental psychology (on which these policy writers heavily rely) that the category of adolescent is constructed. These academics also criticize some consequences, but laud the intentions, of the "child savers" movements of the early twentieth century and the *Juvenile Delinquents Act* RSC 1908 c J-3 that came into force in 1908. They lament that the JDA did not allow for sufficient legal protections for adolescents' rights. They generally insist that, since 1982, legality has been a fair space where the rights of adolescents are protected in Canada. Progress, they argue, marches onward, and they contend in general that, since the 2003 coming into force of the YCJA, legality has become a supportive and even nurturing space for adolescents in Canada. Although they are concerned about the 2012 amendments to the YCJA eroding some of this progress. The dominant narrative is that the system is fairer than it ever was before. And it is a dominant understanding that the law is contained in books and legality takes place in courtrooms.

These academics tend to vilify media and assert the legitimacy of statistical data as a reflection of reality. This policy literature is expressly intended to counteract what it claims is a misapprehension in popular culture: the argument is that adolescents are popularly *mis*understood as increasingly dangerous. The literature relies heavily on the quantitative studies discussed above to refute this. In general, it understands statistical data sets as *the* truth. While understandable given the conditions of possibility in which policy discourse is constructed as a genre, the portrayal of media and popular discourse in policy writing is problematic in that it tends to present media discourse as monolithic, unitary and unsophisticated in a self-serving way that is not consistent with what happened in Ashley Smith's case.

It is difficult to draw a bright line between policy writing by academics and legal documents. The Nunn Commission report, (2006) released shortly before Ashley Smith's death in custody, is a legal document but it is also contributes to policy discourse in the manner of an academic work. It makes recommendations that can be treated doctrinally by courts and legislators as persuasive (not binding) in the same manner as academic texts. The recommendations of the Nunn Commission were in turn written in to the YCJA in 2012. This report is typical, and reconstitutive, of the preponderance of Canadian policy discourse about adolescents: a single white male adolescent is the normative young offender about whom analysis is offered and for whom broad policy change is advocated then made. It only cursorily looks at whether the system is equally inadequate in respect of its treatment of differently situated offenders. It makes no mention of gender disparities in treatment of offenders.[8] While the report makes a passing nod to the fact that adolescent girls and boys are different populations, it sets forth no analysis of whether these populations have different needs or are treated differently, and no reference is made to differences between individuals within these populations: conspicuously absent from the report is an analysis of race and, in particular, aboriginality.[9]

Policy literature about adolescent young women and criminal as well as quasi-criminal regulation is also problematic because it treats the child welfare, mental health and criminal systems separately. The YOA ideologically separated criminal responses to offending behaviour by adolescents from child welfare responses, where, prior to 1984, the regimes were combined.[10] Two legal regimes were created in 1984, and policy writing looks at them separately. However, there is ongoing connection and overlap between systems. Child welfare's protective responses can be *effectively* carceral and the measures taken against adolescents for protective reasons and mental health reasons are often effectively the same geographic space of closed group homes. Further, which adolescents are "in care" and overlaps with those which are criminalized. There is a frequent trajectory of youths "in care" into the criminal justice system. Also because of this regime separation, the child welfare, mental health and criminal justice systems operate administratively separately from one another; consequently, lack of communication between systems is endemic. However, while the discourses of these systems are often mutually unintelligible (relying on different definitions of the subject, divergent solutions and mechanisms), the practical circumstances of adolescent accuseds and offenders, *especially* girls, given their disproportionate social marginality, often involve enmeshment simultaneously with criminal, correctional, health and child welfare systems.

FEMINIST LEGAL STUDIES

Writing from feminist legal theory has helped me move beyond my prior acceptance of certain widely accepted "truths" of existing YCJA policy writing by contributing to my project an understanding of law as a masculinist discourse that assumes implicitly male, white, middle class subjects. Theorization of the relationships between gender, sexuality and the legibility of women's voices to legal discourses from a critical perspective has been undertaken by feminist legal theorists. (Naffine; Conaghan; Rheaume; Dowd, and Jacobs) In general, feminist legal theorists have analyzed and theorized ways in which women and girls have been excluded from the law. Feminist legal theorists have thus contributed theory that explores ways in which legal doctrine is *not* determinative as well as the continued significance of what laws do say to what happens to people. Feminist legal theory also contributes to an understanding of the relationship between law reform and lived experiences as well as to theorization of legal cases as sites for contestation of power between competing meanings and discourses. Feminist legal theory looks critically at the operation of discourses of gender in legal sense-making, theorizes how legal systems and actors are gendered and play a part in the process of gendering and offers insight into how legal relations are understood in gendered terms.

Feminist legal writing raises questions about the race and gender of Agamben's *homo sacer* figure that is discussed below. Ideas from feminist legal theorists about how gender makes available certain subjectivities, and hence certain dominant discursive figurations, that lend themselves to the exclusion of certain subjects. Jennifer Nedelsky, in her work reconceptualizing autonomy as relational, has explored how the law, written *by* a particular, socially located, classed and raced group of white men *for* subjects implicitly assumed also to be men, is ill equipped to deal with the embodied diversity of the human beings subject to the law. (1997) Like Nedelsky, Regina Graycar (1990) Vanessa Munro (2001) and others have critiqued the assumed implicit maleness of the legal subject that is made manifest in law and policy discourse. Critical race theorists like Kimberle Crenshaw and bell hooks have enhanced the depth of this analysis as they critique the assumed race and socioeconomic status of legal subjects as middle class and white. (hooks; Crenshaw) Post-colonial feminist legal scholarship that specifically engages with settler colonialism in Canada also informed my analysis. I found the work of Sherene Razack helpful towards understanding the spatializing of colonial violence against aboriginal people and the conceptualization of aboriginal people as socially dead and how that informs the treatment of the deaths of aboriginal people in police or corrections custody. (Razack)

Of particular relevance to this book are studies that document conspicuous absences of consideration of the agencies of those identified as girls. These include the discussion by Fine of "the missing discourse of girls' desire." (Fine) More recently, Deborah Tolman has argued that a discourse of adolescent young women's inequality remains absent from mainstream discourses of the girl. (Tolman) I draw upon the theorization of agency by Lara Karaian, who links the concept of agencies generally with sexual agency. Karaian's work looks critically at how contemporary discourses around "selfies" and "sexting" and more broadly mainstream discussions of adolescent sexuality constitute teenage girls' unintelligibility as sexual subjects. Karaian provides insight into the cultural and legal disavowal of girls' narratives about digital sexual expression. Karaian concludes that their construction as "girls" undermines the ability of teenage females identified as girls to challenge a normative sexual order in which they are often disciplined and blamed for sexual victimization they endure.

I have also drawn on feminist legal theory in working towards an understanding of the unresolved questions of the relationship of changes in written law to changes to experiences of and constraints on subjects in the juridical field. In this regard, I drew on ideas of feminist legal theorist Lacey on feminist law reform and about tensions between the public and private, affective and rational, dimensions of life when law is considered. (Lacey) Carol Smart's (1995) work that challenges the inherent liberalism of law reform initiatives has contributed to my thinking significantly. In particular, Smart's analysis of the "uneven operation of law" involves a contention that law has different components that are distinct enough that law reform in one area may not affect the operation of law in another. Rosemary Coombe's (1989) work about agency in the juridical field is important to the foundational understanding of the functioning of discourses of law within the legal field that is presented in this book. I enjoy and am grateful for the insightful and inspiring example of analysis of legal cases as intersections or sites for the contestation of meanings, power and discourses, including discourses of gender Rebecca Johnson (2002) provides in her work on the *Symes* case. Like Johnson did with the *Symes* case, I have worked in this book to unpack and distill out different discourses, voices and perspectives present within legal and media texts in relation to Ashley Smith's case. My focus is not precisely the same as Johnson's as my primary interest is not in the contestation of meanings within court proceedings but the overall construction of government and meanings both within and outside of sites of production of formal legal discourses.

THEORIES AND METHODS: THIS CASE STUDY

In this research and my thinking generally, I rely on theoretical foundations found in social constructivist ideas about discourse, power, governmentality and necropolitics as well as agency and related non-essentialist feminist theories about the social construction and performance of gender. I thus assume that it is through discursive processes involving power relations that social agents constitute knowledge, situations, social roles, identities, and their relationships with other social agents. Gender and government are both understood as such discursive processes. Law is understood as socially embedded, constructed through and mutually constitutive of, broader practices of governance of bodies, relationships and states. In the following sections, I outline the theoretical foundations from which the inquiry conducted in this research begins. Then, I discuss the epistemological methodology of critical discourse analysis employed in this study. Finally, I more specifically and pragmatically outline the methods of research used as well as some limitations of, and challenges posed by, those methods.

Defining the Case

The boundaries of the "Smith Case" are easily defined in the formal doctrinal discourse of the common law if the "case" is understood as the inquest decision. However, it is not self-evident, from the theoretical foundations of this book, where her case begins and ends. Theoretical foundations based in social constructivism and governmentality studies complicate the questions of what texts do or do not form part of her case. There has, and will be, only one definitive legal decision issued: the inquest verdict rendered on December 19, 2013. However, numerous texts, including formal legal texts, written texts and visual texts are significant to how different actors engage in making meanings of her life and death that reflect, produce and otherwise engage governance. As discussed previously, I am working from Lauren Berlant's understanding of what constitutes a "case." Berlant contends that a "case" is what an event can become. She writes:

> Usually, when an event happens there are no outcomes; it fades into the ordinary pulsations of living on undramatically, perhaps in memory, without being memorable. When an event occurs out of which a case is constructed, it represents a situation in which people are compelled to take its history, seek out precedent, write its narratives, adjudicate claims about it, make a judgment, and file it somewhere: a sick body, a traffic accident, a phenomenon, instance, or detail that captures the interpretive eye. (Berlant, 670)

The "caseness" of a narrative, actor, or situation frames how it can be used by activists. The complex interplay of a large number of formal legal texts with the interpretive judgment of numerous system actors makes the Smith case an intersection of modes of governance and cultural practices within a variety of formal discourses: mental health, constitutional, correctional, legal, medico-legal and youth criminal justice. (Coombe) As is the case with other discourses, legal discourse is constitutive of actors and they have agency within this constructive process. Legal subjectivities are constituted, using narratives, in social realities. Social actors are not fully cognizant of this relationship and are aware of it to different degrees. I draw on the suggestion modeled by Johnson that legal cases can be studied as sites of "intersection and competition of numerous discourses, each asserting the primacy of its vision." (Johnson xiii) Looked at this way, they are stories filled with bad things that happen but which may lack any single discernable "bad guy": stories of multiple villainies which are not about easily blamed individual villains, but which have some distinct narrative threads.

For the purposes of this research, I define the Ashley Smith "case" much as Foucault defined the "case" of Pierre Rivière in his attempt to reconstruct discursive confrontations and battles, and rediscover the operation of those discourses in the relations of power and knowledge. (1975) Foucault understood the Pierre Rivière matter as a "dossier" or:

> a case, an affair, an event that provided the intersection of discourses different in origin ... all of them speak, or appear to be speaking, of one and the same thing: at any rate the burden of these discourses is the affair on June 3. But in their totality and their variety they form neither a composite work nor an exemplary text, but rather a strange confrontation, a contest, a power relation, a battle among discourses and through discourse. And yet, it cannot simply be described as a single battle; for several separate combats were being fought out at the same time and intersected each other. (1975, x)

Thus, for the purposes of this book, the boundaries of what constitutes the Smith case are delineated in this research itself. I am studying the Ashley Smith case as a social case as embodied in the public talk about Ashley Smith, which is neither the expert Smith case, where she is used as an exemplar for liberal activist apparatus, nor precisely the bureaucratic Smith case as officially resolved by the December 2014 CSC response to the inquest verdict. I adopt the theoretical understanding that the delimitations of cases are constructed during the course of research by researchers. (Ragin and Becker) In this research, the Smith case was delimited after my analysis revealed what features should define the limits of the case. The Smith case as understood in this study is not therefore limited to the inquest decision or to the series of formal legal decisions made about Ashley Smith but rather includes a wide variety of texts that are sources of government in addition to that judgment. It therefore includes texts found in the sites of news media, docudramas, reports and legislative debates. I define Ashley Smith's case for the purposes of this study as the set of *public* texts that purport to define truths about her incarceration and death and delimit the timeframe of the production of those truths for the purpose of this case analysis to the time during which she was publicly presented as a case to be resolved by formal legal systems. This is a period that starts when she first appears in youth court and ends with the response of the Correctional Service of Canada to the Inquest verdict, at which point no further official response to Ashley Smith's life or death is required by law. The Smith case is therefore delimited chronologically as taking place between 2002 and the release by Corrections Canada of its response to the inquest recommendations in December 2014.

POWER AND REPRESENTATION IN DISCOURSE

The thinking about discourses of "girl" that this book develops is based in a social constructivist epistemological frame in which discourse is the principal tool used by social communities in constructing social reality. This research starts from an epistemological assumption that, while "the real" world actually exists, our understandings of the world are always based on human imaginations. Our definitions of phenomena are always constructed, or built, by our imaginations in social interaction. It is accepted there is, as Wittgenstein postulated, no knowledge of the real that precedes cultural constructions (Trigg) and, as Rorty theorized, there is no way for actors to objectively perceive the real unmediated by language. (1979) Social groups construct knowledge intersubjectively, collaboratively creating shared meanings and constructing social facts in the process of this collaboration. As Haraway suggests: "social reality is lived social relations, our most important political construction, and a world-changing fiction." (Haraway, 149)

Discourses are systems of shared meanings through which we explain and define our world and our experiences to ourselves. The constructed nature of discourse and the fact that it mediates our understandings of the real can make it hard to distinguish what is inevitable, or unchangeable from what is contingent, or possible to change. This is the starting point from which I examine how legal, expert and educational definitions of the "norm," of what is "normal" for a girl confine some adolescent young women while completely excluding others. Discourses, as understood in this theoretical framework, are regularized ways of speaking and thinking about the world. (Mills) These systems are the social procedures that organize power and knowledge, thereby creating social facts. Through discourse, power relations produce the subjects who speak. Put another way, this book understands discourse as a set of social "conditions of possibility." (Foucault, 1972) These are the social, cultural and historical conditions, rules and structures under which particular statements become understood as true or false. (Mills, 6) The way we *describe* and *define* reality, while it makes possible an understanding of reality, at the same time narrows our understanding of reality and, even, produces *us* insofar as we understand ourselves and each other.

In describing and defining phenomena in the real, discourses contain constructed representations of those phenomena. Representations are powerful socially constructed images formed using implicit pre-existing, widely-accepted cultural "truths." I rely upon constructionist theory of representation set forth by Stuart Hall that relies in turn upon Foucault's study of discourse not primarily as language but as a system of representation.(1972) I accept Hall's formulation that the process of representation itself constitutes the world it represents. The discourses that are dominant in a culture provide a map that gives meaning to the real – these representations do not simply reflect the real. They constitute a "world changing fiction." Representations not only are *not* the real, they do not even derive their value or power, as Said (1984) argues from analyzing textual representations of the Orient, from being *realistic*. Representations are powerful for their ability to define phenomena and to have those definitions accepted, not for being verifiable in some objectively empirical sense.

I also find helpful Hall's (1996) notion of articulation. Speakers and the texts writers produce employ means of articulation when they try to force objects into categories and to unite, understand

and act as a group. Articulation (or articulated combinations of parts) in discourse is what produces identities, structures and alliances.Articulation involves complex structures and it silences certain statements and obscures differences in order to produce unities. It is an inevitable and necessary element of sense-making, and it also produces tensions and problems.

A generative, "bottom up" understanding of power is foundational to this research. I accept the Foucauldian understanding that power is "multiple, relational, heterogeneous and pervasive." (Mills, 14) I rely on Foucault's formulation of discursive power as generative and diffuse. In this understanding, power relations can be likened to a strategic game. (Burchell, Gordon and Miller) Rather than being dictated by a sovereign from the top down, power is dispersed in society, related to knowledge, and productive rather than repressive. As such, in his understanding of discourse, Foucault makes a direct link between knowledge and power. Power produces knowledge.(Hunt and Wickham) Power produces what is socially understood to be reality, objects and rituals of truth. It is "mundanely productive... not spectacularly conspiratorial." (*ibid* at 81) Power relations involve struggles between discourses for pre-eminence in defining the real.

When discourses define "the real," they make certain things unsayable and constitute subjects' identities. I agree with Judith Butler's (1997) understanding that discourses, in giving actors names, provide us a way in which to exist. Thus constitutive of the real, discourses have power in the face of which actors are vulnerable and only within which our social existence is possible. Discourses limit options by defining them. Discursive constructions — the way things in "the real" are described and defined in systems of power and knowledge — bring about certain events in reality by shaping the conditions of possibility for what can happen in social interactions. For instance, a set of conditions of possibility are defined by various discourses or constructs of the "girl." These discourses are always being generated in social interaction, and each interaction has potential to shape and reshape how phenomena (like girls) are defined. Discourse is what configures the dimensions of the "stamp" of "girl" that is impressed upon adolescent young women. (Lipkin) These conditions are constantly contested; there is no grand plan and while power is not evenly dispersed but clustered in particular locations, there is no conspiratorial junta of designers. Power is diffuse; discourses collide. Discursive social maps and the processes of mapping are always in flux and they are messy.

This approach accepts that in mainstream discourse, terms are often defined in binary opposition. The binary definition of the norm by opposites requires the construction of monsters for the constitution of the norm. "Abnormals," such as mean/nasty/unruly girls, are binary opposites against which the norm of nice/proper girl is defined. As such, the traits defined as aberrant by opposites are constitutive of the norm. Foucault characterizes as intimate the relationship between rationality in the public sphere and the exclusion of certain categories of people as "mad," or incapable of rational thought, rationality needs madness for its self-definition. Foucault (1975) argues that monstrous[11] abnormals are invoked in processes of government to delimit what constitutes the normal and define it by opposites. Monsters are seen as the effect of a simultaneous breach of both law and nature. (Sharpe) Abnormals are monsters whose monstrosity is not visible but behavioural and internalized. By being assumed to breach the "proper" order of both nature and law by failing to enact feminine passivity while breaching legal and social rules, aberrant "girls" are the other against which the norm can be defined.

Narratives

My understanding of narrative is built on social constructivist narrative theory. I am working with an understanding of narrative as one rhetorical mode of writing or speaking. It is a mode that engages with, relies upon and the study of which can reveal, pre-existing discourses in relation to phenomena (like "girls"), as technologies. These technologies invoke, reconstruct, and can alter, existing interactive, social and cultural practices and identities. (Bamberg) Narrative is a genre of text that has a plot, characters, a beginning, middle, and an end. It contains symbolic meanings that are encoded consciously or subconsciously, by its author. (Bhabha) I also work from understandings that narratives are crucial to the construction and performance of legality. Legal narratives are also cultural narratives. Stories that engage pre-existing cultural discourses define cases in law as well as shaping people's understandings of governmentality. Narratives are a key technology by which law is communicated, adjudicative acts are justified, and their principles are explained. (Moran) Like Cunliffe's (2007) study of the prosecutions of Kathleen Folbigg, I work from an understanding that narratives have governmental effects. They function as technologies of government, including as a technology of the self. I also understand that narratives of crime stories play a crucial role in differentiating the criminal from the non-criminal. (Herzog) This book starts from an assumption that narrative accounts give readers access to processes of identity construction by subjects and communities. Telling a story is a way of speaking to someone else about one's self, but it is also speech about the teller's identity as well as the teller's social context and the widely accepted assumptions and discourses circulating in that context. (Chatman; Genette; Josselson) As Catherine Reissman (1993) suggests, researchers should be cautious about interpreting any account of events or of oneself, any story, as the "truth." Riessman emphasizes that "we cannot give voice, but we do hear voices that we record and interpret." On the basis of this epistemological assumption, I do not seek in this book to tell "the" "true" story of Ashley Smith. Were I to try to do so, I would just create another representation of her that would be problematic in many of the ways existing representations are problematic. Ashley Smith's inner world will be forever unknown and unknowable. Rather, what can be known, examined, and understood better, through this book is a narrative of how she is represented by different actors, following different narrative structures, in the case bearing her name. This book is a meta-text. I am seeking to write a story about the stories told, a narrative about narratives.

GOVERNMENTALITY: RISK, SECURITY AND NECROPOLITICS

This study looks at what Ashley Smith's case can reveal about how the modern state is deployed as a matrix of bureaucratic power, in particular when the governed are identified as adolescent girls. Research was conducted into how the conduct of Smith's conduct was operationalized, how power circulates in the contemporary Canadian state, and how discourses of the state, virtue and binary gender hierarchies are governmentalized. In particular, the mobilization of government by a rationalized bureaucratic system is examined. In this study, I build upon the work of Gerlach and Hamilton in their critical theorization of the amorality and even immorality of "monstrous bureaucracy" in the rationalized neoliberal deployment of the power of the state.(Hamilton and Gerlach)

I work from Mitchell Dean's understanding that the concept of governmentality provides "a language and a framework for linking questions of government, authority and politics and questions of identity, self and person." (Dean, 13) Regimes and practices of governmentality are reinforced and shaped by various forms of knowledge. Expert discourses of medicine, psychology, social work and law have power in defining representations of the real. Regimes of practices are dependent upon these expert forms of knowledge.

The concern of governmentality studies is with the government "of human conduct in all contexts."(Dean, 4) The concept of governmentality in this sense relies on Foucault's analysis of modern government grounded in his theories of discursive power. (1982) However, Foucault's governmentality studies were an unfinished project of his later career. It is later theorists who developed the theorization of governmentality that underpins this book. As Burchell, Gordon and Miller describe them, governmentality studies look at a "dimension of historical existence which Foucault did most to try to describe."(1991, ix) I adopt the definition used by Dean, Gordon, Burchell and others elaborating the work of Foucault: "government rationality" and "governmentality" are synonyms. Government can be thought of broadly as the "conduct of conduct." (Graham and Miller) Thus governmentality involves particular mentalities, arts and regimes of government that have emerged since early modern Europe.(Graham and Miller, 2) Government involves regulation by various systems and leaders including processes of government as in the sense "conduct oneself." As Walters writes, sites of governance are spaces where technologies of power and technologies of the self intersect. (Walters, 15)

Foucault's "pastoral" concept of government links everyday subjectivities and practices in local sites with governing. Governmentality studies are not about "strategic relations" between equals/ peers or about states of absolute domination. When government is discussed, it is not just in terms of war and struggle but also of the arts and techniques to deliberately shape subjects' behaviour according to particular sets of norms.(Dean) The place of convergence between techniques of the self and techniques of domination or discipline is governmentality. It is not located in any one regime of law but in interactions that happen in all kinds of mundane as well as grand circumstances: power and relations of power circulate everywhere and converge at particular locations at certain events.

As such, the state of government is not a thing but a practice. (Foucault, 2004) The notion of governmentality is related to the conceptual theorization of legality, as those meanings, sources of authority, and cultural practices that are in some sense legal even if that are not approved or acknowledged by official legal doctrine. (Ewick and Silbey) In this understanding, law is not separate from but enmeshed within broader social discourses and processes. Rather, law and society are mutually constitutive; law is not an external force to which society is subject, but represents a dynamic set of codes, practices, categories and deliberations that both shape and are shaped by broader social, political, and economic logics, contexts and relations.

Government that takes place in mundane sites in opaque ways can be at least as significant as the practices of government in a grander, formal or legislative sense. Law is socially and culturally embedded. Studies about governmentality such as the one undertaken here look at the cultural force of the power embedded in discourse and how that power applies in the criminal justice and correctional systems as well as to people in general, whose actions and identities are constrained by reference to the power of law. Foucault (1991) talks about the importance of "microprocesses" or pastoral power. Later theorists have developed the idea that these microprocesses and the shepherding processes by which they are deployed constitute governmentality. By this, Foucault means the mundane, everyday minor decisions most legal scholarship, for example, doesn't consider. Microprocesses constitute operations of power: those in my study would include specific, day-to-day decisions and actions of individual corrections officers, psychologists and educators in administering routinized sanctions. Governmentality studies try to track power in its many forms: its techniques, its strategies and technologies. (Hunt and Wickham, 45)

This book examines "how, where and with what effect law is produced in and through commonplace social interactions [we can ask].... How do our social roles and statuses, our relationships, our obligations, prerogatives, and responsibilities, our identities, and our behaviors bear the imprint of law?" (Sarat, 20) Put another way, in this book, I study ways in which people's interactions reflect and reproduce the cultural power of law in a wide variety of contexts, like schools and homes and hospitals and media.

In considering this cultural power of law, I work from Ong's understanding of neoliberalism as "a new relationship between government and knowledge through which governing activities are recast as non-political and non-ideological problems that need technical solutions ... neoliberalism as exception is introduced where market driven calculations are ... [used] in the management of populations and the administration of special spaces." (Ong, 3) Neoliberalism refers to governmental approaches that involve radical de-regulation of markets as well as reductions in government spending, privatizations of formerly public utilities and free trade. I rely on risk and security theory in my understanding of the governmental logics engaged in neoliberalism. According to Beck and Giddens, as well as others, in a "risk society" the dominant understanding is that risks need to be contained through scientific, systematized and ultimately actuarial forms of governance. Ericson and Haggerty, in their book *Policing the Risk Society* argue that one key defining feature of the risk society is the use of actuarial knowledge of risk to define and manage danger. These authors link increased bureaucratization of policing and increased surveillance to demands for quantification in assessment of risk. They claim: "in risk society, governance is directed at the provision of security ... [defined as] a situation in which dangers are minimized."

Risk logic frames government as a scientific project. It de-politicizes governmental decisions, and removes moral questions from determinations about what should be done in particular cases. Results are sought to be optimized, risks are sought to be mitigated, and responsibility for the existence and control of undesirable behaviour is displaced onto the citizen. Criminologists such as Hannah-Moffatt theorize that with the flawed logic of risk rationality there is a diffusion of responsibility. In this logic, no one is accountable for results just for responses to particular specific orders, directives or rules. Obedience is a paramount virtue over all others in an inmate, in a guard, and in a low-level bureaucrat, and the key considerations in governance of carceral settings need to be risk and containment.

Security governance, as theorized by Foucault and developed by subsequent governmentality theorists, involves the production of sovereign power through management of populations as "crowds" whereby security is constitutive of the understood freedom of the population and "crowd control" becomes a pervasive goal of the state and populations in this way are treated as "de-democratized, governable social units." (Foucault) Crowds are understood as perpetually both threatened and threatening, and they cannot really act as political subjects. Security of the population is managed in this governmental logic pre-emptively through precautions taken to prevent risks from materializing.

In risk, as in security, logics, the calculus to be undertaken is between trust and a socially accepted level of risk. This drives the production of "inexhaustibly detailed and continuous risk management knowledge." Ericson and Haggerty quote Beck for the proposition that risk society is steeped in "negative logic" in its primary concern with the distribution of "bads" or dangers. Concepts of risk are, according to Ericson and Haggerty, displacing constructions of normality and deviance in managing populations. Actuarial risk calculations seek to produce containment and elimination of risks to maximize the security of society as a whole. Probabilistic thinking and risk technologies operate "in tandem" with foreboding. In this logical system, the "least risky" or "least bad" outcome is optimal. Goods are not sought; rather, bads are sought to be contained. Probability calculations are employed to "tame chance" while they cannot eliminate it. Risk calculi are used to eliminate uncertainties and are future oriented, bringing probability calculations about future possibilities into the present.

Risk logic helps produce regularity and control.

Risk discourse is largely unconcerned with individual morality; it promotes a systemic or scientific macro-morality: a utilitarian calculus of the greatest good for the greatest number. This risk based logic interlocks with the logic of exception that is discussed below. Risk governance is widely understood as prominent feature of late modern governance. The "rational" administrative, organizational and governmental logics of risk are dominant in the early twenty-first century. Looked at in the context of risk society theorizations, the risk-based prison is a Benthamite panopticon. In the logic of risk, the inmate is imagined as a subject that is "panoptically transparent, manageable and contained." Risk governance fosters development of what is sought to be a science of the state. Power is predicated on the classification of agents by certain categorizations, like the coding inmates are assigned in CSC custody. Risk society logic is associated with institutionalization of governance: "institutionalization moves authorship away from the individual. Rather than improvising, people do what the institutional script prescribes. Institutionalization is a process of circumscribing human agency and creating routine enactments." The logic of risk has previously been theorized to be dominant in CSC's bureaucracy, and in particular in its management of woman offenders, especially in the work of Hannah-Moffatt.

Security governance as theorized by Foucault and developed by subsequent governmentality theorists involves the production of sovereign power through management of populations as "crowds," whereby security is constitutive of the understood freedom of the population and "crowd control" becomes a pervasive goal of the state and populations in this way are treated as "de-democratized, governable social units." (Wichum, 165) Security of the population is managed in this governmental logic pre-emptively through precautions taken to prevent risks from materializing.

I find the concepts of biopower developed from Foucault's analysis of the subjugation of bodies and populations, useful to the analysis of the consolidation of sovereign power effected through the use of discipline and incarceration of subjects. Risk logic can be understood to function as a form of biopower by classifying populations. Production of truth claims through the dominant discourse of risk not only shapes how we think and act, it also legitimizes strategies that are applied to overcome undesirable social phenomena, submerging or preventing questions about the motives underlying these claims. Further, production of truths through the discourse of risk can also mask oppressive outcomes risk calculations may have on actors excluded or excepted from the norm as undesirable or risky as well as how populations come to be constituted as populations. By "governing through crime," neoliberal western societies have constructed inmates as an enemy "race." The logic of exception permits various inmates in a variety camps to be expelled from political community. The "war on crime" and linked construction of culture of fear produce criminals who become inmates, both of which are an enemy other to be contained. Simon notes that, in the U.S. context as of the late 20th century, there is a racial "skewing" of burgeoning prison populations whereby "for the first time since slavery, a definable group of Americans lives on a more or less permanent basis in a state of non-freedom."

Simon argues that the strategy in the U.S. of "governing through crime" has produced a "major reorientation of governance" around risk and fear of crime. The racialization of inmates has a dual aspect. They are in many cases people whose embodiment is already racialized: in Canada, they are disproportionately aboriginal and in the U.S., they are disproportionately African-American. Further, even where they do not hail from racialized groups, once incarcerated, inmates become understood as a subhuman race.

While I find Foucault's notion of biopower useful, it is more specifically on related concepts of necropower found in the work of Agamben and Mbembe that I base a good deal of my theorizing in this book. I find the theoretical framework of necropolitics especially useful because it allows for understanding of certain subjects as occupying statuses that are neither fully living nor dead, and it offers an accounting for the power of the state to impose death and death-like status on subjects. Necropolitics provides an analytical framework to aid in understanding how the death of Ashley Smith happened in a series of stages. On this analysis, the day of her actual biological death is perhaps the least contingent, most pre-determined and in many ways one of the less significant events, that contributed to her exclusion from political community. It was this exclusion that started in motion the series of linked events that led to her incarceration and social, political, juridical and biological deaths. I understand necropolitics to encompass the power of the state to impose a variety of forms of "death." Mbembe adds to Foucault's understandings of biopower and sovereignty the concept of necropower, which goes beyond merely "inscribing bodies within disciplinary apparatuses." (Mbembe, 34) Rather, in the era of necropower, weapons are deployed "in the interest of maximum destruction of persons and the creating of death-worlds, new and unique forms of social existence in which vast populations are subjected to conditions of life conferring upon them the status of living dead." (Mbembe, 40) These populations are not disciplined in the sense Foucault talks about with reference to biopower. They are excluded; they are managed. Necropower is the formation of power dominant in what Mbembe calls late modern colonial occupation: governmentality in "management of the multitudes." While Mbembe doesn't speak directly about solitary confinement in correctional institutions, I would suggest that solitary confinement in all its forms and named by all of its euphemisms (e.g. "therapeutic quiet, "administrative segregation" and "suicide watch") is such a death world.

I accept the argument that has been advanced by Giorgio Agamben, Carl Schmitt and Aihwa Ong (Ong, 7) that the state of exception is at the heart of neoliberalism. The fundamental idea is that the state can do anything in the interests of governance, without limits, through the invocation of the state of exception. What Razack identifies as "camps" governed by the logic of exception are various. They are "distinguished by a legally authorized suspension of law and the creation of communities of people without the right to have rights.... [they] are places where the rules of the world cease to apply." (Razack, 7) Razack relies for this proposition on the writing of Giorgio Agamben, who theorizes "the camp as the biopolitical paradigm of the modern." (1998)

Relatedly, I also find useful the concept of "*homo sacer*" as developed by Agamben. In his work, Agamben (1998) looks at the concept of "*homo sacer,*" a liminal being that exists *between* living and dying, people whose lives are easily forfeit, whose deaths are not *murder*. I find helpful Agamben's discussion of the wolf and the ban. He looks at werewolves as those who are "banned" as ancient forms of excluded persons: "the man who has been banned from the city." (Agamben, 63) Agamben identifies carceral inmates as, in some instances, members of the *homo sacer* category, or people who have been banned. Agamben sees the *homo sacer* as an exemplary figure that illumines the logic of exception. In my analysis of the several forms of death to which Ashley Smith is subject through her experiences of social exclusion, including incarceration, I build on Agamben's concept of *homo sacer*, which I argue Smith becomes when she becomes a "terminal" inmate. I also argue that Smith exemplifies the extreme reduction of the logics to which members of western societies are subject.

Further, it is also in part by building on this reasoning that I posit that, to understand the Smith case as a site of contending discourses, we must look beyond the final moments, or even months or years of her incarceration to the conditions of possibility that produced her as someone to become *homo sacer* before she was ever imprisoned. Also useful as a foundational assumption to this book is the theorization by Agamben that, in the logic of exclusion underlying the construct of the *homo sacer*, the political body and the physical body are inextricably linked: politics are at issue in the subjects' biological bodies. (Agamben, 105) This connection is of great importance in explaining what is at stake in the Smith case: the confinement and death of her biological body is inextricably linked to the silencing of her political voice and the voices of other adolescent girls.

According to Razack, states of exception operate in a variety of carceral regimes. Razack builds on Agamben's assertion that the camp has become the rule and our culture is traditionally defined by a logic of exception. Razack argues that it the proliferation of "camps" is a central defining characteristic of the contemporary western "empire" and that the culture of exception core to neoliberalism underpins the eviction of increasing numbers of people from political community. Ferguson's (2014) recent critique of mass incarceration in the United States also develops the critique of the logic of exception that is introduced by Mbembe.

According to Ferguson, the dominant governmental approach in the U.S. is increasingly to lock people away in an attempt to solve social problems. Further, Ferguson elaborates on Mbembe's logic of exclusion: the logic of exception that allows a community to dismiss challenging people who have complex needs and problems that defy easy solution has no obvious stopping point and is consequently very dangerous. In this logic of leaving certain people behind, it is predictable that the community tends to dismiss all problems and to, rather than interrogate conditions creating it, accept misfortune as a natural state of being for those defined or pathologized as unfortunate.

This book does not confine its analysis of governmentality to questions about formal law. Starting from an understanding of governance as culturally embedded, it engages in cultural study of law. Cultural studies of law look at legality in popular culture. Stuart Hall is an early leading thinker in respect of cultural studies of law. Hall examined the social life of law's images and talked about the "rhetorical power of film to affect legal consciousness." (Sarat, 5) As cultural legal studies scholar Sarat describes the cultural studies of law, his project is to 1) treat popular itself as a kind of legal text and 2) address the question of whether and how law-in-media affects subjectivity: does law-in-media "open up new possibilities for understanding will, action and responsibility?" (Sarat, 6)

In this theoretical understanding, media is a site for production of governance. Media do not simply "get the law wrong." What media reports do in discourse is not a question of translation. Media actually participate in the creation of the juridicial field. This book, as does Manderson, takes media and other forms of popular culture seriously as sources of law. Manderson contends that popular culture

> has adopted traditional forms ... [it] emerges as a powerful conservative force with its own concepts of law and justice, its own practices and its own memories ... [it is] *a source of law*, a record and memory of subterranean practices that have not lost their power to constitute legal actions and ideas." (Sarat, 7)

Manderson studies what he sees as law *in* media. He sees media as providing a "site of resistance to formal law ... the effort to preserve or resuscitate an alternative reality." (Sarat, 6) Government and the juridical field as understood in this way is not found only in legislation and courtrooms but also in the news, in movies, in television dramas, in crime fiction and in social media postings. Legality is everywhere and yet its location is not permanently fixed. In particular moments, power acts in particular situations.

In addition to media discourses, expert discourses are also productive of governmentality. It would be difficult to overestimate the significance of expert discourses in late modern governance. Foucault himself drew clear lines linking discipline in the sense of governance and constraint and *the disciplines*. In this book, I start from the theoretical position that the med/psy-discourses exist "on the underside of law" and naturalize the legal power to punish while they legalize the technical power to discipline. Foucault called this the "great carceral continuum" (Hunt and Wickhan) consisting of disciplinary practices that act on the body and on the soul. Hunt and Wickham cite Foucault for the argument that "law comes to be colonized by the new disciplines being invaded by practices of observation and training" and contend that "this is readily evident in contemporary juvenile justice." (Hunt and Wickham, 47) The "paradox of modernity" is that law then seeks to recode the disciplines in the form of law. (*ibid*, 48)

AGENCY

As understood in this research, the concept of governmentality relies upon individual actors having agencies. While Foucault's understandings of discipline and power have been criticized as over-deterministic, subsequent theorists have developed the governmentality framework to account for the possibilities of human creativity and the radical indeterminacy of the moment. Critiques of governmentality scholarship or certainly of Foucault often focused on his failure to account for creative agency on the part of actors. For example, Dean makes clear that the subject governed is an *actor* and therefore the actor is to some degree "a loci of freedom." (Dean, 13) Interpersonally powerful agents are capable of developing "local status." (Thornborrow) This is Thornbor-row's term for actors who are particularly skilled at negotiating interactions and at performances of social identity like gender in ways that allow them to accrue power despite an otherwise low social position.

I understand agents not as passive recipients of predetermined discourses and systems but as interpreting social actors who engage in creative work. They agentically reconstruct discursive practices that set out the juridical field of social practice whether or not they do so consciously. I rely on formulations of agency as an actor's role in *doing power*. For this understanding of agency, I am relying on theorizations of agency in becoming subject as developed by MacLaren, Failer and Shotwell as they write about self creation in oppressive circumstances and especially Mackenzie.(Campbell) For the purposes of this book, I work from a definition of agency as "the temporarily constructed engagement by actors of different structural environments which, through the interplay of habit, imagination, and judgment, both reproduces and transforms those structures in interactive response to the problems posed by changing historical situations." (Emirbayer and Mische, 970)

Agency can be understood as an agent's capacity to act creatively, deliberately and reflexively. However, the freedom of agents to act takes place within contexts. Just as they cannot *know* the real unmediated by discourse, agents cannot *act* except as embedded in discourse. Their self-awareness is constructed in discourse and they remake discourses intersubjectively. Actors have a material-ity that exists prior to discourse. However, *subjects* do not exist prior to discourse. Subjects' reflexive awareness of their power to act is necessarily constrained by their self-understanding. Because actors do not exist prior to discourse, their reflexive awareness of their power to act is necessarily constrained by their self-understanding.

This capacity to act does not exist in the context of a Cartesian mind/ body dualism and conflicts with liberal theories about the individual. As feminist theorists have developed specifically with reference to the effects of gendering on subjectivity, I draw on an understanding that agency is *embodied*. (Campbell, Meynell and Sherwin) Differently situated actors' agencies are constrained in different ways. Variously situated girls have their self-awareness and freedom limited in different ways from more privileged actors especially adult white men, whose masculinity is constructed in such a way as to accord them a great deal of relative social power. In a variety of ways, to varying degrees, many adolescent girls are embodied as agents engaged in navigating the terrain of dominant scripts that place them in a double-bind, or no-win position. At the same time, the capacities that allow someone to amass local status potentially threaten existing systemic hierarchies.

Just as I accept critiques of Foucault's overdeterministic (early) views of agency,[12] I accept that his work left a gap in that it did not sufficiently account for systems and institutional power. Foucault underestimated or neglected the role of law in regulation and the normative content of legal rules. (Hunt and Wickham) In this study, I draw on later theorists who understand law as socially embedded but see its content as highly relevant. Notably among them, Hunt and Wickham criticize Foucault for equating the law with pre-modern forms of power. They contend that Foucault failed to consider the range of laws applying to the mundane, neglecting to consider "everyday" law. (Hunt and Wickham, 71) I draw on Coombe (1989) for a theoretical formulation of agency in the context of legal systems and structures that allows for a simultaneous analysis of both "big" and "little" power. This book applies theoretical governmentality question asked by Hunt, Wickham and Walters in reference to legal studies of a particular event: I ask how law is implicated within social relations, neither assuming the power of law nor its ineffectiveness.

As understood in this study, the state is not privileged as the central site of governance but it is still an important locus of power. The discursive content of formal law is relevant in interaction with other forms of governance. The ideas of neoliberal politics and hierarchical binary gender relations are institutional rationalities mobilized in governance. I adopt Coombe's claim that systems and structures and agency and practices *all matter* to call for "critical empiricism" in legal scholarship. There are links between the subjective consciousness of actors and the structure of legal discourse; the error of liberalism is in assuming a complete and autonomous subject that exists prior to discourse. Coombe's theory of practice allows for understanding of what she terms the "pervasive structurality of experience without denying human agency and creativity." (Coombe, 83)

The written language of law has an objective reality because actors within systems feel bounded by it, and it has a materiality because actors performing adherence to it create barriers for actors who violate it. It is the socially constructed realities that come to surround law and not legal language itself that limit the possibilities of interpretation. (Coombe, 108) So, it is the "particular conditions of a historically specific interpreting community" that shape governance in the juridical field. Those interpreting conventions undergo ongoing transformations and are produced in enactment and re-enactment. The written language of the law is important as a tool manipulated by its users. It can be turned by historically oppressed groups on their historical oppressors with success. (*ibid*, 94-95)

My understanding of narratives is linked to the understanding of agency from which I work. I rely on Judith Butler's theorization of narrative agency. (2005) Because our agencies are always already shaped within the constraints of contexts that are continuously engaged in shaping them, one's narrations of oneself are always partial. Narrations are always interrupted by the existence before one comes into being of the conditions of possibility one inhabits. Multiple narratives of one's self, and, specifically here, of the Ashley Smith case are possible and all accounts are always fiction, however, narration is necessary because: "only the narrated self can be intelligible, survivable." (Butler, 34-35) As Butler puts it:

> "I" does not mean we cannot narrate it; it only means that at the moment when we narrate we become speculative philosophers or fiction writers ... prehistory interrupts the story I have to give of myself, makes every account of myself partial and failed, and constitutes, in a way, my failure to be fully accountable for my actions, my final "irresponsibility," one for which I may be forgiven only because I could not do otherwise. This not being able to do otherwise is our common predicament." (Butler, 78)

Thus, this book looks at narratives produced in Ashley Smith's case as constituted stories involving power. In doing so, it contributes to the field of critical inquiry that looks at the operation of law as governance. (Hunt and Wickham) In this understanding, power is understood as a process. Social hierarchies and structures continue to be real because they are continuously re-enacted and reconstructed. In consequence, each social interaction, each moment, is both inside discourse and still filled with possibilities. The possibilities an agent can realize are limited by their consciousness which is in turn interrupted before it begin by the existence of their subjectivity within pre-existing discursive frames.

FEMINIST THEORY

Gender is an important dimension in the matrix of power that constrains the actions and consciousness of actors. My understanding of the agencies of girls as they are governed is complicated by theoretical insights feminist theorists have had into the role played by discourses of gender in producing peculiar difficulties faced by marginalized agents when they act. As discussed above with reference to agency in general, I understand that girls in part know themselves in dominant discourses through definitions set forth by adults, usually adult males, who seek to define their reality.(Irigaray) As critically unpacked in Gilbert and Gubar's (1979) *Madwoman in the Attic*, masculinist discourses (like fiction written by men, or the narratives in criminal cases) tend to imprison female actors in binary narrative structures that accord them subject positions of "angel" or "demon."

It is particularly difficult for actors identified as girls to exercise their agencies where they are tasked with navigating the juridical field. Girls navigating governance frameworks are exercising agencies in ways that are complicated by blankness and silences around the particularities of their experience, as is discussed in Chapter 2. As feminist legal theorists have posited, there are manifold and complex ways in which women and girls have been excluded from participating actively in legal processes and in the formation and application of law. (Naffine: Conaghan; Dowd; Jacobs, Rheaume) When adolescent females act in juridical space, they are acting in a space that is defined by and for middle class adult white men. They are strangers in this space: representation and articulation of their presence and action is difficult in the ways that representation of and by subaltern ethnic groups, presents problems. (Spivak) Further, this book builds on theoretical foundations laid by feminist and girls' studies theorists, who have analyzed silences around girls' agencies in other contexts. (Karaian; Fine)

These understandings of gendered agencies and the social roles of formal law in turn rely upon non-essential, social constructivist understandings of gender. Relying on a social constructivist epistemology, I start from non-essentialist, constructivist theories of gender and identity. An important starting assumption is that social power relations and knowledge about girls produced in interlocking discourses have shaped what "girl" means as an idea, discourse and cultural figure. (Little and Hoskins) In starting from this assumption, I draw on the work of feminist discourse theorists (Sawicki; Haraway; Butler).

I understand that the self, in being constituted in discourse, is not an extension of an inner essence or a particular (male/female) sexual body. I rely on Butler generally and Haraway's "Cyborg Manifesto" to deconstruct the notion of the integrated, stable, authentic female identity. There is a close relationship between social discipline and the body. This book builds on the understanding that the disciplinary power of the discourse of femininity on the female body of adolescent young women circulates, fixing at particular moments at particular events or intersections. (Bartky) Government as understood by governmentality theorists is actively engaged in constructing gender. Representations of the girl contain and reinscribe existing cultural power relations. The notion of girl is socially constructed in different ways, some of which are dominant or hegemonic, and those constructions have material consequences for adolescent females who are — or are not — identified as girls.

Gender as a discourse is naturalized and both produces and restricts an agent's mode of being. The discursively produced identities of girls involve and invoke the body. Subjects labeled as — or seeking to be identified as — girls, actively perform actions and discipline their bodies, even surgically altering themselves, to conform to what a "good" girl should do and be. Behaviours and other aspects of conduct together produce certain characteristics that are in turn taken as evidence of a naturalized female essence and a difference between men and women that is binary. While the feminine is regarded as the more 'natural' gender, as women are seen as linked more than men to biological aspects of their embodiment being successfully feminine requires artifice. I accept Butler's theorization of gender and even sexed bodies unstable identifiers, as "imprinted." (Riviere) Masculinity and femininity are disciplines of the body requiring socially mandatory *work* for their production. Gendering is therefore a powerful and pervasive method of social control. (Balsamo)

Multiple and overlapping identities of "girl" are naturalized, gendered representations produced and articulated in discourse. Discourses of the girl reflect and reinscribe certain power relations. Discourses of the girl are naturalized so that "girlhood" shapes an agent's mode of being in particular ways. Those agents who are unsuccessful in performing femininity - or refuse to do so - are seen as un-natural. In the western neoliberal cultural mainstream, while the construct "girl" is discursively constructed as *inferior* to "man" and "boy," girls are also *threatening*. Feminist discourse theorists posit that as a result of their construction in opposition to the normative: "boys," "girls" are perpetually in need of containment and control. As a result, adolescent young women/ girls become subjects as they are *subjected* to particular disciplinary techniques and receive a great deal of disciplinary attention.

The performance of feminine gender by adolescent young women has broad social significance. It is important for social reproduction that adolescent young women play along with ascribed nurturing roles. "Proper" mothering and constrained sexuality are important pre-requisites for hierarchies to be reproduced. Failures or refusals of certain adolescent young women to perform their gender acceptably and/ or traditionally within prescribed parameters, are seen as threats to social order.

The naturalized identity of girl is not single-stranded. Rather, it is intersectional with other aspects of social identity. Differently situated girls experience situations differently. Discourses of the girl are specific manifestations of certain patterns in power relations at particular times. This theoretical foundation allows for troubling of monolithic category of girl and the production of analysis that gets beneath the girl/boy binary. No one is ever just a "girl" without some sort of qualifier. Every actor occupies other social locations, including their racialization, sexual identity, social class and religious or ethnic heritage, all of which are constitutive of what is meant by girl. Indeed, middle class socioeconomic status and racialized whiteness are always already constitutive of the "girl" when the figuration is invoked without qualifiers. The implicit blankness of "girl" without a qualifier (like "black" "aboriginal" or "third world") actually refers to a particular (white) racialization and (middle class) social location understood to be the norm.

Processes of production in interlocking discursive sites shape and continue to shape what identities are available to adolescent young women and in what ways. As Driscoll points out, the construct of girl is produced in a number of intersecting locations.(Driscoll) Schools, hospitals, courtrooms, prisons, mental health therapy contexts, and homes are spaces where individual identities and discourses of the girl inter-weave. Representations of the girl are involved in the deployment of government by the modern state.

METHODS

I work with intersectional methodology (Johnson) to analyze interlocking regimes of oppression that are active in late modern Canada by looking at how they *intersect* in an event in which a problem is constructed to be governed. This problematization is presented by Ashley Smith's case. More specifically, this book critically unpacks dominant discourses about Smith as girl in the juridical field (including legal, media and expert sites) and how the interlocking logics of governmental frameworks deployed in in a variety of sites rendered the possibility of Smith's political subjectivity, including her agency and in particular, her female sexual agency problematic and even unwritable and unknowable.

This book attempts to understand socially produced meanings. of Ashley Smith as "girl." It takes Ashley Smith's case as a partic-ular ""event" where conflicts, confluences and tensions between existing ways of become visible. (Hunt and Wickham, 21) It asks what combination of circumstances, what power relationships, and what institutional accretions of power in seemingly unrelated fields gives rise to a particular outcome. (*ibid*, 7) In seemingly unrelated fields gives rise to a particular outcome. And, it inquires into what Lauren Berlant calls the "caseness" of Ashley Smith, asking of what general type various figures of Ashley Smith are constructed as a case. This is a social constructivist study that deploys the tool of critical discourse analysis to make visible the implicit ideological content of articulations in discourses of Ashley Smith. Other important methodological tools on which I rely are the concepts of representation, figuration, articulation and the tool of critical discourse analysis as an analytical exercise. In this book, I work with the concept of figuration. (De Laurentis) Figuration is the process by which a representation is given a particular form: "a figure is the simultaneously material and semiotic product of certain [discursive] processes." (Casteneda, 3-4) A figuration is "a specific configuration of knowledges, practices and power." (*ibid*) Accordingly, I qualitatively study texts from media sources and official legal texts to determine what figurations of Ashley Smith emerge in these cultural domains.

This book looks at complex sets of conditions interacting. Critical discourse analysis is employed as a critical and interpretive methodology to reveal operations of power in places where familiar social, administrative and political discourses tend to mask or normalize it. (Shapiro, 1) It is a way of studying the contingencies and past events that produce constructs thought to be immutable and inevitable in the present — at how conditions of possibility develop that show the sometimes discontinuous and chaotic becoming of the present. Thus, the book studies figurations of Ashley Smith as girl as technologies of power that emerge in three discursive sites: formal legal documents, docudramas and print media texts.

What this methodological orientation can reveal is insight into how a set of systems and rationalities came together in manifold small ways to produce Ashley Smith's case. It creates an account of local production of governance in specific sites. It examines and diagnoses specific conditions enabling the maintenance of certain power structures of legitimacy and authority. This study looks at figures of Smith and of the "girl" that emerge in texts produced in her case as technologies of power. I adopt Foucault's (1988) understanding of technologies of power as "technologies ... which determine the conduct of individuals and submit them to certain ends or domination, an objectivizing of the subject." It explores, troubles and complicates what these figurations do as technologies of power. My analysis develops knowledge about systems of power and specifically exposes the operations of power in the Smith case where familiar discourses obfuscate them. (Shapiro) I look for the governmental *work* in relation to organizing social power being done by and through the related figurations of Ashley Smith as girl that emerge in her case.

I use critical discourse analysis to look at how Smith is described and how existing social structures of governance are articulated through those descriptions. Critical Discourse Analysis (CDA) is a methodological framework for conducting research into how discourses function as instruments of power and control. CDA looks at social structures and processes involved in text production. It is an analytical way to make visible relationships of causality that are otherwise opaque and to see links between texts and broader social and cultural power relations and discursive processes. (Fairclough) CDA makes visible interlocking webs of domination, power, discrimination, and control that exist in language. (Wodak) It is a framework for looking at discourse as tool in the social construction of reality. (Van Leeuwen; Jewitt) CDA relies on a basic assumption that there is a dialectical or mutually constitutive relationship between events and the discursive context in which they are embedded. (Phillips and Hardy) CDA looks at the production of reality that is performed by discourses and at how ideologies and existing relations of power are presented in and maintained by discursive sites studied. I draw on major contributions to the development of CDA by Norman Fairclough, who developed methodological tools for looking at discourse as a social practice that contributes to the maintenance and reproduction of existing social practices.

I conduct a qualitative critical discourse analysis of the ways in which Ashley Smith is represented and analyze the figurations of her as "girl" that emerge in three discursive sites involved in her case. I seek to discern in texts the "dialogical struggle (or struggles) as reflected in the privileging of a particular discourse and the marginalization of others." (Phillips and Hardy, 25) The focus of this analysis is on how power is connected to meanings and how discursive constructions of an event produce a social reality that is taken for granted. I would like to make visible the taken-for-granted assumptions about "girls" that are opaquely present in discourses about Smith's case, and to specifically diagnose how these discourses obscure from view and divert attention away from her agency.

To describe this research on a more technical level: the study qualitatively analyzes how Smith is represented and emerges as a figure in a variety of texts from each of the following three discursive sites: formal legal documents, docudramas and print media texts. Texts from each of these sites were qualitatively analyzed for thematic commonalities in figurations of Smith and of dominant and counter discourses of girls in each site. This includes study of included images because images are understood in this CDA epistemological framework to be texts: cultural productions and not transparent recordings. This analysis involves critical assessment of whether and to what extent the figurations of Ashley Smith in these different sites overlap and intersect. Texts are also read for their silences.

I look at what texts studied exclude, what they include, what available facts or data they take to be relevant and what inferences are drawn. I look at the texts in respect of what possibilities and potential meanings they make visible and which possible stories they ignore, dismiss or obscure. I engage in micro-analysis of language used, specifically in reference to descriptions of Smith as "girl" and at how language is deployed to constitute and re-constitute the strategic purposes and semantic themes of the text. I look at the treatment of expert discourses and at who is privileged to speak. The cohesion and coherence of the texts produced about Ashley are studied to reveal their implicit logics. I identify dimensions constituting discourse, looking at semantic, linguistic and the strategic dimensions of the texts studied. I study how micro-elements of texts link to macro discourses.

Messages in the text are studied for their cues to existing social relations, specifically locating, identifying and making visible in the texts cues to existing discourses of what is constitutive of a "good" or "normal" girl.

RESEARCH DESIGN

First, I looked at formal legal documents produced in reference to Ashley Smith's case. These include several reports from various bodies, including the New Brunswick Ombudsman, (2008) several by the Corrections Investigator for Canada and the University of Toronto Faculty of Law's International Human Rights Program. (Mundhane) I also examined documents produced in relation to the inquests. One significant document was the December 2013 inquest decision. I also read decisions and court orders issued in relation to a series of motions made by CSC and a group of health professionals seeking to keep documents and witnesses out of the inquest testimony. I obtained these documents using CanLII as well as Google searches in addition to browsing Federal governmental websites of CSC, the website of the office of the Correctional Investigator and the site of the "Falconers" law firm, which represented Ashley Smith's family in the inquest and civil suit in relation to the Smith case.

Second, I looked at docudramas concerning Smith, with a focus on those that brought Ashley Smith's case into widespread notoriety. These included CBC's *Out of Control* and *Behind the Wall* as well as a documentary on CBC's *The Current* in 2012 called, "Ashley Smith and Mental Health in Canadian Prisons."

Third, I looked at a large number of print media articles about Ashley Smith's case. I looked at many articles from a range of print media outlets in each time period. I looked at national papers of record, local media sources and also more tabloid forms of journalism from across the political spectrum. Media sources I drew from included the *Toronto Star*, the *National Post* and the *Globe and Mail*, CTV News, Sun Media network papers as well as local papers in Smith's home region (New Brunswick) and the community (Kitchener) in which her death took place.

In addition to doing multiple searches on the Google news and scholar search engines, I did several searches on the news database Factiva, looking at newspapers (Date range from October 2007 to January 2014). This search yielded over 5000 news stories. A series of attempts were made to first recover all available documents, to find all of the "talk" about the Ashley Smith case in the genres described. Because her case was ongoing for seven years with regular, daily coverage in print media across Canada, after a preliminary review of all available articles, I determined it would be unwieldy to study in detail all articles available. To make the search more manageable, I removed duplicates and focused the queries on certain time periods. I honed in on times where the number of articles spiked, and which marked turning points in the case. Based on my preliminary research, I determined that three distinct time periods are representative of shifts in the discourses around her case. These are the immediate media response to her death (October 2007 to June 2008), media coverage of her first inquest (2010-2011) and of the second inquest as it wrapped up and was met with an institutional response (2013-2014).

For all of the texts studied, I undertook a preliminary read-through or viewing to get a gestalt sense of the variety of figures of Ashley Smith circulating throughout the case. Then, after this preliminary review, I re-read the documents and coded for the following focal points in descriptions and definitions of Ashley Smith: mental illness, child, girl, woman and inmate. From this coding and my qualitative analysis of the documents, I discerned chronological trajectories in the growth, flourishing and falling away of certain configurations of Ashley Smith as case or instance of a particular "type" of subject. The analytical chapters that follow discuss the patterns and trends in those representations and the figures of Ashley Smith that coalesced.

NOTES AND LIMITATIONS

Three aspects of the Ashley Smith case posed methodological challenges for me in undertaking this study. First, a large number of texts by or about Ashley Smith that are referred to in various other texts about that case are not publicly available. These include many records of discretionary decisions and reports produced official sites in relation to the case. They also include self-expressive materials reportedly in Ashley Smith's youth file, such as her journals. Various stakeholders in the Smith case ostensibly have these documents, and are keeping them from being released for a variety of reasons that align with their interests in outcome of the case. However, while this would pose significant methodological challenges for certain studies of the Smith case, it is inherently unproblematic within the research design of this book, because what I am studying is the case as a matter of public discourse, and what I am doing is reading those public texts against the grain. Consequently, the subject of this study is inherently defined by what is publicly available.

Second, simultaneously yet quite conversely, there are an abundance of public texts that have been produced in official and media sites about the case. In consequence, I had to spend months reviewing thousands of documents in order to put together my analysis, and even so it would not be practicable to exhaustively itemize each and every text produced. I had to make decisions about what to focus on.

Third, it was not just the volume of texts but their content that had to be managed in my research. Of course, my own particular social history and positionality leave me vulnerable to being emotionally disturbed by the subject matter. Because of my past experiences as an adolescent, I was acutely conscious throughout this research of the dangers of over-identifying with the deceased subject and I strove to do her case justice by ensuring that it was not subsumed within my own narratives. Further, because of my current social position as a law reform lawyer and activist, I was concerned throughout this research about how to navigate change movements with integrity. However, the subject matter of the Smith case would be challenging for any researcher. The task of watching and re-watching video footage of a young woman being confined, injected, restrained and ultimately dying was exhausting. Grueling too was using the pause feature on the media player to ensure I had the various time signatures noted, as was poring over the hundreds of incidents and many reports. Consequently, my research took longer than I had anticipated. I had to take breaks. I had to go outside.

ENDNOTES

---

[1]One non-academic analysis of Ashley Smith's case that bears mentioning comes from her mother. Coralee Smith's statements about what happened to her daughter are not academically theorized but are broadly consistent with the findings of this research. Ashley's mother Coralee said that Ashley "was not suicidal until she faced an ever growing series of sentences for misbehaviour inside prison walls, sentences that she eventually realized (perhaps correctly) would never end." Canada East News Service. "Ashley Smith was Destroyed by Prison System: Mother" (5 February 2012) http://www.journalpioneer.com/News/Local/2012-02-05/article-2886595/Ashley-Smith-was-destroyed-by-prison-system%3A-mother/1.

[2]There is a lengthy procedural history to the prosecution of Kelly Ellard which is detailed in the final 2009 decision on her case rendered by the Supreme Court of Canada R. v. Ellard 2009 SCC 27 (CanLII). Reena Virk's murder has become the subject of a popular novel by Rebecca Godfrey, *Under the Bridge* (Toronto: Harper Collins, 2005) and Hollywood has purchased the movie rights.

[3]R. v. Todorovic 2009 CarswellOnt 4353 (SCJ). For media coverage, see especially Maria Jimenez, "The Last Days of Stephanie Rengel," *Toronto Life* (December 2009) online: http://www.torontolife.com/features/last-days-stefanie-rengel/?pageno=1 Toronto Life.

[4]For discussion see *R. v. Steinke*, 2008 ABQB 201. This is a decision on the change of venue application; it is in the name of the co-accused but refers also to Richardson and references media coverage/ statements. There is also a brief decision on the publication ban in her case: *R. v. JR* 2010 ABQB 38 CanLII.

[5]The Canadian Civil Liberties Association had status as a party at the Ashley Smith inquest. The CCLA's submissions focused on the use of solitary confinement and the need for stronger oversight and accountability of federal prisons.

[6]The ages that counted as adolescence varied in different provincial and territorial jurisdictions under the JDA, and were different for boys and girls in Alberta. The upper age for adolescence was usually 16.

[7]Under the YOA and YCJA, a "young person" or adolescent, is aged from their 12th to the 18th birthday, unless they have done something for which the legislation allows or requires them to be treated as an adult.

[8]In fairness, there is one sentence, however, about different charge rates for girls and boys on page 162 of the report.

[9]This is particularly glaring given the disproportionate overincarceration of aboriginal people, and especially aboriginal young women and girls, across Canada. See Elizabeth Fry Society Fact Sheets "Aboriginal Women": "In 2004-2005, Aboriginal women made up 30% of the women in federal prisons. In provincial jails and detention centres in Saskatchewan, women compose 87% of the female prison population, 83% in Manitoba, 54% in Alberta, and 29% in British Columbia." http://www.caefs.ca/wp-content/uploads/2013/04/Aboriginal-Women.pdf

[10]The *Juvenile Delinquents Act* S.C. 1908 contemplated that all criminally accused adolescents were "misguided children" in need of protection. It allowed for dispositions that resulted in the holding of adolescents for things as vague as "sexual immorality" and it was commonplace for adolescents subject to JDA sentences and others who were being cared for by the child protection system to be held together. For discussion see e.g. Bala, Nicholas and Anand, Sanjeev. *Youth Criminal Justice Law*. 3d. Ed. Toronto: Irwin Law, 2012 at 9.

[11]Haraway builds on Foucault's understanding of monsters as follows: "Monsters have always defined the limits of community in Western imaginations ... on the natural and supernatural, medical and legal, portents and diseases — all crucial to establishing modern identity." (Haraway, *ibid*) This is a bit different from Stuart Hall's "moral panic" framework where folk devils are considered to be the ill against which society must protect itself to assuage its anxieties, but it's a related and complementary understanding.

[12]It is notable, however, that Foucault's own views of agency grew less deterministic later in his career. It may also be that critiques of his thinking being overdeterministic are based on a misapprehension of his work, at least in part. Foucault disputed the possibility of a single, grand resistance, but he did write that there are points where resistance is possible all over the power grid. Foucault, Michel, *The History of Sexuality. Volume 1*, Translated from the French by Robert Hurley, New York: Vintage Books, 1990 (originally published in French: Foucault, Michel, *La Volenté de savoir*, Paris: Gallimard, 1976) at 95-96.

3. Inmate Smith

Necropolitical Success

"He's in prison now, being punished: and the trial doesn't even begin till next Wednesday: and of course the crime comes last of all."

"Suppose he never commits the crime?" said Alice.

"That would be all the better, wouldn't it?" the Queen said...

Alice felt there was no denying that. "Of course it would be all the better," she said: "but it wouldn't be all the better his being punished."

"You're wrong there, at any rate," said the Queen. "Were you ever punished?"

"Only for faults," said Alice.

"And you were all the better for it, I know!" the Queen said triumphantly.

"Yes, but then I had done the things I was punished for," said Alice: "that makes all the difference."

"But if you hadn't done them," the Queen said, "that would have been better still; better, and better, and better!" Her voice went higher with each "better," till it got quite to a squeak at last.

Alice was just beginning to say "There's a mistake somewhere—"

—Lewis Carroll, "Wool and Water," *Through the Looking-Glass and What Alice Found There* (1871)

INTRODUCTION

Ursula K. LeGuin's (1974) short story "The Ones Who Walk Away from Omelas," according to Ferguson, (2014) can be read as a philosophical parable about a bargain offered to a society by interlocking utilitarian logics of exception, security and risk. The logic of exception has been theorized by Ong (2006) as being central to neoliberalism. In this logic, through use of exceptional spaces, including prisons, populations governed by neoliberal technologies are dependent upon the existence of other populations excepted from those technologies. LeGuin's story is a tale of a Utopian city that relies for its people's safety and contentment upon the confinement of a child in a locked room. The story asks whether the suffering of one person can be justified if it enables the contentment of many. It also implicitly raises the question of to what extent there may be flawed assumptions beneath the logic that the happiness of the people in general relies upon the suffering of the one incarcerated child. I excerpt it below at length.

> In a basement under one of the beautiful public buildings of Omelas, or perhaps in the cellar of one of its spacious private homes, there is a room. It has one locked door, and no window. A little light seeps in dustily between cracks in the boards, secondhand from a cobwebbed window somewhere across the cellar. In one corner of the little room a couple of mops, with stiff, clotted, foul-smelling heads stand near a rusty bucket. The floor is dirt, a little damp to the touch, as cellar dirt usually is. The room is about three paces long and two wide: a mere broom closet or disused tool room. In the room a child is sitting. It could be a boy or a girl. It looks about six, but actually is nearly ten. It is feeble-minded. Perhaps it was born defective, or perhaps it has become imbecile through fear, malnutrition, and neglect....
>
> The door is always locked; and nobody ever comes, except that sometimes — the child has no understanding of time or interval — sometimes the door rattles terribly and opens, and a person, or several people, are there. One of them may come in and kick the child to make it stand up. The others never come close, but peer in at it with frightened, disgusted eyes. The food bowl and the water jug are hastily filled, the door is locked, and the eyes disappear. The people at the door never say anything, but

the child, who has not always lived in the tool room, and can remember sunlight and its mother's voice, sometimes speaks.

...They all know it is there, all the people of Omelas. Some of them have come to see it, others are content merely to know it is there. They all know that it has to be there. Some of them understand why, and some do not, but they all understand that their happiness, the beauty of their city, the tenderness of their friendships, the health of their children, the wisdom of their scholars, the skill of their makers, even the abundance of their harvest and the kindly weathers of their skies, depend wholly on this child's abominable misery.

... At times one of the adolescent girls or boys who go to see the child does not go home to weep or rage, does not, in fact, go home at all. Sometimes also a man or woman much older falls silent for a day or two, and then leaves home. These people go out into the street, and walk down the street alone. They keep walking, and walk straight out of the city of Omelas, through the beautiful gates. They keep walking across the farmlands of Omelas. Each one goes alone, youth or girl, man or woman. Night falls; the traveler must pass down village streets, between the houses with yellow-lit windows, and on out into the darkness of the fields. Each alone, they go west or north, towards the mountains. They go on. They leave Omelas, they walk ahead into the darkness, and they do not come back. The place they go towards is a place even less imaginable to most of us than the city of happiness. I cannot describe it at all. It is possible that it does not exist. But they seem to know where they are going, the ones who walk away from Omelas.

In this chapter, I conduct a critical discourse analysis of representations comprising the official story about Inmate Smith.[1] It will be argued that the CSC bureaucracies received in Inmate Smith an unmanageable inmate already rendered socially dead by her prolonged period in youth custody and transfer to adult corrections.

Forms of governance that are raced and gendered ideologies of others that allow some people to be categorized as neither alive nor dead were actively involved in Ashley Smith's death both before and after her transfer to CSC custody. What is horrifying here is not that any one person in particular or any group at CSC calculated a plan to kill her: they almost certainly did not. Rather, systems of power in place brought about her administrative death, and those systems have eluded scrutiny and accountability for it.

There is not just one Inmate Smith: overlapping, in some ways contradictory and messy, but nonetheless analytically similar figures that foreground Ashley Smith's status as a carceral subject emerge from texts produced in a range of official sites. These sites include various bureaucratic locations found locally within correctional institutions as well as at CSC's regional and national offices. The official story about Inmate Smith and the way she was governed by the state reveal the operation of interlocking processes where logics of risk and security become totalizing.These logics over-whelm other possibilities for action in the patterns of negotiations between formal legal rules and system actors' agency in criminal justice and correctional systems. (Coombe) Critical analysis of the Inmate Smith figure reveals the Smith case as an instance where interlocking logics of security and risk are operationalized in a rationalized bureaucracy that not only depoliticizes but also, as Hamilton and Gerlach have previously argued, amoralizes gover-nance. The CSC apparatus of governance is shown to be a monstrous bureaucracy which, like other rationalized neoliberal structures of governance "are inefficient, amoral, and even immoral, more concerned with maintaining procedure than with producing just outcomes." (2010, 396)

THREE CONFIGURATIONS

Three distinct figures of Smith as a carceral subject emerge in official documents produced by various bureaucratic systems and agents, including CSC at certain chronological periods in the case. First, Ashley Smith is configured as a youth with complex needs when she is at odds with the educational system and before the New Brunswick youth courts. Once she is placed in youth custody, which was when Smith received her first significant closed-custody prison sentence, (Richard, 2008) representations of Smith transform into depictions of "YP" (Young Person) Smith the official term for youths held in custody facilities. This construction shifts once again when Ashley Smith is transferred to adult custody. It is on her 18th birthday, July 29, 2006, that the application to transfer Smith to the adult system is filed (Richard, 2008). After this transfer, she is officially represented as an "offender" or "inmate."

Period 1: A Challenging Youth with Complex Needs

The first official legal texts about Ashley Smith's life represent her as a "challenging youth with complex needs." (Richard, 2008) These texts are produced by police, education officials, and probation officers as she enters her teenage years in reference to allegations about her disruptive behaviours at school. The reference to her as a challenging youth is also found in official texts made retrospectively, written after her death and gazing backwards to the time of her youth in New Brunswick. In these texts, although those interacting with her in the community and the juridical field would have understood her as female, because the youth system in Canada is gender "blind," Ashley Smith is officially configured without a gender. It is in March 2002, shortly after Ashley Smith turns 14, that she receives her first youth sentence. This sentence is handed down for her involvement in several minor offences that are not specified in the report of the New Brunswick Ombudsman (Richard, 2008). She is sentenced to a one-year term of probation and enrolled in an Intensive Support Program. By December 2002, Ashley Smith's enrollment in public school is terminated and she is transferred to the alternative system. During this period, Smith is banned from Moncton city transit, runs up her family's long distance bill upwards of $1,000 per month, is considered by officials to have had little positive interaction with her peers, and is suspended for 4 weeks from alternative school. (ibid)

Challenging Youth Smith is characterized at one point during this period as a young person with mental health issues. In early 2003, when she has just turned 15, she is sent for a psychiatric assessment. However, it is determined that Smith poses a risk to security at New Brunswick's Pierre Caissie Treatment Centre and she is thrown out early on March 30, 2003. She had completed 27 days of her recommended 34-day assessment. She was discharged "since she was seriously disrupting the assessments of the other youths." (Richard, 16) During her stay, Smith receives "psychological, psychiatric and educational assessments" (Richard, 17) and is variously diagnosed with personality disorders." She is recommended for individualized counseling in the community by a psychological expert and to take "follow-up" medication. (*ibid*) This discharge seems, at first blush, counter-intuitive: what the rationale for the discharge says is that Ashley Smith is too troublesome to stay in a mental health facility. According to Correctional Investigator Howard Sapers, this discharge is a critical missed opportunity. (Sapers, 2008) I argue that this discharge is an event that signals a logic of exclusion at work in necropolitical processes in the mental health system. Ashley Smith is excluded from treatment for stated utilitarian reasons connected with the general security and management of the Pierre Caissie facility and not relating to her health and functioning.

Period 2: YP Smith

On October 21, 2003 Ashley Smith is remanded to custody and begins her prolonged "experience within" the youth custodial apparatus. (*ibid*, 18) Her incarceration is for violating her probationary conditions by throwing crab apples at a postal worker. (Richard, 2008) Smith's remand into custody formally reconfigures her as a carceral subject, a "Young Person" (YP). This stage lasts from April 2003 until October 2006. Despite having initially been sentenced to a short period of time in custody, she remains "either a part-time or full-time" prisoner at the New Brunswick youth prison for three years. (Richard, 17) Because the labeling system in the YCJA refers to all young people incarcerated through its machinations as "young persons," official texts do not refer to her as a girl: YP Smith remains throughout this period officially genderless, although her female embodiment presents administrative complexities and monetary expenses not associated with male YPs.

The *Youth Criminal Justice Act* sets out the generally understood conditions of possibility under which Ashley Smith was charged, tried, convicted, sentenced and held in custody until she turned 18. The stated purposes of the YCJA are complex but purport to be centred on the rights and well-being of youth.[2] However, while it is generally accepted that the YCJA governs adolescents in Canada, it is also subordinate regulations, administrative rules and practices shaping the conditions of possibility under which YP Smith was defined, disciplined, punished and contained.[3] Once she becomes a YP, formal legal and institutional conditions of possibility interact agencies of actors in those systems to produce the denotation of Inmate Smith as risky. This first sentence puts in motion the sequence of charges for disciplinary offences that ultimately lead to Smith's death. It is the designation of her as YP Smith that underlies her punishability by means of criminal sanction for a series of administration of justice offences relating to her non-compliance with rules while in custody. Very little — if any — of what Ashley Smith was subsequently charged, or otherwise sanctioned, for doing, would be considered criminal conduct were it not committed by someone already constituted as a carceral subject.

YP Smith faces more than 800 incident reports during her time in youth custody at the New Brunswick Youth Centre (NBYC), and 50 more criminal charges.[4] In these incidents, YP Smith is frequently restrained and segregated. For example, on June 1, 2004, while segregated, YP Smith "smeared feces throughout her cell, covering the cell window which obstructed supervision checks." (Richard, 21) When staff are cleaning the cell, YP Smith "became non-compliant with staff and attempted to exit the cell, which lead to her being physically restrained by staff." (*ibid*) Smith then proceeds to cover her window and the cell camera with torn cloth; she is then placed "in a body belt restraint" and subjected to a "pat search." Another example of restraint and segregation used occurs on June 26, 2004. While she is segregated, YP Smith refuses staff demands that she remove items she has placed over her cell window and camera. In consequence, "staff were authorized to place Ashley in a restraint belt called the 'WRAP'" and YP Smith remains immobilized in this state for "approximately 50 minutes." (*ibid*, 22) Still another example of the use of segregation and restraint against YP Smith is documented on March 1, 2005. The NBYC Superintendent authorizes staff to pepper spray Smith after she refuses their request "to leave the shower area and return to her cell." YP Smith is then found "in possession of a piece of metal, possibly a razor blade" (*ibid*, 23) Once subdued, YP Smith is transferred to segregation "where the decontamination process (applying copious amounts of water to the eye area) was commenced." (*ibid*) Yet another example is presented by an incident reported on January 27, 2006 when YP Smith, not segregated at that moment "became extremely vocal towards staff; yelling names, and throwing items around in her cell." (*ibid*, 22) She then refuses to hand over utensils to correctional staff, stating she would only do so if she was transferred back into segregation. She also threatens to self-injure "or trash ... her cell if her requests were not met." (*ibid*) YP Smith then self-injures and "began walking around in her cell naked." Management transfers YP Smith back to segregation. Of course, the examples above are illustrative only. This is not an exhaustive list.

Walking around naked, refusing to return utensils, shouting loudly, covering a window with cloth, and refusing to get out of the shower are not behaviours that would lead adolescents in family homes to be arrested. Even smearing one's feces around one's room, while certainly not socially acceptable and definitely unusual, is only *criminal* behaviour because Inmate Smith is already a carceral subject. Considered in the context of Smith's many complaints about not being provided with adequate sanitary supplies such as tampons and toilet paper, the feces incidents could be re-read as acts of frustration, resistance or protest. Looked at in the context of Levi's analysis of how Auschwitz inmates endured petty cruelties that, taken together, stripped their humanity from them (Levi),[5] these actions can be re-read as reflections of a dehumanizing context rather than simply pathologized as evidence of YP Smith's unmanageability.

The fact that YP Smith is already in custody is foundational to her disobedient and unruly conduct being defined as criminal in *all* subsequent incidents. In an escalating pattern, YP Smith on several occasions accumulates three or four new charges in a day. She does so without ever physically hurting anyone but herself. YP Smith accumulates "upwards of eight hundred" documented incident reports and 501 institutional charges "over a three year span." (Richard, 19)

Disciplinary infractions are translated by NBYC staff into criminal charges in accordance with their operating policy framework. In turn, these charges lead to new convictions for YP Smith on every available occasion. It was the New Brunswick Ombudsman who concluded that it was YP Smith's official status as an inmate that was a necessary condition precedent to her further criminalization: "One could conclude that Ashley became a punishable young offender in prison." (Richard, 47) Indeed, it was through YP Smith's status as a carceral subject that she became a punishable subject legitimately subjected to discretionary discipline and punishment. It was in turn through this discretionary discipline that YP Smith's punishment became exponential and serial: each act became a serial act, taking on a different, and ever more serious consequentiality because it was in a series of unrelenting resistant acts.

For example, consider two largely typical "days in the life" in the official record of YP Smith during this period. On April 28, 2003, YP Smith is involved in four "incidents" that stem from charges in relation to other incidents. These incidents involve her not-complying with orders to co-operate with being transported to and from court to face other charges. Two reports document YP Smith's refusal to abide by the Sheriff's requests. The third concerns her refusal to be strip searched upon returning from court. The day's fourth incident relates to her being "overheard telling another youth that she was going to inflict self-harm with an earring." (Richard, 19) Consider this other "day in the life" two and a half years later. On September 28, 2005, YP Smith accumulates three incident reports. One report does not specify how, but indicates she refuses to comply with orders and becomes aggressive towards staff. The other two reports are about YP Smith's self-injury. (*ibid*) Notice how official responses to YP Smith are virtually identical on both occasions. The official response to YP Smith's conduct is not adjusted to her needs or adapted over time. It remains unreflexively ineffective.

In large part because the Smith Inquest dealt only with her time in custody as an adult, there is little detail about her youth court record available to review. What is most readily available from the NB Ombudsman's review of her youth record, are statistics.

Interestingly, despite being assumed to be pathologically resistant, YP Smith offers little resistance within the processes made available by the court. YP Smith pleads guilty to the administration of justice offences with which she is charged 90.07% of the time. She pleads not guilty 9.93% of the time. She appeals verdicts 11.43% of the time. This means that YP Smith rarely contests new charges against her. Even when she does not plead guilty, this is to no avail. Her few pleas of "not guilty" result in no acquittals. She is found guilty of every charge she faces. (Richard, 46-47) YP Smith's court record does not evidence much engagement on her part with processes of the justice system, or meaningful consideration by the justice system of what remedial measures might encourage or support changes in her behavior. Obviously, if the goal of the incident reports, charges, and behaviour management strategies was to change YP Smith's conduct, they failed. However, it is not obvious that this was the goal.[6]

It is also in prison, and by virtue of the starting condition of possibility that YP Smith is a carceral subject that Ashley Smith becomes a punishable *adult* offender. On January 29, 2006, Smith turns 18. On this day, she is segregated in solitary confinement at NBYC. The passing of this birthday gives the justice system new power over her future: as of this date, any future convictions entered against her will be dealt with by means of an adult sentence. (Sapers, 2008)

Even so, the wheels of the legal system grind slowly. Even after she turns 18, and a transfer application is made, YP Smith's charges and incident reports keep piling up in youth custody until they reach a climactic end in October of 2006. On October 19, YP Smith refuses to comply with a strip search. Eight correctional staff are sent in to restrain her while a nurse cuts her clothing off with scissors. (Richard) Two days later, on October 21, 2006, YP Smith is tasered for not complying with orders to get off her bed, where she is standing while holding "two cups filled with an unidentifiable liquid substance." (*ibid*, 28) Three days later, YP Smith is again tasered and this time also pepper sprayed after "allegedly refusing to back away from her cell door." (Richard, 53) On the same day, YP Smith is sentenced for still other charges accumulated while in youth custody. This sentence is to an "additional 348

days of custodial time added to the already existing 1,455 days."
(Richard, 29) A judicial determination is made that Smith should
be transferred to adult custody to serve this sentence. Since the
sentence exceeds two years, YP Smith is transferred to the federal
adult correctional system. This transfer can be understood a necropolitical action that substantially contributes to bringing about
Ashley Smith's juridical death. By means of this determination,
she was exempted from protected statuses of "child" or "youth"
and excluded from the rehabilitation-focused principles of the
YCJA. This period of youth incarceration, and the transfer determination fall outside of the defined scope of the inquest inquiries.
Yet it is during this period that the momentum of accumulating
youth charges produces Ashley Smith's "rep," her relegation to
an adult penitentiary. Ultimately, the conduct of her conduct, the
arts of government employed, in the YP Smith period produce her
as a terminal inmate who would be understood by Agamben as
homo sacer, a subject outside of society, living in a state of "bare
life" (*zoe*) outside of the law, whose death would not be murder.
(Agamben) Before YP Smith is ever placed into CSC custody, the
careening runaway train of the incidents and charges in her case
seems to foreshadow her biological death.[7]

C. *Period 3: Inmate Smith*

The third distinct period in the official story of Ashley Smith's
case relates her configuration as an adult inmate in federal Corrections (CSC) custody. This period has its own chronological
trajectory, from October 2006 to October 2007, that moves from
her incarceration as an adult towards consolidating the juridical
death, and ultimately bringing about the biological death, of Inmate Smith. The Inmate Smith period can thus itself be subdivided
into three periods. These periods are not altogether discrete: they
overlap but are marked by points of analytical significance along
acontinuous trajectory of increasingly rigorous and effective necropolitical exclusion of Ashley Smith. Inmate Smith starts by being a
member of a large subset of inmates upon her transfer. Gradually,
she becomes officially understood as a member of a much smaller
subset of terminal inmates. The necropolitical process by which
this reconstitution takes place begins quickly upon her labelling

with a maximum security designation and assignment to solitary confinement. Finally, she becomes a member of an even smaller subset when bureaucratic dissolution of her bodily integrity and autonomy to a point where she exists as *homo sacer*, a banned, contingent body in a death-world. In this trajectory, Inmate Smith's biological death is the final point on a long necropolitical journey of dehumanization.

The figure of Inmate Smith dominates in CSC texts where forms of expertise that claim knowledge of the best, least risky security protocols are privileged. The "truths" of formal legal discourse, such as a criminal record and correctional designations such as an offender's coding or designation, are deferred to in these texts. The figure of Inmate Smith is also prominent in media texts dating from prior to CBC's release of its *Out of Control* docudrama, discussed in detail in Chapter 5, and especially the early media reports emerging out of the story of the front line CSC security staff being charged with negligence in relation to her death.[8] In media sites, including reports of her death in 2007 and 2008, the inmate figure also dominates. There, Ashley Smith is largely referred to as a "dead inmate." She is represented in various ways that are consistent with journalistic conventions of identifying actors by age and geographic "home." She is described as being from Grand Valley institution and hailing from New Brunswick.[9] In media texts in this period, Inmate Smith is peripheral to a narrative about prosecution of guards accused in her case that generally characterizes this prosecution as unjust. As an illustrative example, consider the following: "Smith, who was pronounced dead in hospital, had been serving a six-year, one-month sentence for offences committed as a young offender and began serving her sentence on Oct. 17, 2003. She would have been eligible for release in November."[10]

3.(a) Adult Carceral Subject

Once she becomes an adult carceral subject and transferred to CSC custody, Ashley Smith is officially labeled an "offender" or an "Inmate Smith." The *Corrections and Conditional Release Act* (CCRA) SC 1992, C.20 is the statutory framework within which the CSC defines "inmate" at s.1:

"inmate" means

(a) a person who is in a penitentiary pursuant to

(i) a sentence, committal or transfer to penitentiary.

For CSC's local and national bureaucracies, Inmate Smith's gender and embodiment make her an administrative headache from the beginning of her incarceration as an adult. She bears certain differentiating criteria that make her unusual for the type "inmate." Statistically, the usual or archetypal inmate in North America is of a working class man. Ashley Smith's embodiment does not fit readily into this stereotype. Inmate Smith is a woman whereas most inmates are men, and she is younger than most inmates.

Inmate Smith and her troubling attributes are a cumbrous burden on the daily grind of the prison apparatus. Because the YCJA is formally gender blind, YP Smith officially acquires a gender when she enters adult corrections and becomes a woman inmate. Gender is explicitly and overtly relevant to the conditions in which Inmate Smith is held; the everyday conditions in which she lives in CSC custody are fundamentally gendered. Different rules are applied to her than to male prisoners as part of CSC's "women-centered-approach." (Rush to Judgment, 34) For example, surveillance and searches of her must be carried out in the presence of women guards. This adds an administrative burden not imposed by men.

Many criminologists have criticized the CSC's "woman centred" approach as based in a risk-based model that focuses on responsibilization and control. (Hannah-Moffatt) Women inmates are tasked in this logic with "taking responsibility" for their "choices": in de-contextualized responses to their actions while inmates' conditions of incarceration are determined not with reference to their rehabilitative needs but rather what will be least disruptive to the functioning of the institution. This management model produces a disjuncture between the colloquial understanding of a maximum security designation as a reflection of dangerousness and the basis for the institutional coding of maximum security. While it stands in for dangerousness in popular understanding, the official designation of "maximum security" may or may not mean violent, dangerous or at risk of escaping. It may just as likely mean an inmate is understood to self-harm or is designated by relevant corrections officials as mentally ill. Consequently, the gendered space of incarceration for women by CSC overlaps significantly with the death-space of solitary confinement. Woman prisoners are confined to the death-world of solitary confinement for a wider range of reasons, and per capita more often, than are men.

Under this "woman-centred approach," as one of very few woman inmates, Inmate Smith is inherently problematic and a drain on resources for CSC from the beginning of her incarceration. Women are vastly more expensive to hold in prison than men. In 2010-2011, according to Canada's Ministry of Public Safety, it cost $214,614 to house a woman inmate (on average: a maximum security woman inmate would cost far more) and $95,034 for the average male inmate. (Public Safety, 2012) Mundane aspects of women's incarceration are made more bureaucratically complex by rules crafted to protect women from abuse, for example, rules that require female guards to be present when they are searched. Inmate Smith's most banal physicality: her menstrual cycles, her need for female undergarments, her large physical size that is discordant with the stereotypically diminutive stature expected of women, are challenging for CSC to address. This complexity is amplified at the macro-level because security logic is inherently gendered as a masculinist discourse of patriarchal protection. (Buss et al.) Inmate Smith fits neither stereotypical expectations of inmates nor of women and is in consequence difficult for the prison system to manage as an "offender" and for a variety of actors to imagine as a "victim" or person to protect.

Definition, classification and coding of Inmate Smith involved many interpretive moments in which institutional actors exercised agencies Inmate Smith is assigned a Maximum Security designation. She is sub-categorized as a "high risk female inmate," or a "high risk female offender." (CSC Press Release, 20 December 2013) The deployment of this categorization profoundly affects the manner in which she is governed. Descriptions of Inmate Smith sometimes refer generally to her lengthy record but more often to her riskiness; they rarely if ever mention the crimes for which she was originally incarcerated. Also left unstated, and unclear, is to whom or what she poses a risk. Codes and charges assigned to various "incidents" obscure the banal triviality of the acts involved. As was the case while she was in youth custody, examples of the trivial incidents giving rise to charges are legion during this period. The accumulation of her charges in youth custody and the hundreds of incident reports in adult custody involved daily, moment-to-moment microprocesses of governance in the interpretations and discretionary behaviours of guards. Equally, the weight of these texts, once amassed in large numbers as a record, in turn shape the discretion of guards, who seek to act pre-emptively to prevent Inmate Smith from breaching the security of the institutional population.

As in the YP Smith period, it is in application and invocation of a complex web of legislative, regulatory and administrative details through official texts that the official story of Inmate Smith takes shape. The *Corrections and Conditional Release Act* (CCRA) SC 1992, c. 20 is the formal legislation governing how CSC officials deal with "incidents" arising and "offences" committed, in prison. In principle, this *Act* is focused on managing risks posed by inmates to one another and to the broader community. (CSC Press Release, December 20, 2013) What measures are considered to be necessary and proportionate depends on whether an inmate is considered by prison officials to be a safety threat to themselves or others, making risk management the *Act's* primary objective.[11] The risk rationality in which the CCRA was steeped at the time of the Smith case has been further entrenched in statutory drafting in the years since her death.[12] In addition, section 87 of the CCRA requires that all decisions (including transfer decisions) taken by the Correctional Service consider the health status of an inmate.

Subordinate official texts, such as regulations, guidelines, directives and "management models" guide how bureaucrats are to interpret and implement the legislative regimes set out in the statutory laws. These regulatory texts are meant to be interpreted and applied in a manner consistent with the statutes. Relevant regulatory texts include the *Corrections and Conditional Release Regulations*, SOR/92-620 as well as several CSC Commissioner's Directives concerning "uses of force;" and SITREPS — Situation Reports (Sapers, 2008) — which are circulated to all managers throughout the organization. These SITREPS are of great importance to the case because, according to Sapers, Inmate Smith figured prominently almost daily. (*ibid*) Another key instance of official representation of Inmate Smith is that of "offender Ashley Smith" in the CSC Response to the Office of the Correctional Investigator's Deaths in Custody Study

Management of Inmate Smith, and other woman inmates, is to be done in accordance with CSC's *Situation Management Model* (SMM). There is a textual gap between the categories available to assign to Ashley Smith and the assignment of her to those categories. Semantic indeterminacy is evident despite the felt boundness of guards by the formal legal tests in place: discretion is involved. Even where guards feel they have no choice but to take particular actions in relation to Inmate Smith, it is they who "sign off" on the orders. Judgment is exercised by CSC officials in various levels of management positions as well as police and judges in a myriad of moments in the hundreds of incidents and charges in the Smith case. For example, the decision to transfer YP Smith to adult custody was a discretionary judicial determination. Charges for assaulting a peace officer were laid against Inmate Smith after altercations with guards when she refused to disrobe or leave a room were defined as "incidents" by interpretive judgment exercised by staff. Framing of her resistance to being brought to court to face charges on several occasions as assaults on police officers and security incidents were also judgment calls. Finally, every time a judge found her guilty of new criminal charges, the guilty finding and the sentence were both contingent on the judge's discretion within limits imposed by law.

The logics of security and risk that lead to Inmate Smith's designation as dangerous are self-confirming. System actors mobilize certain logics when exercising their discretionary judgment. CSC culture and policies produce certain discursive conventions. These texts are written in a particular language, referring to pre-existing policies and procedures, with specific forms of coding and risk assessment that are prescribed by CSC conventions. It is not just the formal legal texts but also the cultural practices of actors that constitute conditions of possibility at the meso-level of analysis. The controlling discursive paradigm of the SITREPS reports about Inmate Smith is risk rationality that focuses on minimizing potential "bads" or harms by containing security threats posed by inmates. In general, Inmate Smith's treatment in custody was not justified in the language of discipline. Government in the Foucauldian sense is not an art concerned with the conduct of her conduct by imprinting technologies of the self onto her. Rather, Inmate Smith was simply immobilized and contained. Words and images are used that maximize sterility of interventions by staff in the context of the custody of Inmate Smith. The paradox of Smith's agency being contained within a frame of offending trapped her into deeper and deeper enmeshment in closer and closer regulation of her every move.

I argue that the solitary confinement imposed on Inmate Smith is what Agamben describes as the "ban," a continuing and definite exclusion of the carceral subject from community, an exclusion even amongst the excluded: the removal of the carceral subject from *bios* (social existence) within the prison population and its relegation to *zoe* or "bare life." (Agamben) In keeping with its commitment to security through risk rationality, the CCRA specifically provides for solitary confinement. The Act authorizes "administrative segregation" for security reasons at s. 31. The notion is that segregation, or solitary confinement, is to be used if an inmate jeopardizes security. Administrative segregation is *not* defined as punitive in formal legal texts or in official statements of CSC. To quote a CSC spokesperson, administrative segregation is "not a form of punishment," but rather a means "to help ensure the safety of all inmates, staff and visitors." (CBC News, 8 September 2013) It is to be used only when "there is no reasonable alternative and for the shortest period of time necessary." (*ibid*) Administrative segregation is defined as a security measure in adult corrections and the equivalent, "therapeutic quiet," is a security measure in youth corrections.

Inmates are coded with respect to being "maximum," "medium" or "minimum" security. They are coded pursuant to regulations to the CCRA. Solitary confinement cells in Canadian custodial facilities are given a variety of names, none of which refer to discipline or punishment of the prisoner they contain. The same geography of limited space (a small room with no windows and few items of furniture or amenities) is used to contain inmates in solitary confinement or segregation in Grand Valley Institution, in the Saskatoon Regional Psychiatric Centre, the Young Offenders

Centre in New Brunswick, as well as all of the other institutions in which Ashley Smith was held in her time in custody. These small, locked rooms for solitary confinement of prisoners are referred to euphemistically as "administrative segregation," "observation cells" and "therapeutic quiet." All of these terms actually mean the same thing; to ensure security and management of risks, the same logic is applied and the same rooms, the same death spaces, are used to hold inmates who have been disruptive as are used for those on suicide watch.

While maximum security is understood colloquially to refer to a person's dangerousness, the determination by bureaucrats as to whether a subject should be labeled maximum-security is, according to the tests set out in applicable regulations, made in reference to the risks they pose to themselves as well as others. This determination is made pre-emptively and does not necessarily refer to a past event. The decision whether to code an inmate "Maximum Security" is a determination based on a CSC Institutional classification system that involves a discretionary process. The stated aim of this classification is "to provide the safest and least restrictive environment possible." Federally-sentenced female offenders are to be classified and housed in environments that are commensurate with their assigned security designation.(Luciani, Motiuk and Nafekh) Longstanding concerns have been repeatedly raised about the overuse of the maximum security designation and solitary confinement against woman prisoners, and are identified in the 1996 Arbour Report as systemic "shortcomings... of the most serious nature."

Both Inmate Smith's maximum security classification and her relegation to solitary confinement are official designations that are not what they seem. While they sound like references to dangerousness on her part, they actually reframe her "high needs" as institutional risks. (Hannah-Moffatt, 2011) CSC has acknowledged, but rejects, the critique that the 'maximum-security' designation is applied inequitably to women, over-estimating the risks they pose and imposing unnecessary restrictions. In response to this critique, a CSC study examined the question of gender differences in security classification by comparing maximum-security female to maximum-security male offenders. This study did not find significant gender differences in the use of maximum security designations, but it did find that the assignment of risk could be assessed based on "suicide potential," that woman prisoners were more likely to have "high needs" and that "high needs" inmates were more likely to be understood as "high risk," especially if they showed "suicide potential." (Blanchette and Motiuk)

As a technology of power, the Inmate Smith figuration legitimates the means of governance focused almost exclusively on containment and security. Discursive work done by the figure obfuscates the underlying incidents giving rise to her "maximum security" designation and make invisible the escalating pattern of a series of minor infractions and are deployed to characterize Inmate Smith as risky.

The response deemed most appropriate to Smith's conduct in the context of her construction as risky would consist of increased containment and isolation. When transferred to CSC custody, Inmate Smith was constructed as risky on the basis of her youth corrections file, meaning that the high risk Inmate Smith construction preceded all reports and charges made about her while she was in CSC custody. The cumulative effect of these legislative and regulatory categories was to produce a weight of institutional discourse that constructed Inmate Smith as a dangerous person in need of containment. Inmate Smith is a figure on which hundreds of further incident reports and charges laid in Corrections custody were based. Security protocols were enacted as responses to refusals to comply by a featureless/ blank inmate with no appreciation for her particularity. The figure of the dangerous inmate in need of containment for security reasons supports regimes of rigid enforcement of rules against such an excluded and unmanageable being.

While it emerges from, and is articulated in, official documents in ways that reinforce, the internal logic of the correctional system, the figure of Inmate Smith is not inevitably deployed in support of maintenance of the correctional system and institutional status quo. After the death of Ashley Smith, representations that coalesce into substantially the same figure of Inmate Smith are also prominent in critiques of the correctional system. For instance, Sapers critiques the "governance model for women's corrections" in place in CSC by mobilizing the representation of Ashley Smith as an inmate. (2008) Sapers identifies problems which led to the death of Inmate Smith as "a preventable culmination of several individual and system failures within the Correctional Service of Canada. These failures are symptoms of serious problems previously identified within Canada's Federal Correctional system and are not applicable only to Ms. Smith." (2008, 4)

In this understanding, the caseness of the Smith case is broadly relevant: what happens to Inmate Smith is a generalizable case of what might happen to any female inmate, and perhaps even any inmate, who becomes unmanageable in CSC's "care and custody." The patterns in treatment of woman offenders revealed by analysis of the Inmate Smith figure have the potential to confront clusters and structures of macro power and to question, if not even perhaps refute, logics that Sapers has argued, both in advance of and in response to the inquest verdict, need to be changed (Sapers, quoted in *Toronto Star,* 19 December 2013). A March 2014 post on left-leaning independent news website Truth-out.org, for example, uses the Inmate Smith figure to bolster a claim that "solitary confinement becomes the perfect metaphor for the neo-liberal subject." (TruthOut) Further, use of the Inmate Smith figure, for example, is now being sought to be made of this figuration in the Glen Wareham case. (Stone, 4 July 2013) This is a case of a male inmate who died in CSC custody in which the deceased's family members are suing Corrections for wrongful death, citing Inmate Smith's case as fundamentally similar to that of Wareham. Similarly, the Inmate Smith figure has been used to call into question the suicide of Edward Snowshoe, who, in 2010 at age 24, died by suicide in CSC custody at Edmonton Institution, a maximum-security federal prison, after spending 162 days in segregation. (CBC News 11 July 2014)

3(b) Terminal Inmate: Homo sacer

Shortly after becoming configured as an adult Inmate in October 2006, Ashley Smith comes to be understood as an unusually unmanageable inmate. In the context of governance by a rationalized bureaucracy, unmanageability on the part of a subject is a major crisis for the system. While the Inmate Smith figure remains ubiquitous in official texts, it is clear from communications between

CSC staff and management, as well as from the volume of texts produced about her, that the system is struggling to maintain the representation of Inmate Smith as ordinary. A tension between the exceptional and ordinary, always endemic to bureaucracies, which works to transform the particular into a case of a general type, is clearly evident in the Smith case. The cumulative weight of Inmate Smith's record begins to guide discretionary decisions to pre-emptively limit her potential to cause problems for the institution. As noted above, Inmate Smith is labeled "high needs," is assigned a maximum security designation and, largely pre-emptively, consigned to segregation status. During the Inmate Smith period, while official documents label and code her as an inmate like many others, it is obvious from the volume of documents being generated that containment of Inmate Smith is proving tremendously resource intensive. Incidents involving her are triggering requirements for the production of hundreds and even thousands of reports by front line staff which are then circulated to management. From May to October 2007, according to Sapers, Inmate Smith is mentioned in "hundreds" of daily CSC report, or "SITREPS," 22 of which mention repeated ligature-tying and self-harming incidents. (Sapers, 2008)

By late 2006 or early 2007, in the theoretical framework of necropolitics, Inmate Smith can be understood as a "terminal" inmate; alternatively, on Agamben's formulation, she can be understood as banned or *homo sacer*. She has been dehumanized into someone who is, in many respects, socially and juridically already dead. Micro definitions that constitute her banal physicality and survival behaviours as well as her resistances as "incidents" and responses by guards as "uses of force" produce Inmate Smith's status as a terminal inmate. There is a great deal of continuity between the youth and adult systems in respect of how the systems coded, made sense of, and responded to, Smith's conduct. While the adult correctional system is formally "separate and apart" from the youth system and transfer of YP Smith did change her circumstances in removing her from a facility containing other young people to adult facilities, other aspects of her conditions of incarceration are strikingly similar in the adult and youth systems. Just as YP Smith had accumulated hundreds of incident reports and criminal charges in youth custody so did Inmate Smith attract hundreds of incident reports and scores of new criminal charges. As before, records of these incidents rarely, if ever, reference her harming others but rather tend to involve defiance, self-harm or general unruliness that would not be considered criminal if undertaken by an actor not already framed as a carceral subject or inmate. Over the 11.5 months Smith was held in the adult system, "[she] was involved in approximately 150 security incidents, many which revolved around her self-harming behaviour," which consisted of "superficially cutting herself, head-banging or, most frequently, fashioning a ligature out of material and then tying it around her neck." (Sapers, 2008) The construction of her basic survival behaviours as new disciplinary incidents is a denial of Inmate Smith's autonomous existence, and a relentless erosion of her bodily integrity.

A difference between the Inmate Smith and YP Smith periods is that the youth system, perhaps because it had the benefit of recourse to the "safety valve" of the ability to transfer Smith to adult custody, did not seem to struggle quite as rapidly or as much with how to contend with her. In contrast, the adult correctional system quite rapidly spun out: it is evident that the cumulative weight of the hundreds of disciplinary infractions incurred by Inmate Smith in adult CSC custody within weeks began to exhaust guards and the system itself. Mandatory compliance with general systemic rules by guards was producing a totalizing regime of surveillance and of containment. This regime was incredibly resource intensive, expensive and exhausting. While reconfiguration of Inmate Smith as an adult took place at a discrete moment in October 2006, there was continuity in the totalizing paradigm of surveillance in which she was enmeshed through her time in youth corrections to her time as an adult inmate.

Official documents from the Inmate period of the Smith case show the day to day conditions in correctional institutions to contain messy enactments of struggles between local and systemic power hierarchies. During this period, it is evident in official texts that Ashley Smith is successfully frustrating attempts by front line staff and management to manage her. There is also clearly an institutional struggle between front line CSC guards, the management of particular institutions and central CSC management about how to deal with Inmate Smith. Concerns are raised by CSC management about failures on the part of guards to formalize their interventions, and on the part of local managers for excessively formalizing their responses. For example, the "Rush to Judgment" report depicts certain local-level managers at various institutions as "cowboys" dismissive of the institutional rules and safety protocols, (Rush to Judgment, 27) who were intervening by disciplining Inmate Smith antagonistically and inappropriately often. On December 13, 2006, when Inmate Smith was housed at Nova Institution, front line staff were informed that the institution's Warden and Deputy Warden had been called in to conference calls with CSC national headquarters to discuss high numbers of Uses of Force (UOF) involving Ashley Smith.(Rush to Judgment, 20) Sapers notes that CSC breached its own rules concerning how to house and contain inmates in the Smith case insofar as: " the use of institutional transfers; the use of administrative segregation; interventions involving the use of force; the provision of health and mental health services; and, staff responses to medical emergencies."(2008, para 11)

Guards were asked, when dealing with Inmate Smith to observe a protocol of "keep[ing] the communication 'matter-of-fact.'"(Rush to Judgment, 18) Guards were censured for being too emotionally engaged in communication with Inmate Smith, both for being too sympathetic and too angry. The bureaucratic admonition to remove emotionality from guards' interactions with Smith is a struggle. It is not once but repeatedly that guards are asked to "remove the personal" and "remove warmth"[13] when dealing with Inmate Smith. This enforced impersonalization, descriptions and coding of Inmate Smith slipped into dehumanization. In addition to the instruction that guards act "matter of fact" in response to her self-harm, a directive was later issued to the effect that guards were not to intervene unless she stopped breathing. Acting Grand Valley Warden Cindy Berry testified at the Smith inquest that a directive had been issued to guards to stay outside of her cell unless she was in "medical distress." (CTV News 30 September 2013)

Clearly, a concerted programmatic effort was undertaken by CSC management to ensure that front line guards and local-level managers would perform as uncritical functionaries when implementing directives and rules. Some criminologists have argued that correctional staff unconsciously adopt the risk rationale integral to the logic of the correctional system. (Hannah-Moffatt) This would imply that staff are not aware, let alone critical, of the operating logics they are tasked with following. However, the ongoing and persistent conflict between front line staff and central management in the Smith case calls into question to what extent adoption of this thinking is unconscious or complete. It appears that guards were well aware, and critical, of the systemic logics they were required to implement. The non-compliance of the front line staff with management directives on multiple occasions indicates that the system is much messier and agents within the system harder to manage than this contention of unconscious adoption would suggest. (Gerlach, Hamilton, Sullivan and Walton)

Evidence of the difficulties presented to staff and various levels of management by the task of containing Inmate Smith is presented in an email to front line staff from low-level management sent in November, 2006:

> all staff that have dealt with Ashley should be recognized for their efforts in dealing with a very difficult offender. It is very draining both emotionally and physically to deal with this type of offender. All staff did a terrific job in maintaining a safe and secure environment in less than desirable conditions. Well done. (Rush to Judgment)

The dispassionate official records about Inmate Smith conflict with the understandings of Inmate Smith present in the oral culture of the front line guards. Amongst these actors, Inmate Smith was spectacularly notorious. Even when she was first transferred to CSC custody Inmate Smith was preceded by her reputation, as, according to the Rush to Judgment report " the most difficult inmate in the system," which together with her designation as "maximum security," marked her immediately as a difficult inmate. Similarly, in "Behind the Wall," Ashley Smith is referred to as having come to Saskatoon with a "rep" amongst guards as "the most difficult female inmate in the system. (CBC 2010) Reference to Inmate Smith's "reputation" amongst front line CSC guards is found later in descriptions the "A Rush to Judgment" report in excerpts from official CSC communications. To quote: the institution "never had an inmate so problematic as [inmate Smith] in the ten year history of this institution." (Rush To Judgment, 39)

While texts about Inmate Smith produced in official corrections Canada sites meticulously document her days in scrupulous adherence to various policies, violations of Ashley Smith's rights were at the same time, as Sapers notes, "routine." These are documented as "use of force" incidents and Sapers also makes numerous allegations that things like forced injections with anti-psychotic drugs body cavity searches and failures to appropriately report uses of force were also routine. (Sapers; Beaudry) Antipsychotics were repeatedly administered notwithstanding the fact that, in all the documents I have reviewed, I have not seen a single one in which an expert ever diagnosed Ashley Smith as psychotic.

Clearly, Inmate Smith was exhausting system resources. In 11.5 months in Federal CSC Custody, Inmate Smith was moved 17 times amongst three federal penitentiaries, two treatment facilities, two external hospitals, and one provincial correctional facility. According to Sapers, "nine of the ...17 moves of Ms. Smith were institutional transfers that occurred across four of the five CSC regions. The majority of these institutional transfers occurred in order to address administrative issues such as cell availability, incompatible inmates and staff fatigue, and had little or nothing to do with Ms. Smith's needs." (Sapers, 2008, 5) The series of transfers between CSC and mental health institutions reveals a sequence of security-based attempts to exclude Inmate Smith from the jurisdictions and concerns of a variety of institutions. Further, it reveals the often messy interaction and overlap of disjointed bureaucracies within CSC: the bureaucratic workings of local institutions in various regions of Canada as well as CSC's centralized national management. Different units within CSC were evidently trying to divest themselves of the problems, costs and exhaustion caused by this troublesome inmate.

The sheer geographic range of these transfers is in part produced because Inmate Smith is female and there are few facilities available for woman inmates. Her gender therefore is engaged in the processes that compound the effect of necropolitical actions that bring about her social death. Far from her home and family in Moncton, Inmate Smith becomes unrooted, banned, losing her social identity in being unmoored from community. At a practical level, these transfers result in the impractibility of Inmate Smith having any visitors, visitors who in turn could have acted as non-expert advocates on her behalf or witnesses to her struggles. More abstractly, they produce Inmate Smith as politically locationless, eroding her membership in any form of community. Indeed, they produce Ashley Smith for the bureaucratic CSC systems in which she is enmeshed, as a sort of fetish object, unmoored from her index offence, origins or identity outside of prison. These transfers can also be analytically understood as seventeen *unsuccessful* attempts by various entities within the correctional system to divest themselves and the system of the management woes Inmate Smith's presence is causing. What follows is a list of the specific transfers of Inmate Smith:[14]

•Oct. 31, 2006-Dec. 18, 2006 Nova Institution for Women, Truro, Nova Scotia(Dec.19, 2006 enroute to Regional Psychiatric Centre, stopover at Joliette Institution, Joliette, Quebec)

•Dec. 20, 2006-Apr. 12, 2007 Regional Psychiatric Centre, Prairies, Saskatoon, Saskatchewan

•Apr. 13, 2006- May 10, 2007 L'Institut Philippe-Pinel de Montreal, Montreal

•May 10, 2007-Jun. 2, 2007 Grand Valley Institution for Women, Kitchener, Ontario

•Jun. 7, 2007-Jun. 11, 2007 Grand River Hospital, Kitchener, Ontario

•Jun. 11, 2007-Jun. 18, 2007 St. Thomas Psychiatric Hospital, St. Thomas, Ontario

•Jun. 19, 2007-Jun. 26, 2007 Grand Valley Institution for Women, Kitchener, Ontario

•Jun. 26, 2007 Grand River Hospital, Kitchener, Ontario

•Jun. 27, 2007-Jul. 26, 2007 Joliette Institution, Joliette, Quebec

•Jul. 26, 2007-Aug. 24, 2007 Nova Institution for Women,

Truro, Nova Scotia
- Aug. 24, 2007-Aug. 27, 2007 Central Nova Correctional Facility, Dartmouth, Nova Scotia
- Aug. 27, 2007-Aug. 31, 2007 Nova Institution for Women, Truro, Nova Scotia
- Aug. 31, 2007- Sep. 6, 2007 Grand Valley Institution for Women
- Sep. 6, 2007 Grand River Hospital, Kitchener, Ontario
- Sep. 6, 2007-Sep. 21, 2007 Grand Valley Institution for Women
- Sep. 21, 2007 Grand River Hospital, Kitchener, Ontario
- Sep. 21, 2007-Oct. 19, 2007 Grand Valley Institution for Women, Kitchener, Ontario

Dispersal of responsibility for Inmate Smith does discursive work in permitting and legitimizing the way in which she was dealt with in Corrections Custody. While Sapers does not theorize the construction of Inmate Smith, he does make the observation in his 2008 "A Preventable Death" report that "nobody seems to have taken charge of Ms. Smith's case at the correctional service despite the ongoing awareness of senior staff that Ms. Smith required special care and that the efforts that had been made were inadequate and ineffective." (Sapers, 2008, 19) This disengagement is understandable when considered in the context of the relentless series of reprimands front line staff contended with when they did engage with Inmate Smith. It was in their interests to participate in a pattern of avoidance. Guards faced censure, termination of employment and even arrest if they did not comply with the bureaucratic rules imposed on them. Beneath the depersonalization deliberately effected in the CSC texts about Inmate Smith is a rationalized bureaucratic logic that involves dispersal of responsibility for this troublesome inmate. In official texts, it is evident that Inmate Smith is a problem for the system but she is no one's problem in particular. Further, Inmate Smith is a problem to remove, or, failing that, to contain, not to solve. This dispersal of responsibility across the institutions and across time through use of coding supports the institutional transfers to which Inmate Smith was made subject.

(c) Juridical Death and Bodily Contingency

After hundreds of incidents in which Inmate Smith is determined by CSC guards and management to be extraordinarily difficult and burdensome for CSC bureaucracy, representations of Inmate Smith gradually transform from a figure of a terminal inmate likely to become juridically dead to a figure of a contingent subject whose bodily autonomy is completely compromised and who inhabits a "death world" of perpetual segregation. In this death world, she exists, from the perspective of the CSC bureaucracy, as a biological being who is socially and juridically dead already. Inmate Smith has, by spring 2007, become so closely surveilled that her movements are tabulated and restricted even at the most banal levels, with her daily bodily functions being recorded and her use of toilet paper rationed. As was the YP Smith figure, during her incarceration in CSC custody, the figure of Inmate Smith is mobilized as a tool for containing, excluding, dehumanizing and establishing Ashley Smith's status as socially dead. Once Inmate Smith is confined to solitary on a longterm basis, she is the subject of unbearable scrutiny. The lights are never turned off. She is bathed in dim fluorescent light and under the view of cameras 24 hours a day with no human contact except through her meal slot. As the CSC Guards' union says, Inmate Smith "was constantly accumulating data." (Rush to Judgment, 10) Every action she undertakes leads to her further enmeshment in surveillance and containment. Her daily bodily behaviours become the obsession of the state. Bureaucratic exhaustion creates ridiculous amplification of the work of the state at an exponential level.

Even Inmate Smith's simplest bodily acts lead to her being written up and accumulating data. She is considered disruptive when asking for a tampon, asking for pen and paper, asking for a blanket, eating, refusing to eat, taking medication, refusing medication, disrobing, refusing to disrobe, asking for toilet paper, and refusing to use toilet paper. Miniscule agentic acts, such as asking for a tampon, which could be read many different ways, are not seen as basic survival behaviours but rather as acts of defiance — and maybe her very survival is defiance — that bring down institutional responses: "uses of force" and forced injections. Acts in which Inmate Smith harms herself result in her being placed on

"24 hour suicide watch," which in turn only escalates the level of surveillance to which she is subject. Isolation and surveillance, as before, do not ease but exacerbate, Inmate Smith's problematic conduct. In this period, Inmate Smith's self-harm, including especially ligature tying self-strangulation, escalates, with front line staff having routinely to "to forcefully remove ligatures from her neck sometimes as many as six or seven times a day."(Rush to Judgment, 8) For months, Inmate Smith makes multiple attempts at self-strangulation and, for months, she is prevented from biologically dying by the interventions of guards.

However, in the midst of all of this extremely detailed scrutiny of her bodily functions, there is no reference to any masturbatory or otherwise sexual behavior by Inmate Smith. Given that she was young, alone and ostensibly very bored, and in light of the fact that one of the things for which she had been received as "challenging" as a teen had been her consumption of questionable online materials for a fee (the nature of these websites has not been disclosed[15]), it would be surprising if she did not masturbate during all of her years in solitary confinement. The absence of any reference to sexual behavior on her part, and the insistence on the part of Dr. Rivera and others that her self-strangulation was not auto-erotic are conspicuous. Perhaps she simply did not masturbate. However, it is not clear whether she in fact did not masturbate, whether guards decided to, for reasons of discretion, decline to mention masturbation on her part, or whether references to it have somehow been removed from the record. In the context of such detailed attention to the minute details of Inmate Smith's physicality, the silence of official records about her sexual behaviour and sexuality seems to call out for some kind of explanation. Perhaps the stereotypical construction of "girls" as without sexual desire prevented those surveilling Inmate Smith from recognizing auto-eroticism in her acts. Perhaps because Inmate Smith's physicality did not correspond to prevailing stereotypes about what is sexually appealing in a young woman, surveillance of her movements lacked a voyeuristic appeal and the possibility of her sexual agency was overlooked. Or perhaps front line guards, who appear to have cared about her, discretely turned their gaze away from her most intimate acts and refrained from documenting them, which, if it did happen, would have been an agentic and resistant act on their parts. This analysis cannot conclusively determine whether any of these explanations is correct. In any case, the official story of Inmate Smith renders Ashley Smith's limited range of sexual agency invisible.

Similarly, the repeated strip and cavity searches to which Inmate Smith was made subject in custody are nowhere characterized as sexual assaults notwithstanding the fact that there are very specific (and heteronormative) regulatory limitations[16] on who can perform strip searches. The very existence of these regulations confirms the obviously intimate, sexual dimensions of the touching involved. Because she would have been socially, and administratively, received as gendered, sexed and with sexuality, it seems strange, and strangely deliberate, that there is no official recognition of Inmate Smith's sexuality. What is clear from all of this, is that there is a concerted programmatic effort in the official texts about Inmate Smith to "unsee" — and thereby deny — her existence as a sexual being.

Inmate Smith is transferred away from Saskatoon's Regional Psychiatric Centre to the Pinel Institution in April 2007. When the time Ashley Smith spent as a carceral subject is looked at in the context of its totality, it seems entirely inappropriate to focus on a brief period at the end of it in ascertaining what killed her: from 2003 to 2007, a gradual progression into dissolution of her autonomy takes place. The dissolution of Inmate Smith into a contingent body takes place as security and risk logics driving decisions about how to manage Inmate Smith exhaust themselves and system resources wear thin. The series of transfers has not worked. Management takes further steps to rid itself of the problems posed by Inmate Smith: directives are made to guards to limit their engagement with her. The reconfiguration of Inmate Smith into a contingent being has clearly coalesced, by the time at some point in 2007 that the following direction to guards is ordered by the Acting Warden. Front line staff are ordered not to intervene, nor even to enter her solitary confinement cell, unless she stops breathing.[17]

The way CSC was seeking to manage Inmate Smith by this point was untenable within the liberal rights-framework limits imposed by formal law. While the rule of law framework, and the CSC managers acting as custodians of it, obsessively required Inmate Smith as well as front line staff to "comply" with its imposed rules and directives, CSC Management did not follow its own rules in the management of Inmate Smith. She was held in segregation for longer periods than permitted by law. CSC violated its segregation policy under Commissioner Directive 709 and failed to conduct 60-day mandatory regional segregation reviews of Inmate Smith's status. Her complaints, to which CSC management were legally obligated to respond, were not addressed in a timely fashion. The series of transfers violated her *Charter* rights. While CSC 's officials invoked formal legal texts when convenient, CSC management ignored them when it was not.

A programmatic effort undertaken by the CSC bureaucracy to limit Inmate Smith's contact with front line staff had the effect of limiting possibilities for her expressions of agency. With no contacts with family, staff or treating mental health professionals except through a meal slot, Inmate Smith could not express agency by inciting conflicts with front line staff or patterning other interactions with them. Nor is it realistic to argue that, at this point, she could have derived much benefit from therapeutic or otherwise assistive interventions offered to her through a meal slot. In the context of the non-intervention order directed to guards, Ashley Smith was limited in her options for agentic expression to surrendering into passivity or continuing to enact resistance via self-harm that produced a stoppage in her breathing. In this way, it can be argued that institutional logics operating in the CSC bureaucracy as well as bureaucracies in youth courts, youth corrections, and even schools led to concerns about high costs, extra work and possible sanctions in relation to failure to those costs and that work combined with the self-generating momentum and self-fulfilling inevitability of surveillance regimes, produced Inmate Smith as a contingent body, a *homo sacer* figure. These logics drew actors within a variety of systems into institutional and management processes from which they could, but largely didn't, deviate. In these processes, Ashley Smith as a person became farther and farther removed from consideration and Inmate Smith as a figuration of a difficult inmate became more and more confined in a space between alive and dead.

Dissolution of Inmate Smith into a contingent body in the official story about her is never seamless; there is a struggle that takes place in the institution on a daily basis in which her dehumanization is not invariably confirmed and re-enacted. While the overwhelming trend of institutional decisions about Inmate Smith was towards taking necropolitical action, systems and actors did not function monolithically. The Inmate Smith figure helps reveal multiple agencies, tensions between official discourse and actors, and resistances and struggles in the system. Where bureaucratic discretion was exercised in the assignment of coding and official definitions to Inmate Smith's behaviours, some guards evidently disagreed with strategies for dealing with Inmate Smith imposed by management. These guards resisted, and disobeyed, the official plans for how she should be addressed. They were disciplined by management. Once Inmate Smith died, these same front line guards were sanctioned, fired and scape-goated. CSC Guards' Union lawyer Howard Rubel presented evidence at the Smith inquest that several front line guards were disciplined because they entered Smith's cell. For example on January 24, 2013, a front line correctional officer who cut a ligature from Smith's neck on an occasion prior to October 19, 2007, testified at the Inquest that he was reprimanded for so doing. Acting Warden Berry acknowledged at the Smith inquest that guards were disciplined for entering Smith's cell even in instances where her face was purple and she was gasping for breath. Rubel contended in closing submissions at the Smith Inquest that guards, despite their failure to remove the ligature and prevent her death, even disobeyed the non-intervention order in Smith's videotaped last moments by entering her cell when she was still breathing. (*Canadian Press*, 26 November 2013)

Inmate Smith officially complained many times about her treatment in custody. According to Sapers, Ashley filed grievances at Nova Institution. She asserted that: "Excessive force was used against her- She wasn't permitted writing paper or writing instruments. She wasn't permitted sufficient toilet paper for hygiene purposes. She was not permitted soap in her cell, was only given finger foods, and was only given a small piece of deodorant on her finger at a time. While menstruating she was not permitted underwear or sufficient sanitary products to meet her hygiene needs. In August 2007, during the first month after Inmate Smith is transferred to Grand Valley Institution for Women, she submits seven complaints about what she alleges to be unjust segregation and undue treatment. CSC denies all seven of these complaints. (Sapers, 2008) Nonetheless, in September 2007, Inmate Smith makes one last attempt to engage with system rules in order to seek fairer treatment by putting one final "complaint in the sealed envelope and placing it in the receptacle located on her unit." (Sapers, 2008) It is in the middle of December, 2007, two months following its submission, that CSC Management opens Smith's sealed complaint. (*ibid*) By then of course Inmate Smith is dead.

Critical discourse analysis of official texts about Inmate Smith from this period reveals extreme absurdities of bureaucratic governance of this "unmanageable" carceral subject. The stifling nature of the institutional context and definitional apparatus in which she was embedded ultimately assign consequences for Inmate Smith's every action, even the most banal. Incredibly, several levels of bureaucratic management and even the Government of Canada become concerned with the bodily functions of Inmate Smith; the most mundane aspects of her beingness become elevated to being the business of the state. Texts from this period reveal the entangled ridiculousness of a contemporary bureaucratic apparatus. The imperative to take total control of the carceral subject makes everything she does relevant. The operationalization of this system of control becomes farcical while the bodily autonomy of the carceral subject is removed. Once Inmate Smith is held in solitary confinement, understood to be "high needs" and gained a "reputation" for being unmanageable, data accumulates whenever she acts, In the context of the bureaucratic entanglement in which Inmate Smith was enmeshed at this point, her death is not only a predictable outcome but the sole likely result: it is highly unlikely this situation could have reasonably ended other than with her death.

Analysis of the video of Inmate Smith's biological death reveals at the micro-level in the moment of her death how the judgment of front line staff was paralyzed by orders from management and ultimately by security logic. This footage, which CSC fought hard to suppress, as will be discussed later in this chapter, depicts the death of Inmate Smith while several front line guards stood watching. It is scrupulously recorded with a time signature running on the film; the video recording starts at 6:45 a.m. on October 19, 2007. Testimony at the inquest indicates that guards had gathered outside Smith's cell for at least ten minutes prior to starting the videotape. (CBCNews 22 January 2013) When the film begins, Inmate Smith is lying in a small corner of floorspace in her solitary cell, between the bed and the wall. Smith is positioned face down, gasping for breath, from asphyxiation by the ligature she had tied around her neck. It is certain from the footage that at least four guards (and at times five in addition to the one holding the camera) are gathered, standing continuously at the door to Inmate Smith's cell for at least ten minutes with the camera rolling. What they ostensibly do not know is that they are watching her die. The guards' surveillance and inaction continue even while the gasping stops and Inmate Smith's face turns visibly blue. They do enter the cell several times but do not assist her or remove the ligature from her neck for at least 10 minutes.

Narrative comments by guards that accompany the video footage taken while Inmate Smith lies dying consist of impersonal, matter of fact comments directed to Ashley Smith such as "It's been long enough. You need to take that off" and, calmly, without emotion: "Ashley" and hushed reassurances to one another such as "we don't have to do anything." (Behind the Wall) These comments are easily comprehensible as guards' enactments of the behaviours they have been instructed to display. Perhaps they are also reminders by the guards to themselves or for posterity of prior directives not to intervene made by the managers who are the expected audience of the video. The guards' attention to their audience calls attention to the subject position they occupy, a position not dissimilar to that of Inmate Smith. They are confined by a set of rules, closely surveilled but not assisted, by several higher levels of CSC management. This video, understood as a text produced under certain conditions with certain purposes is like a hall of mirrors. It presents an ominous enactment of a response to the question "who watches the watchers?"[18] and also to Coralee Smith's parting question aired at the end of the "Behind the Wall" documentary: "who gave that order [not to intervene]?" They are watched through the looking glass framed by logics of risk and security. This reading of the video suggests that while an order was, in one sense, given by a particular bureaucrat, in turn, this bureaucrat was only one in a series of reflected images of authority that together make up a mirror maze where no agent is reachable, tangible or responsible. Regardless of who actually gave the order, it was made not just possible but predictable in a rationalized bureaucracy and budget cycle guiding that bureaucrat as much as it did the guards, and anyone involved in the criminal and carceral institutions in which Inmate Smith was confined, by everyone and no one in particular.

The tenor of the guards' comments changes about 12 minutes into the video when they enter into the cell a second time and begin CPR. One cries out that she is inadequately trained for the task, swearing and saying she has not had CPR training for eleven years. The institution is scrupulous about recording of all that transpires but not, has not, clearly, paid comparable attention to preparing of staff to help in emergencies. Emergency workers arrive at 7:10 a.m. and take over chest compressions. The 25 minutes depicted in the video are a microcosm of what happened in Inmate Smith's carceral life every day: surveillance, inaction, no assistance, avoidance. By the time the recording stops, Inmate Smith is dead.[19]

The gears of CSC systems do not cease to grind in their paradigmatic patterns after Inmate Smith's death. The 2014 response of CSC to the inquest recommendations rejects two key imperatives and refuses to place limits on the use of solitary confinement while it also rejects the admonition it should be subjected to external scrutiny. It also, while enumerating without reiterating them, claims that the bulk of the other inquest recommendations have already been addressed in the time since Smith's death. (CSC, 2014) This is entirely consistent with the earlier response of CSC to Sapers' 2008 Report on the death of Ashley Smith, which took the form of a checklist. Sapers complained this response was cursory and not comprehensive. His key concern raised was that "recommendations that go to the very core of accountability and governance within federal corrections — e.g. oversight of women's corrections at the national level, external monitoring of segregation, expert chairing by an independent mental health professional of national boards of investigations involving suicides and incidents of self-injury — continue to be rejected or supported only "in part" by the Correctional Service."[20] From the perspective of critical discourse analysis, it is not a minor detail that the response took the form of a spreadsheet and that its contents claim the production of the spreadsheet itself was a significant step towards responding to concerns arising from Inmate Smith's death: "The posting of this document is an important step in publicly sharing the initiatives that the Service is pursuing to address the issues identified in the Office of the Correctional Investigator study on deaths in custody." Further, responses that deal with improvements to its infrastructure are clearly non-sequitors that fit the CSC's own pre-existing agenda to bolster its funding and facilities.[21] CSC suggests that the issues identified in Sapers' report could be partially resolved by improvements to their surveillance technologies and facilities and proposes, as a solution, construction projects that could be undertaken to facilitate for guards and management better surveillance of cells.

WHAT IS LOST

In the configuration of the beingness of Ashley Smith into the figure of Inmate Smith, certain aspects of her embodiment, history and particularity are privileged while others are made invisible, and lost. As discussed, in the recounting and deployment of her official "record" and her "maximum security" designation, the minor and mundane underlying factual circumstances of the incidents that gave rise to the incarceration of Ashley Smith are minimized. A view of the rapid trajectory of a teenaged actor from throwing apples at a postal worker and stealing a CD into solitary confinement in an adult prison is artificially obscured by the official description of her charges in her criminal and correctional records. Contextual contribution of corrections procedures to Ashley Smith's record by corrections' systems is lost; after she is transferred to adult custody, her youth is made invisible and her mental health concerns are not part of the official record. Finally, the carceral context foundational to and productive of Ashley Smith's escalating pattern of offences officials is erased.

The Inmate Smith figure fits well with narratives about unruly inmates having to be managed by a bureaucratic system that assesses risk and manages security. It bolsters the credibility of expertise in management of such a system, both by scientific analysis and knowledge of rules that apply in its operations. The existence of such unruly, incorrigible, risky and unmanageable actors accords easily with narratives that affirm the legitimacy of a robust carceral apparatus and applaud the work of corrections officers and systems. The truth claims it enables about Inmate Smith are self-confirming. The system is legitimated by reports of her unruliness. Broadly, the structure of carceral exclusion and logic of exception are confirmed to be necessary by her conduct while confined. The Inmate Smith figure has effects in producing a need to neutralize, and punish, Ashley Smith. It makes possible the transformation of a failure to return a hairbrush into a criminal mischief charge and self-harm incidents into assaults. It transforms mundane, even banal bodily functions, into the business of the state. The snowballing series of charges keeps Correctional facilities in business; the NYBC onsite court turns short-term carceral subjects into long-term and repeat carceral subjects.

As constructed in official texts produced during her life, Inmate Smith is a figure who is responsibilized for her "bad choices" yet is not seen as a world-creating actor. Her resistances are read as misbehaviours that constitute non-compliance. These behaviours are understood as deliberate but never thought to *make sense*. In a 2006 "Management and Reintegration Plan for Ashley Smith," a psychological expert author, speaking to mental health criteria for capacity, states "she [Ashley Smith] is capable of engaging in purposeful behaviour ... Ms. Smith is aware of the behaviours in which she engages and is able to apprehend the probable conse-quences of her actions." (Rush to Judgment, 19)

In the official discourse, Inmate Smith is an actor who "makes bad choices" but her actions are not meaningful. It is significant that the figure of Inmate Smith is understood to have *some* agen-cy; she can be disobedient and obedient. While the figuration of Inmate Smith makes unthinkable or at least irrelevant certain aspects of Ashley Smith's agency, the agentic potential Inmate Smith is considered to have is in a "choice" whether to "comply" with authority. The accepted official psychological assessment of Inmate Smith was that she was a noncompliant subject "intent on playing games." (Perkel, 25 March 2014) A 2003 report made by a psychiatrist at Restigouche Hospital sets the stage for and sums up this construction of Inmate Smith's agency "Ms. Smith clearly understands her responsibilities and their consequences and can control her actions when she chooses to." (*ibid*)

Further, the bureaucratic admonition to blindly follow structured rules and to prefer the lesser risks of inaction over the risks of action interrupts the judgment of and confines the subjectivity of the guards much as it does Ashley Smith. Inmate Smith resists the logic of compliance as a governmental technology of the self and in her resistance is confined by it too, trapped in a cycle of ever-increasing sanctions for rule-breaking, while the same logic traps the guards into watching her die. In failing to account for agency as other than non-compliance or compliance, this binary logic allows for no subject positions between rule follower and rule breaker and no interactions that are not hierarchical.

THE INQUESTS

While it never completely disappears, the Inmate Smith figuration has become dissonant with widely-held understandings of Ashley Smith that have emerged since her death. The "official story" about her death that emerges within routinized documents produced by CSC is no longer commonly believed. The trajectory of the development of the Ashley Smith case is not consistent with the portrayal of the interaction between purportedly sensationalist media and rights-driven, emancipatory, dispassionate legal processes claimed by mainstream policy literature. Inmate Smith, in life, was relegated to obscurity, to confinement with her complaints about her treatment ignored and none of her convictions newsworthy or noteworthy in the legal system. While her conduct in life produced, and was in turn structured by, a routinized, formal official response, the event of her death provokes a very different sort of official and social response. Her death becomes a case of legal and social significance. This altered response does not come first from official sources. It is not policy investigation or legal advocacy but investigative journalism that ruptures the trajectory of the case and draws critiques of the way Inmate Smith died into the public consciousness. Even before Inmate Smith becomes celebritized, it is journalistic agents who raise questions about guards failing to intervene in the event of Inmate Smith's death and move the story into widespread disrepute. Before 2010, in these media reports, the case is framed as one of rogue bad actors in the correctional being fired and criminally charged.[22]

Public attention is drawn to the Smith case as investigative journalists begin to inquire into what made possible a young person's journey from incarceration for throwing apples and stealing a CD to death in solitary confinement over the course of four years. This journey drives the investigative energy of the media. In 2010, the release of CBC two docudramas "Out of Control" and "Behind the Wall," and a revelation in media reports of a finding in Dr. Margo Rivera's report about Ashley Smith's death that it "is unlikely that Inmate Smith committed suicide" (Makin, 29 October 2010) are pivotal moments where the Inmate Smith figure loses its traction as an explanatory frame. It is with reconfiguration of Ashley Smith from a blank inmate into *somebody's* middle class white child in the CBC Docudrama "Out of Control," as will be discussed in the next chapter, that the Smith case starts attracting a high degree of public scrutiny.

The conditions of possibility of the Smith inquest combined with strategic decisions on the part of CSC counsel also contributed to transformations in widespread understandings of the case. Ironically, CSC's tactical decision to fight relentlessly to keep investigative scrutiny away from its management and practices also contributed to popular rejection of the Inmate Smith figure. The ways in which meaning was officially made of Ashley Smith's behaviours were to a large extent deliberately hidden from scrutiny after her death. CSC responses to allegations that they had breached their own institutional policies in keeping Inmate Smith in solitary confinement for prolonged periods were consistently met with retrenchments of systemic defenses: in its response to Sapers' concerns about Inmate Smith's death, CSC (2009) refused to acknowledge its failure to uphold its own segregation policy. In the first inquest, at the behest of CSC Counsel, presiding coroner Dr. Bonita Porter refused to look at the data accumulated by CSC in the nine months preceding Ashley Smith's death. This decision was quashed by the Ontario Divisional Court on Judicial Review in *Smith v. Porter (Judicial Review)* 2011 ONSC 2844. Dr. Porter stepped down and a new inquest was convened with Dr. John Carlisle presiding.

In the second inquest, counsel for CSC made a series of motions that were an aggressive legal tactic to deal with the crisis presented for its systems by the Smith case. Counsel used the inherently legalistic tool of motions to entrench a tactical position that what transpired with Inmate Smith in CSC custody was ordinary, routine and normal and therefore not worthy of scrutiny. Motions were made to keep sealed Smith's psychiatric and medical records detailing her forced restraints and medications administered to her while incarcerated sealed; motions were made to keep the videos depicting Smith's death out of the inquest evidence and to keep the public from viewing them.[23] Motions were made by her treating physicians in facilities outside of Ontario to keep those medical records out of the proceeding, allegedly for (convenient) jurisdictional reasons. The summons to witness of CSC Commissioner Don Head was sought to be quashed.[24] All of these motions were ultimately unsuccessful, but they did present expensive and time-consuming barriers to getting official "data" about Inmate Smith into evidence. The motions not only did not work: the plan to normalize CSC's treatment of Inmate Smith and shield their systems from scrutiny backfired. These heavy-handed legal tactics contributed strongly to the tainting of the Inmate Smith figure, to widespread awareness of the facts of the case, and to public dissonance with the narratives presented by CSC about her death.

Resistance by CSC to the fact-finding project of the inquest was no doubt expected to be more effective. The meso level apparatus of an inquest as defined in the *Coroners' Act* RSO 1990 c. C-37 has limited power. The Ontario *Coroner's Act* structured the inquiry that took place after Ashley Smith died. This *Act* sets up inquests as blended medical and legal processes, legal in their form but presided over by a medical doctor,[25] for officially determining what caused deaths, including when prisoners die in custody.[26] The Ashley Smith inquest is significant doctrinally to the interpretation of this legislation in that it has opened up questions about what is the proper scope for the inquiry that takes place in a coroner's inquest. The Smith inquest involved significantly more testimony and a wider chronological scope of inquiry than inmate inquests generally do. There was also conflict in the course of the inquest over the extent to which the Ontario coroner could access records produced by medical professionals working with CSC outside of Ontario. Nonetheless, the jurisdiction of the inquest was to look at how and why Inmate Smith died, not how inmates are treated by CSC generally.

The inquest verdict is comprised of jurors' determination as to the cause of death combined with recommendations. An inquest decision does not provide a narrative of what took place or insight into the internality of the deceased. While provocative and arguably supportive of a broader interpretation of the role of coroner's inquests, the unprecedented homicide verdict in the Smith inquest has no direct material effect in formal legal arenas. It is true that no prior inquests about the deaths of prison inmates in Canada have resulted in a homicide verdict unless another prisoner is the one considered responsible for the death. However, no institution or actor is sentenced, charged, fined or sanctioned by the verdict. The verdict neither binds the state to take action to remedy nor to undertake a general inquiry into CSC practices, whether in relation to women offenders or generally. In fact, the government has declined to do either. Equally, the inquest verdict does not promise to bring about social change or changes to CSC practices although CSC settled an $11 million civil suit brought by Ashley Smith's family members for an undisclosed but certainly substantial amount and estimates indicate CSC spent in excess of $5 million on the preparation and presentation of the inquest case, CSC management has signaled it intends to spend little money or energy on institutional change.[27]

Yet, the verdict of homicide is important. It challenges what are assumed to be the parameters of possibility of what inquests can do. No prior inquest into the death of a prisoner in Canada yielded a verdict of homicide that impugned someone or something other than another prisoner as being at fault for the death. The inquest had a different outcome than even advocates for the Smith family imagined possible. In materials filed for the CSC motion to quash the summons of its Director, the respondent counsel for the Smith family *conceded* that the verdicts available to the inquest jury were not determined, suicide or accident. Homicide was not mentioned.[28] The homicide verdict is a bold, activist assertion by the inquest jury. It is an unprecedented re-assertion of Ashley Smith's citizenship, of her membership in *bios*, or political community, a refutation of her status as *homo sacer*.

INMATE SMITH AND MACRO-POWER

Representations coalescing into the figure of Inmate Smith can be understood as microprocesses of governance. They engage in the enactment and reconstitution of power relations in discursive, conventional and institutional sites. The figure does governmental and discursive work in legitimating certain kinds of interventions and bolstering the credibility and authority of certain types of expertise. CSC management claims that the responsibility for its violations of its own policies and meso-level operating constraints fell on Inmate Smith's bad choices, as well as on failures of front line staff. It has embraced framings of Inmate Smith as an unusually seriously mentally ill person, all of which displace responsibility away from their systems and preserve the existing carceral regime. Nonetheless, the figure is a technology of governmental power that is not always used in the same way, and sometimes has been articulated by liberal and other reformers in ways that are potentially emancipatory.

At the macro-level of analysis, the figure of Inmate Smith both reflects and has potential to confront modalities of governance. The figure of Inmate Smith can reveal exclusionary practices in government of adolescents, imprisonment, and solitary confinement, and help in deciphering and confirming problems with underlying governmental logics at work in contemporary practices of imprisonment. The figure of YP Smith can be used as technology to refute commonly accepted core claims about the youth criminal justice system that are fundamentally inconsistent with the official understandings of Ashley Smith as an inmate. Representations of YP Smith in official documents seriously undermine widely accepted and commonly understood claims about the nature of the youth criminal justice system. The individualized approach claimed to be undertaken in the YCJA is not consistent with the governance to which Ashley Smith was subject. Sanctions for her actions were endlessly repeated despite being obviously counterproductive in changing her behaviour. There is nowhere evidence of a serious inquiry into what interventions or techniques of governance might help her to become a contributing member of society upon release. Rehabilitation and eventual reintegration of Inmate Smith into society are nowhere referenced and it is not evident that they were contemplated. YP Smith is constructed as dangerous and requiring forms of containment that limit her interactions with other people, including guards and mental health personnel. What upset, angered or otherwise motivated YP Smith, which would have to be considered in order for sanctions to be "meaningful," is not considered in official texts.

After her death became publicly known, the figure of Inmate Smith became increasingly articulated by parties seeking to effect broad systemic change. For example, the figure of Inmate Smith has been mobilized by progressive advocates seeking to reduce and even eliminate use of solitary confinement in Canadian prisons.[29]

The prison is not a space of lawlessness, but rather a messy space where the power of a variety of formal legal discourses is deployed alongside other technologies. Management, system agents and even Inmate Smith in her filing of complaints as interpreting social actors invoke and manipulate the formal discourses of the law. Formal legal discourse influences what happens to Ashley Smith, but does not simplistically determine how she is treated. Consider the transfer application. In that instance, the formal law about under whose jurisdiction an 18 year old inmate falls is rigidly followed. However, throughout the case, a wide range of other legal rules are disregarded and ignored where they are inconvenient to, or inconsistent with, what bureaucrats seek to do. Rules about reviewing inmate's status are deflected by series of transfers enabling CSC to keep her in solitary confinement; timely responses are not given to grievances; forced injections are administered.(Sapers, 2008, 2.1.3.) Guards clearly felt bound by orders and rules even to the extent that this sense of obligation paralyzed them into non-intervention at the time of Ashley Smith's death.

Carceral bureaucracies ignored legal limits imposed upon them in many instances. Management of YP Smith by youth corrections in New Brunswick and then of Inmate Smith by CSC consistently violated her rights and operated in violation of statutory laws, guidelines and procedures even while it took place in an abundance of legalism. Although the power of law was referenced unendingly in reports about her and charges against her, Inmate Smith's *Charter* rights to security of the person, liberty, to be free from unreasonable search and not to be unlawfully detained were violated; her right to have her grievances heard and responded to was violated; she was tasered, pepper-sprayed, beaten, forcibly injected with psychotropic drugs when she wasn't psychotic, and held in solitary confinement for extended periods without proper reviews. Formally accorded legal rights were overwhelmed by the logic of exception in this interplay.

This analysis of texts about the Inmate Smith figure reveals a level of bureaucratic surveillance of the most banal domains of Ashley Smith's existence that is intense to the point of untenably expensive absurdity epitomized by detailed documentation of her daily bodily functions, and the imposition of an administrative limit of her use to four squares of toilet paper. In this surveillance, the bureaucratic gaze finds what it is looking through in the process of constructing juridical acts in Inmate Smiths' most basic physicality. The operation of biopower in the form of necropolitics in the bureaucratic management of Inmate Smith as a carceral subject reveals the fundamentally compromised bodily integrity of the "contingent body" of a carceral subject and the fundamental immorality in a liberal rights framework of the bureaucratic management of the banal details of Inmate Smith's life, which forecloses any possibility of her bodily autonomy. (Gerlach, Hamilton, Sullivan and Walton) The death of an exceptionally unmanageable, inconveniently female, unusually large, inmate is a predictable, expected and economically even desirable outcome of interlocking risk rationality, security-focused governance and the neoliberal logic of exception in the rationality of necropolitics.

The "individual and system failures" described by Sapers in the Smith case can thus be re-read not as anomalous but predictable outcomes of application of the totalizing logics of risk and security through a bureaucratic apparatus. (Rigakos) Configuring Ashley Smith as a "maximum security" and "difficult" inmate allowed CSC to domesticate, categorize, statistically report and tabulate her conduct. In this configuration, a single inmate's life and death are too easily rationalized as an acceptable loss.

The close reading of discourses circulating in the Smith case undertaken here reveals that, in failing to respond adequately to the medical emergency on October 19, 2007 in which Inmate Smith died, (Sapers, 2008, 3) guards were not "bad apples" engaged in rogue conduct. Their inaction is one strand in a complex and many-stranded web of decisions excluding Smith from political community, education, medical treatment, and even the broader prison population.

However, because Inmate Smith's death mandatorily triggers an institutional response, it does interrupt the grinding of bureaucratic processes. It publicly reveals tensions and chinks in a messy and disjointed system. While it resolves immediate management problems for systems, it also opens up a forum for contestation of official definitions of Inmate Smith and official narratives of what took place. The denial of CSC's obstructive motions, the expansion of the scope of the inquest and the ultimate verdict of homicide in the Smith Inquest also show the radical contingency of the present and the power of the intervention of interpreting human actors. Uses to which the video footage and other constant surveillance were put in those proceedings, in media texts and in ongoing debates are not closed or simply determined by the uses for which they were produced.

The dispersal of responsibility that led to Inmate Smith's death is constructed in the rationalized economy of a bureaucratic hall of mirrors. Docudrama footage of obscured faces of guards failing to intervene as Inmate Smith lies dying, as well as in the masked faces of several unidentified, interchangeable, guards saying "you will comply" to her in an earlier incident provide images of the dehumanized reflected "faces" in the carceral funhouse. Front line guards are under constant surveillance in much the same manner as the inmates. The failure of guards to act in Inmate Smith's dying moments is only a final re-enactment of a routine process in which guards' judgment is overridden and paralyzed by fear of discipline from management, overall security is paramount and each inmate is inconsequential. Her death is a positive outcome from a budgetary perspective for CSC and mental health systems. It resolves management problems she posed to, and alleviates burdens imposed by the costs of that management on, bureaucratic systems of governance.

The agentic potential of CSC guards in choosing to follow or resist orders is lost in their security-based reasoning and the logic of risk governance. Routinized coding and defining of Inmate Smith as unmanageable and noncompliant prescribes certain solutions that involve blindly following rules. It is by following this logic under surveillance that all are led into the trap of accumulating charges in which Inmate Smith was caught, and also into a discursive trap in which those guarding her and even those managing the guards were caught. If the ultimate value is in following rules, guards, wardens and managers equally cannot, or if they can, they *do* not, let their human judgment override them in seeking more creative ways to address her or even by intervening to save her life. What is lost in the monstrous bureaucratic (Hamilton and Gerlach) relations between inmates, guards and management is not just Ashley Smith's world-creating agency. The dangers of these logics also threaten guards', wardens' and CSC managers' agentic potential. Ultimately, the Omelan bargain we have been persuaded to agree to by notions of security and the broader good menaces us all.

ENDNOTES

---

[1] In this chapter, I refer to Ashley Smith as Inmate Smith when I am describing or relating this official story. I refer to her as Ashley Smith when I am discussing her "caseness."

[2] According to its Preamble and its Declaration of Principle in s. 3. Also, The UN *Convention on the Rights of the Child* is referenced in the preamble to the YCJA. The YCJA is supposed to guide decision makers in handing down "meaningful consequences" to adolescent offenders, as well as reducing what was considered to be Canada's over-reliance on incarceration for youth. Decision makers in the juridical field are admonished by this law to consider the underlying reasons for criminal

offending by youth are addressed in order to ensure appropriate intervention is provided and adolescents in custody are reintegrated into their communities upon release.

[3]Throughout this period, and throughout her life, Ashley Smith was a subject to whom the meso-level apparatus of protections afforded by the *Canadian Charter of Rights and Freedoms* applied. Of particular relevance, procedural rights are afforded, cruel and unusual punishment is prohibited There are other procedural rights accorded by the *Charter* that are relevant to the many legal proceedings that took place during the Smith case, including the right to counsel (s.10(b)) and the right not to be arbitrarily searched (s.9) or detained (s. 11) as well as the right to counsel in legal proceedings concerning him or her. Further, Section 12 prohibits "[c]ruel and unusual treatment or punishment" of prisoners. and deprivations of liberty except in accordance with law are prohibited by the *Charter*. Relatedly, Constitutional supremacy means that these rights trump any actor or administrative system, and that officials cannot act arbitrarily or without legal justification.

[4]According to Sapers (2008) Smith incurs 50 criminal charges while in the NBYC. Richard counts "upwards of eight hundred documented incidents" involving sanction of YP Smith for negative behaviours during the over three year period she was in the youth system (Richard, 2008, 19).

[5]Levi, Primo *Survival In Auschwitz: The Nazi Assault on Humanity* New York: Simon and Schuster, 1996. Levi's analysis of life and death in an extermination camp is useful to consider when contemplating the banality and burdensome weight of accumulating sanctions to which Ashley Smith was subject but it is important not to over-state parallels between the forms of imprisonment currently occurring in Canada and Nazi concentration camps.

[6]This disconnect is underscored by the problematic location of the officially impartial courthouse where Smith acquired most of her convictions: it was located on the grounds of the NBYC. This location and the abundance of convictions problematize the claimed neutrality of the court processes as between the CSC and the offender.

[7]For discussion see e.g. Bala, Nicholas. The Development of Canada's Youth Criminal Justice Law. In K. Campbell (Ed.) *Understanding Youth Justice in Canada*. Toronto: Pearson Education Canada, 2005. Under the former youth justice regime, Canada received criticism on the international stage for being the world leader amongst industrialized western nations

in per capita incarceration rates of its youth. This pattern was intended to be corrected by the YCJA and statistics say that the legal regime change has had an effect in reduced Canada's "over-reliance" on incarceration for adolescents. From a utilitarian perspective, legislative change has led to Canada locking up statistically fewer adolescents. However, perhaps this does not get to the root of the concerns raised internationally about Canada's excessive reliance on youth incarceration: the official story of YP Smith brings to light the continued reliance of our nation's systems of governance on an expensive, non-rehabilitative, approach to unruly young people: confinement and containment.

[8]See e.g. Canadian Press "Fourth Prison Employee Charged in Connection with Death of NB Woman" (1 November 2007); Also see reference to the "19-year-old New Brunswick woman" " New Brunswick Guards Accused of Negligence Back in Court in March" cbc News (6 February 2008).

[9]See e .g. "Prison Employee Charged in Connection with Death of N.B. Inmate" Canadian Press November 2007. "19 year old inmate Ashley Smith of Moncton, N.B."

[10]Canadian Press "Fourth Prison Employee Charged in Connection with Death of N.B. Woman" (1 November 2007).

[11]An enumerated list of disciplinary offences as well as the procedure for CSC's Formal Disciplinary Process is found in s. 40 of the CCRA.

[12]Any doubt as to whether risk management was the primary factor to be considered in interpretation of the CCRA was cleared up by a 2012 amendment, which added s. 3.1 to the law. This section provides that: "the protection of society is the paramount consideration for the Service in the corrections process."

[13]In an email sent to CSC managers eight days before Ashley Smith's death, Grand Valley acting warden Cindy Berry criticized the guards for "not removing warmth" from their interactions with Inmate Smith.

[14]For a good interactive infographic see "Ashley Smith's See-Canada-Tour" Canadian Press: http://cponline.thecanadianpress.com/graphics/2013/ashley-smith/index.html.

[15]On the CBC Timeline, it is stated, for example: "Ashley starts running high monthly long distance charges, ranging from $200 to $1,600 per month. She would spend a lot of time on the Internet, looking at inappropriate material" http://www.cbc.ca/fifth/blog/the-life-and-death-of-ashley-smith.

[16]Per Commissioner's Directive 566-7, "16. Notwithstanding s. 49(4) of the CCRA, a male staff member will, under no circumstances, even in

an emergency, conduct or witness the strip search of a female inmate, but will contain the situation until such time that female staff members arrive to conduct and witness the strip search."

[17]As cited previously: "they were frequently disciplined for making that call — at Berry's behest — even in cases where Smith's face had turned purple and she struggled for breath" http://www.ctvnews.ca/canada/ ashley-smith-inquest-warden-didn-t-know-of-guard-s-confusion-about-entering-cell-1.1476269#ixzz34G18ZTLc.

[18]"Who watches the watchers?" or "Who watches the watchmen" Quis custodiet ipsos custodes? is a Latin phrase generally first attributed to the Satires of Roman poet Juvenal (Satire VI, lines 347–8), which is literally translated as "Who will guard the guards themselves?" The question is also often associated with the philosophy of Plato.

[19]Much has been said about the usefulness of this video to the Smith Inquest and to the publicization of her case. Although it was mandatorily produced by CSC, massive efforts were undertaken to suppress it. Video footage of Ashley Smith's death is similar in this way to other official representations of her: they bear numerous interpretations and articulations and their uses are not easily predictable.

[20]Office of the Correctional Investigator (OCI) Initial Assessment of the Correctional Service of Canada's (CSC) Response to the OCI's *Deaths in Custody Study, A Preventable Death* (Report into the Death of Ashley Smith) and the CSC National Board of Investigation into the Death of an Offender at Grand Valley Institution for Womenhttp://www.oci-bec. gc.ca/cnt/rpt/pdf/oth-aut/oth-aut20090911ia-eng.pdf.

[21]For example: "CSC is pursuing funding to implement short and long-term strategies developed to address the specific service, support, and accommodation needs of women offenders with mental health and behavioural needs." (Rec. 1 OCI, Rec. 1 CSC) http://www.csc-scc.gc.ca/005/007/ rocidcs/grid3-eng.shtml.

[22]For an illustrative example see " Ont. Prison Workers Fired Over N.B. Inmate's Death," CBC News (17 January 2008).

[23]The full judgment of Dr. Carlisle on the motion concerning the sealing order is available at: http://www.falconers.ca/documents/RulingonSealingOrderandSubmissions.Oct232012.pdf.

[24]To view the CSC-produced documents in which this was sought see: http://www.falconers.ca/documents/AnticipatedevidenceofDonHead.pdf.

[25]Sets out the jurisdiction for inquests in s. 16.

[26]s. 10 of the Act requires at (4).

[27]The recommendations in the inquest judgment in respect of systemic change to CSC operations are largely reiterative of recommendations made in other inquests and in repeated reports by Sapers. CSC Commissioner Don Head told the inquest jury not to "bother making costly recommendations" in testimony at the proceedings See Stone, Laura. " CSC Spent Over $5 million on Ashley Smith Inquest" *Global News* (22 January 2014) http://globalnews.ca/news/1097960/csc-spent-at-least-5-million-on-ashley-smith-inquest.

[28]http://www.falconers.ca/documents/FactumFinalApr1511.pdf At paragraph 39 of Factum of the Respondents/ Appellants.

[29]Media coverage of the constitutional lawsuit launched against the Attorney General for Canada to challenge indefinite use of solitary confinement in prisons, in BC in 2014 by the BC Civil Liberties Associationhttps://bccla.org/wp-content/uploads/2015/01/2015-01-19-Notice-of-Civil-Claim.pdf has shown photographs of Ashley Smith, for instance. Also consider for example the 2013 CBC "Ideas" documentary on Solitary Confinement http://www.cbc.ca/news/canada/solitary-confinement-a-growing-issue-in-canadian-u-s-prisons-1.1699487.

4. Child Ashley

Recuperation

INTRODUCTION

*My person was hideous and my stature gigantic. What did
this mean? Who was I? What was I? Whence did I come?
What was my destination? These questions continually
recurred.*
—Mary Shelley, *Frankenstein* (1818, Chapter 15, 5)

Mary Shelley's *Frankenstein* is a story about an intelligent, over-
sized and impetuous "youngster" whose parentage and bearing
are not "normal," who does not fit within the normative paradigm
of what it means to be a child and who becomes despondent, violent and self-destructive after being excluded and rejected from
membership in human community. Shelley's creature struggles for
approval and acceptance but is understood as a monster. Once
excluded, the creature becomes violent. Shelley's story tracks the
difficulties on the part of a misfit monster who is unimaginable
within the category of child, and the creature's experiences of
rejection, isolation and dissonance.

There are many parallels between the figure of Child Ashley and
Mary Shelley's classic Romantic monster. In this chapter, as I did
in the preceding chapter with reference to Inmate Smith, I look
at a figure of Ashley Smith that coalesces from a number of texts
in the case. This chapter focuses on figures of Ashley Smith that
foreground and privilege the aspect of her being a "child." I look
at variations on how Ashley Smith was configured as a child at

117

different points in the Smith case, and by whom. First, she was seen as a misfit, risky child, and specifically a risky girl,[1] then, at least by CSC guards, as someone childlike "gaming" the system and finally, only after her death was she seen as a properly, normally constituted, "good" girl subject or child victim. In this chapter, I look at how Ashley Smith's dissonance with, and inability to fit within, the classed, raced and gendered categories of child (and girl) bring about her social death long before she finally biologically dies in CSC custody. I argue that Ashley Smith's monstrosity within culturally accepted discourses of the girl and child contributes significantly to her exclusion from political community and necropolitical actions taken in the juridical field. In looking to answer questions about who and what killed Ashley Smith, we should direct our attention to confining gender codes and racialized thinking which provide the exclusionary logic that constructs Ashley Smith as monstrous and marks her for incarceration from the category of child. In this chapter, I focus on what brought about her social exclusion, which preceded and in large part precipitated her juridical and biological deaths.

Figures of Child Ashley that emerge in the Smith case function as technologies of governmental power in strategically intentional as well as unintended ways. Figures of Child Ashley that emerge in the Smith case function as technologies of governmental power in strategically intentional as well as unintended ways. I argue that articulations of "Child Ashley" by progressive reform efforts as deployed "on behalf of Ashley" potentially undermine their own ostensibly recuperative and emancipatory political purposes. They re-inscribe white supremacist, confining boundaries of discourses of gender and childhood on which they draw. It is those same boundaries that marked Ashley Smith for exclusion, incarceration and ultimately death.

Looked at in this way, the Smith case is a case of an adolescent young woman governed by very repressive discourses of gender, childhood and whiteness. The Normal Child Ashley figure leaves unchallenged the masculinist angels-and-demons narratives of the law. It is a governmental technology articulated by a variety of actors and institutions in discourse in the construction of the Smith case as a particular sort of social problem, a problem of mislocation in which the wrong person (an innocent middle class white girl) has been mistakenly placed in a venue properly constructed to confine and contain more stereotypically abnormal (aboriginal, working class, male) prisoners.

The figure of Child Ashley as a "normal" child victim lost in the system was a powerful discursive technology articulated at certain critical points in the Smith case to effect the celebritization of Ashley Smith and strategically draw public attention to her death. In this chapter, I look at the deployment of words and images in constructing the Child Ashley figure. I track the emergence and flourishing of the figure and note its gradual relegation to less prominence than the Patient Smith figure. I look critically at the sites in which the figure appears. Further, I analyze pre-existing cultural and formal legal discourses of the child with which this figure intersects and at constellations of macropower with which it is engaged. I argue that Ashley Smith's biological death is the most predetermined event in the Smith case: it is the social deaths effected by her unthinkability within the category "girl child"[2] that exclude her from political and human community and the juridical death that contains her away in solitary that are more significant: her biological death is an almost inevitable after thought. To prevent similar deaths in custody, I therefore contend that change must be made to the confining discourses of gender and childhood.

TRAJECTORY: SITES, EMERGENCE AND FLOURISHING

There are three overlapping but distinct constructions of Ashley Smith as a child over the course of her case. First, during her life, she is understood as a risky child. Then, following her death, she is reconfigured in some texts as like a child "playing games." The configurations of the risky and gaming child are mutually confirming and supportive. It is the third reconfiguration, Ashley Smith as "normal" child, that effects a rupture in representations of her. This transforms her transformed dramatically from an abnormal girl into a proper, normal, noble girl victim. This transformed representation of Ashley Smith dominates texts generated in the Smith case for a brief time in 2010, and has significant governmental effect. It is ultimately superseded by the representation of her as a mental patient.

It is Normal Child Ashley that emerges as the pre-eminent figure of Ashley in the Smith case around early 2010, at the time of the "Out of Control" CBC Docudrama. (2010) This docudrama signals a pivotal moment of rupture in the case where the official configuration of Ashley Smith as Inmate Smith — the figure that has supported the official narratives told by various authoritative sources in the bureaucratic apparatus since her incarceration began — loses its legitimacy in the public imagination. The Child Ashley figure is originally constituted in this docudrama as well as in certain news articles from early 2010 until the conclusion of the inquest in 2013. Patient Smith replaces the Child Ashley figure in the media by at least early 2011. However, throughout the remainder of the case, the Child Ashley figure circulates in certain texts and statements of lawyers, social advocates, Ashley Smith and the Smith family, including her mother Coralee Smith. This Child Ashley figure produces other figures, especially family members, for Ashley. The Child Ashley figure is often found in texts explicitly or implicitly crafted by agents and groups who understand themselves to "speak for" or advocate on behalf of Ashley Smith. In these texts, Child Ashley is a figure articulated to mobilize public and official sympathies on Ashley Smith's behalf. Although it is clearly eclipsed in dominance by the figure of Patient Smith by the beginning of the second inquest, throughout the remainder of the Smith case, the child construction stays present. Indeed, as will be discussed in Chapter 5, configuration of Ashley Smith as a child is in many ways not only compatible, but complementary with construction of her as a vulnerable, valuable person with mental health problems.

ASHLEY THE IMPROPER AND RISKY GIRL

At the time of her death, Ashley Smith was not, in formal legal discourse, a child. As discussed in Chapter 3, immediately upon turning 18, Ashley Smith was divested, through a formal legal process (a transfer hearing), of the status of being a youth or child at law. This resulted in her removal from youth custody to the federal penitentiaries administrated by CSC. While "child" has particular social meanings, it also has overlapping and somewhat conflicting meanings in formal legal discourses. Under various provincial and territorial laws in Canada, for the purposes of child protection, a child is defined as someone under the age of majority; where Ashley Smith grew up, in New Brunswick, child protection legislation defines a child as "someone actually or apparently under the age of majority," namely 18 years of age.[3] However, under Canadian domestic law, for the purposes of criminal liability, under the YCJA, a child "means a person who is or, in the absence of evidence to the contrary, appears to be less than twelve years old."[4] For criminal purposes, children under the age of 12 are individuals who cannot incur criminal liability. At international law, under the *United Nations Convention on the Rights of the Child*, however, a "child" is defined as someone 17 years or under. For the period during which Ashley Smith was in conflict with the criminal law, she was considered to be a "young person" (between 12 and 17 inclusive). As discussed in the previous chapter, a formal legal construct, "young person" is a genderless figuration the from the YCJA and other youth-related legislation which seeps into broader public discourse. Smith, at age 19, imprisoned in high security adult penitentiaries, did not fall officially within the status of child under any legal definition available.

Despite her official status at the time of her death as an Adult Offender or Inmate, throughout her engagement with the prison industrial complex, system actors at different levels of the CSC bureaucracy, New Brunswick child protection system and mental health professionals all made sense of Ashley Smith as a risky "child" in various ways. Variations on the figure of Child Ashley are present as a subordinate construction of her to the official Inmate configuration in texts and statements produced throughout her case. At the front-line level, prison guards generally appear to have unofficially understood her as a child and had varying degrees of comfort with that.

However, before she turned 18, before Ashley Smith became a carceral subject (thus during the "challenging youth with complex needs" period discussed in Chapter 3), the educational and child protection systems of New Brunswick did accept that Ashley

Smith was a legal child and more specifically they read Ashley Smith as an *abnormal*, risky girl. She was labeled a "bully" and her initial exclusions from school were attributed at least in part to "bullying behaviour." (Richard, 2008 at 17) During her life, psych-professionals who she consulted and was referred to did not understand Ashley Smith as primarily a person with mental illness, as will be discussed in Chapter 4, but as a tyrannical child, a child with behaviour problems. The tyrannical child is someone not properly constituted as a child but who nevertheless acts in some ways like one. It is an *overgrown* child who is impossible to manage or control through the usual means and needs to be restrained through control and confinement.

Throughout her life, albeit with some exceptions, Ashley Smith was generally understood as a "normal" youth by psy-experts in the sense that she was read as not legitimately in need of mental health care. According to her mother Coralee Smith's testimony at the Smith inquest, Ashley Smith was understood by psy-experts prior to her incarceration as an immature, but not mentally ill, teenager. Coralee Smith told the inquest jury that Ashley saw a psychiatrist who decided Ashley was "just a normal teenager." "I'm too fat and I have acne," was Ashley's take on the session, according to Coralee Smith's testimony. (Perkel, 20 February 2013)

That the phrase "large, tyrannical child" repeats in the testimony of mental health professionals treating Ashley Smith is not a coincidence. It is a diagnosis. Psychiatrist Dr. Jeffrey Penn's notes brought forward in testimony in the second inquest read: "This young woman is essentially a large tyrannical child who can't tolerate limits, feels estranged and isolated from peers, unloved, unliked, and often hopeless." (Perkel, 25 March 2013) This label of Smith as a "large, tyrannical child" also appears in testimony from psychologist Dr. Allister Webster from the second inquest, who, referencing Penn's notes, called Smith: "a large, tyrannical child who can't tolerate limits." As Penn said in testimony at the second inquest, "tyrannical child" is a reference to "what a psychiatrist named Dr. Avner Barcai had decades earlier described as the "fearful-tyrannical child." (Blatchford, 25 March 2013) According to psychiatrist Dr. Avner Barcai who coined the term, the "tyrannical child" is a type of personality-disordered *adult* subject who believes irrationally in his or her own omnipotence, has fantasies of power and has lived with caregivers incapable of setting limits on him or her. (Barcai) The labeling of Smith as a "tyrannical child" in this construction is actually not easily reconcilable with her young age. It disqualifies her from childhood. A "tyrannical child" is a diagnosis devised to be applied to an adult improperly acting like a child, not for a youth who is misbehaving.

The offending child or masturbating child and madman are two of what Michel Foucault understands as "monsters." According to Foucault, the monster operates as a master category for defining and justifying contemporary forms of exclusion, erasure, surveillance and control. (Sharpe) The "tyrannical child" who is defined by his or her inability or unwillingness to accept authority and be maturely or "appropriately" adaptively compliant can be understood as an abnormal within the category of monster as theorized by Foucault. However, it is not a monstrous child. It is a monstrous adult acting improperly *like* a child. It is someone who, for some reason, does not deserve the protective label of child, someone acting irresponsibly and immaturely without being entitled to the excuse for doing so of being a child. Labeling Ashley Smith as a "tyrannical child" by psy-experts does constitutive work in claiming from the authority of scientific objectivity that Ashley Smith is a thoroughly unlikeable subject undeserving of help or attention. As an unmanageable subject not worthy of experts' time, Smith is by default consigned by psy-experts to solitary confinement while she is in CSC custody. Thus, through representation of Ashley Smith in expert discourse, she is constituted as irredeemably socially dead and legitimately the subject of juridical exclusion as a terminal carceral subject.

ASHLEY THE GAME-PLAYING CHILD

A variant on the Child Ashley figure that is found in texts and statements produced by CSC actors is the "game-playing" child. Psychologist Dr. Allister Webster said of Ashley Smith in testimony at the second inquest that there was a "power struggle" between Ashley Smith and CSC staff and calls this struggle "the game... She expected that CSC would always be the adult and come in and help."(Jones, 4 March 2013) In the "Rush to Judgment" report put forward by the Correctional guards' union, Ashley Smith is represented as a "likeable" "needy," "social" and "playful" child. In this text, she is represented as interactive with guards, and manipulative within those interactions. This Report was put forward in 2008 by the union in a context of "pending criminal charges against three correctional officers, and the constant threat of reprisals by CSC" (Rush to Judgment, 5) in defense of those among its members who had disciplined by their employer and criminally charged with negligence in relation to Ashley Smith's death. The Report's explicit purpose was to " set the record straight" about her death and to propel "senior management to assume its proper share of responsibility for this incident." (*ibid*)

The chief characterization in the "Rush to Judgment" report of Ashley Smith is as a "child" playing a "game" — "the choking game." To quote an anonymous guard cited in the report: "The thing with kids in care is that sometimes the only physical contact kids get is when they cause trouble. This girl was also bored out of her mind. She was constantly accumulating data. Yet you couldn't let her out ... she would inevitably create an incident."(Rush to Judgment, 9) Representations of Ashley Smith as like a child "playing games" bolster the expertise of prison guards and fit well with the idea that she is being "cared for" in a manner that is discordant with mainstream understandings of what is meant by imprisonment.

It is significant that it is primarily front line guards who perceived Ashley Smith as game-playing. Calling her resistances "games" is a compassionate, dismissive and paternalistic, way of characterizing them as something less sinister or intentional than manipulations or defiances. On the other hand, while it is compassionate, it allows Ashley Smith something other than willfulness. Her resistances are not understood as politically rational or rebellious in this formulation. Interestingly, it does acknowledge her resistances as agentic in a partial, limited way. The construction of Ashley's interactions with guards as "games" is a representation of her interactions with systems and actors in the correctional system as dialogic, or at least proto-dialogic. While Ashley Smith was, as inmates generally are, upon her incarceration, socially dead in the context of the broader society, she had a social existence within the prison. She was not dead to the front line staff who, like the prisoners themselves, spend their everyday lives present within the prison, even though they do not inhabit the prison full time. The euphemistic "game" language being used by guards to describe a power struggle between themselves and an inmate appears to be not just for her benefit but for theirs as well. It is evident that these guards understand themselves to be "good guys" and think of themselves as helpers to the inmates they supervise. "The funny thing is that I liked Ashley," said one correctional officer as reported in the "Rush to Judgment" report. "She had her good qualities. She was funny. When she was choking herself I was heartbroken. I asked her, 'Why now?' and told her I would treat her the way she treated me. She seemed to respect that. In reality, this girl was living in a cell in which all the floor tiles were removed, all the light fixtures were gone, and the sprinkler had been covered." (Rush to Judgment, 8) While guards may have indeed been, or had self-interested reasons to portray themselves as, empathetic with Ashley Smith and to characterize their relationship to her as one of care, the representations of Ashley Smith constructed in guards' testimonies and statements do not seem merely superficially compassionate. To all indications, many guards genuinely felt compassionate, friendly and even attached to Inmate Smith. It is also reasonable to surmise that the human feelings between guards and inmate were reciprocal and largely mutual, that Ashley Smith liked some of them and did not like others.

In this Game-Playing Child configuration, Ashley Smith is not entirely passive or unagentic. Rather, her agency is understood in terms that see her using the system and its actors to meet her needs, including a need for attention and amusement. In that reading, her actions were not malicious, or 'bad', but intentional, calculated, and a rational response to the situation in which she found herself. While this construction of Ashley Smith's agency is not as 'bad' it is however also not conceived of as meaningful, not to be taken seriously, not political, and not mature or "adult." A power struggle between front line guards, the bureaucratic rules of management and Ashley Smith is transformed into something lighter: a game. Another reference from the "Rush to Judgment

Report" is illustrative:" This correctional officer understood that Smith wanted staff to enter the cell. "She would say, 'I want to fight. I want to play with you guys.' But I never had to go in that cell. I had her under control. She said to me 'I don't like it when you're working here. I like to make you angry, but I can't.' She was like a little kid." (Rush to Judgment, 9)

While the figure of "game-playing" Child Ashley is deployed in ways that contrast with understandings of her as 'bad', it is simultaneously used ways that undermine the seriousness and political nature of Inmate Smith's predicament in custody. Discursive work is involved in making the conduct in which she engaged at the end of her life seem less urgent and serious and obscures the reality that the stakes to this "game" involved her life or death. Game metaphors ("the choking game") used to describe her resistances obfuscate the serious nature of the life-and-death struggle for existence in which Inmate Smith was engaged and gloss over the injuries she was incurring. Problematically, this configuration obfuscates ways in which management, guards and others tasked with her care, such as psychiatrists, abused the rules in relation to her. This figure is, in many instances, articulated on behalf of those tasked with dealing with Inmate Smith at the front line level, and is articulated as a technology to recast the relationship between prisoner and front line CSC staff to be one of caring and nurturing contact.

This "game-playing child" figure fits with narratives of care, supports arguments that the guards were highly skilled professionals doing their best in a challenging environment, and bolsters the union's claim that a relationship of care exists between guards and inmates in CSC facilities. Vincent and Zlomistic reference CSC "belief that Ashley was playing "a game" with prison guards, enjoying the attention that came with them continually running into her segregation cell."(Rush to Judgment, 29) Games are dialogic, challenging and may be productive of enjoyment or fulfillment by people engaged in them — at least on the part of the winners. They are situations in which all players agentically participate. The configuration of Child Ashley as a "game-playing child" supports the construction of Ashley Smith's relationship with her guards as one of care and is a defense against allegations of their inhumane treatment of her. The use of these game metaphors reveals differences between Ashley Smith's relationships with guards and with CSC management. It also reveals insights into the complex human-ness of social interaction and relationships sought to be managed in a carceral setting. While it is jarring and perverse from the perspective of an actor located in mainstream society, outside of the prison industrial complex, to see this relationship as one of care, it is important to note that this is how the guards understand themselves. It is evident from the "Rush to Judgment" report, from the video footage from Ashley Smith's April transfer to Pinel from Saskatoon Regional Psychiatric Centre to Pinel[5] and from the tearful testimonies of front line guards at the inquest that human feelings of affection, anger, friendship and a surrogate sense of family existed in the relationships between Inmate Smith and front line guards.

Further, there are other implications to power in the deployment of game metaphors in relation to Ashley Smith. In neoliberal societies, "games" and "sports" are socially acceptable contexts in which play can get rough and people can get hurt without recrimination. Calling Ashley Smith's interactions with guards a "game" goes a long ways towards explaining away her injuries and "time outs" in solitary confinement as legitimate. Also, games are a rule-bound activity. The notion that Ashley Smith and the front line CSC guards were engaged in a game implies that they were operating on the basis of some shared set of rules and indeed suggests that guards were in control of a situation they clearly were having difficulty managing. Games have winners and losers. The assertion by guards that they were engaged in a game with Ashley Smith implies that the guards and Ashley Smith were employing strategy and intentionality. Games also involve chance. Their outcomes are not predetermined. The guards' use of gaming metaphors, while it supports the suggestion that they were ultimately in control of Ashley Smith, reveals that gaining such control was a daily struggle and was not a foregone conclusion. Finally, the game metaphor also bolsters the legitimacy of the guards' role and supports the implication that it is ultimately they, not management or psy-experts who have the crucial expertise as to how to deal with prisoners and manage prisons.

The assertion of care and friendship between guards and prisoners that the Game-Playing Child figure of Ashley Smith asserts is not entirely disingenuous. The figure reveals how the messy complexities of human relationships in all their personalized ugliness and beauty are difficult for CSC's bureaucracy to contain and manage by rationalized, impersonal means. Indeed, the "game-playing child" figure bolsters a narrative structure in which it can be understood that not *just* Ashley Smith but also front line prison guards are victimized by their subject positions as low-level functionaries in relation to the prison industrial apparatus. The "Rush to Judgment" characterizes Ashley Smith as one of many victims in the case, including front line CSC officers:

> in addition to Ashley Smith, there are many other victims in this story. The people who worked diligently to save her life, despite management impediments, are being made to bear the consequences of her death. The Union of Canadian Correctional Officers will never accept this rank injustice. (Rush to Judgment, 41)

RECUPERATION: ASHLEY THE NORMAL CHILD

As of early 2010, in many media texts, Child Ashley is configured as a "normal" girl with normal implicitly — and explicitly at times — standing in for white, middle class and properly feminine. Normal Child Ashley is someone who was, as Jiwani argued was the understanding of Kelly Ellard, not to be dismissed as inevitably destined for prison and other forms of exclusion but rather someone who, prior to incarceration, was a "saveable white girl." (Jiwani) The figure of Child Ashley is often represented as normal or average case of a type of Canadian middle class white child. In being paradigmatically normal, the figure of Normal Child Ashley reveals widely accepted assumptions about what constitutes middle class whiteness and fills in the form of what is often understood to be an empty category. There are about 5,000,000 children under age 14 in Canada, about 40% of whom could be considered "middle class." (Statistics Canada, 2011) In the Normal Child Ashley figuration, great discursive effort is expended to reconfigure hers from a case of a blank and dangerous run-of-the-mill inmate into an innocent, victimized, middle class child who did not belong in prison, from one of *them,* into one of *our* children. The recuperative reconstitution of Ashley Smith as a normal middle class girl is made possible by her biological death: her resistant agency is no longer troubling that categorization by resisting it. A normal child is configured as a social category in opposition to a properly constituted inmate. In this configuration, Ashley Smith is not, however, recast as one of *us.* This important distinction is explored in more detail below.

The preponderant representation of Ashley Smith in the CBC's "Out of Control" docudrama is as a normal child from a normal, or good, home: even a suburban princess. The normalcy of Child Ashley is established in large part by emphasis is placed on her "normal childhood." The assertion of the normalcy of this childhood has become the dominant understanding of her early life to the extent that the Wikipedia article about the Ashley Smith inquest opens its biographical segment by saying "Ashley Smith had a normal childhood in Moncton." On the online CBC Timeline of the Ashley Smith case, the text states: "Ashley had a normal childhood. She liked camping at the beach, kayaking, and riding her bike." (CBC Timeline) Emphasis is placed on the assertion that Ashley Smith's normal childhood happened in the context of a normal family. It is this normalcy that implicitly underpins the reconfiguration of Ashley Smith as a good girl, an adolescent who is not bad but *troubled.* The narrative begins by characterizing Ashley Smith as "a troubled little girl who cried for help." Early in the docudrama, the scene takes viewer through a look at the "nice, neat home" of Coralee and Ashley Smith. Narrator Hana Gartner says in voice over "the story begins not where you think it would be begin, but in a nice, neat home with parents who really care." Ashley Smith's mother Coralee Smith is quoted: "we are talking about a child." The staging of the "Out of Control" documentary shows at length an image of flowers in a windowbox outside what is ostensibly her family home and refers to "the child [Coralee] wants to remember." It goes on to describe Ashley Smith as a child who "still played with dolls" and spends time interviewing Coralee in her daughter's room, which she calls a "grown up room," but the cinematic gaze is cast tightly not on the room as it stands but on a box of dolls that have been placed in storage in a closet. Gartner, the director of the docudrama then calls the room "a child's room." The camera pans Ashley Smith's room including the dolls in it, making reference to the dolls while her mother says "people said she was not a girly girl, but she had dolls ... she was a princess." The "Out of Control" docudrama's narration goes on to say "she was barely a teenager" and to characterize, in passing, Ashley Smith's conduct as "teenage defiance."

Similarly, *Toronto Star* reporters Donovan Vincent and Diana Zlomistic represent Ashley Smith as a "middle class kid" in their 2013 e-book *The Life and Death of Ashley Smith*. (Vincent and Zlomistic) This is another important text in constructing the normal Child Ashley figure. The text puts less emphasis on the paradigmatic normalcy of Ashley Smith's family than does the "Out of Control" docudrama. However, this texts emphasizes Child Ashley's normalcy as someone going through a "natural" developmental stage. For example, the text states as follows "Ashley ... was going through the natural transformations of adolescence." (*ibid*, 2) Also, like the "Out of Control" docudrama, this book foregrounds representations of Ashley Smith as a very young child. Photographs included in the text of the book are baby photos, (*ibid*, 9) a picture of Child Ashley doing the dishes while wearing a frilly apron at age four, (*ibid*, 9) and school pictures of her aged 14 and younger. There is one photo of her at 15 holding a basketball and standing beside her dog "at the family home." (*ibid*, 12) This photograph diverges from the rest because it features Child Ashley in a less stereotypically feminine pose, wearing less stereotypically female clothing, and it is one that, quite unusually amongst the portrayals of Ashley Smith in photographs circulating in the media, reveals her tall stature and strong appearance. While this visual text does not emphasize her femininity, it does stress the normalcy of her social location in what appears to be a middle-class suburb, doing what "normal" middle-class kids do.

Media texts in which the normal child figure dominates seem intent on assigning fathers to Child Ashley. According to Vincent and Zlomistic, prison guard Gaetan Desrochers developed "a kind of father-daughter relationship" with Ashley. (*ibid*, 27) Journalist Hana Gartner in her narration of the CBC "Out of Control" documentary misidentifies Coralee Smith's "family friend" Herb Gorber as Ashley's "father" and does not refer to the fact of her adoption. This has complex consequences. On the one hand, this misidentification simplifies the narrative about Ashley Smith's family life. At the same time, it confirms Child Ashley's home life as "normal" and provides a benign, caring, white patriarchal authority figure by whom she is claimed as a legitimate child. However, this misidentification also produces something for other media sources to expose as scandalous and provides the foundation for later stories that critique the credibility of the putative normalcy of Ashley Smith's family, and, by implication, of her.

Descriptions of Child Ashley in the *The Life and Death of Ashley Smith* e-book represent her as feminine, angelic — or at least harmless — and white. She is described as "the brown eyed, milky skinned cherub ... snuggled under a handmade pink flannel quilt." (*ibid*, 7) Emphasis is placed in this text on her young age at first incarceration. To quote from the Vincent and Zlomistic book a phrase that also became a news headline and a shared rhetorical device: "she packed for jail like a kid going to camp." (*ibid*, 13) In this book, Ashley Smith's friend from her time at NBYC, Jessica Fair, is quoted by Vincent and Zlomistic as saying "she was a baby at heart. She was never a violent person." (*ibid*, 15)

Of course, I am not suggesting that Ashley Smith was not young when she first entered prison; she was. It is significant however, that the years she spent in prison are erased in this configuration. She did become a legal adult, even if she did so in custody. Child Ashley is being represented as someone even younger than she was.

Other media texts where the normal Child Ashley figure is constructed similarly foreground innocence, childishness, compliance and femininity, as in this 2013 *Toronto Sun* article:

> The proud mother painted Ashley as a happy homebody who adored quilts, the colour red, riding her bike and playing with her sister's kids...."You never saw that girl without a smile on her face. Most of her life was smiling and happy," insisted Smith. "At home, Ashley was a mom's girl. It was always, 'Yes, Mom.'"(*Toronto Sun,* 20 February 2013)

As with the misidentification of Herb Gorber as Ashley Smith's father, this romanticized portrayal of Child Ashley as uniformly compliant and always smiling both supports the contention that the official construction of Inmate Smith was out of step with reality and, at the same time, by overstating its narrative of Ashley Smith's normalcy, provides a basis for the Child Ashley configuration to be "exposed" or refuted. This construction of quilt-loving, smiling and happy Child Ashley is favourable to a (literally) incredible extent that is completely discordant with any official text about her authored during her life. This portrayal sets the stage for investigative journalism to expose its overstatement as fallacious.

In the "Behind the Wall" docudrama, produced somewhat later than "Out of Control" (in November 2010), while the child Ashley figure does not prevail, it is present, and typically set up through opposition to the Inmate Smith figure in official discourse. The Child Ashley figure is used in opposition to the figure of the "most difficult inmate in the system." Nurse Bracken, interviewed in the docudrama, calls Ashley Smith a "little girl." In this same docudrama, Coralee Smith characterizes Ashley Smith as a "child victim" and is quoted as saying that Ashley Smith "could be anyone's child." Of course, by "anyone's child" the contention here is not actually that Child Ashley could be *anybody's* child but that she could be the child of someone who matters, of a white, middle class, socially significant, viewer of the docudrama, a child of someone like Nurse Bracken herself, university educated, middle class and white.

In addition to media texts, the Child Ashley figure circulates in texts generated by people purporting to be advocates for Ashley Smith throughout her case, by lawyers for the Smith family as well as agents of progressive politics such as advocates for woman prisoners (notably the Elizabeth Fry Society) and advocates for children's rights. Advocate and Executive Director of the Canadian Association of Elizabeth Fry Societies (CAEFS), an advocacy group for women in prison, Kim Pate says of Ashley Smith: "She looked far younger than her 19 years." (Kevin Newman Live) Pate also repeatedly made statements that are engaged in the constitution of the Normal Child Ashley figure, saying for example, "She was quite typical of an adolescent. A bit feisty." (MSN News 15 October 2013) Other advocates from the same organization made similar claims. For instance, Vincent and Zlomistic report that "Ashley was an immature 19-year-old" according to Elizabeth Fry lawyer Breese Davies. (Vincent and Zlomistic, 25) Similarly, lawyer Richard Macklin, making submissions for Ontario's Child and Youth Advocate said "Ashley Smith was a child... Ashley Smith was a child.... It was the security focus that led to her undoing" at the inquest. (Canadian Press, 26 November 2011)

We are invited through the docudramas to position ourselves as parents or family member to Ashley Smith. She is "just a kid." Viewers are not invited in to understanding of Ashley Smith as a possible alternative self in another possible world. She is not configured as a valuable, complex actor in her own right. Rather, her value is relational. She is a good mother's child, Coralee's child. Ashley Smith is not the protagonist in texts where the Child Ashley figure dominates. She is peripheral to the main action, which is a story about adults who care for Ashley and want answers about what happened to her.

While the Child Ashley figure raises public sympathy for the Smith family, it simultaneously claims her and forecloses the possibility of identification with Ashley Smith. She is always and inevitably someone's daughter, sister, niece or granddaughter. Counsel retained by and advocates speaking "for" Ashley Smith and the Smith family controlled the narrative of what is claimed to be Ashley Smith's voice and directed attention away from the conflict between Ashley Smith, her adoptive mother, and her other family members, that contributed to her placement in foster care before she was incarcerated. This construction never asks the viewer to consider the possibility of asking the question "what if *you* were Ashley Smith?" The Child Ashley figure does not ask us to identify with her (as one of us) but to *own* her, or control her as ours. The Child Ashley figure shifts the social problem defined by the Smith case from management of an inmate to (parental) control of recalcitrance.

TROUBLING THE "NORMAL CHILD"

Assertions of Ashley Smith's social class, family status and whiteness are closely bound up with posthumous recuperation of her as a "normal," in the sense of normative, asexual or sexually virtuous, and good, child. The taken-for-granted social category of *normal* child can be troubled as always already gendered, classed and raced. As discussed previously, Batacharya and Jiwani recently explored the profound extent to which the "normal" and "saveable" girl in contemporary mainstream Canada is raced as white. (Batacharya; Jiwani) Research and theorization from the disciplinary field of child studies provides historical context for the social category of childhood.(Kehily) The protected category of "child" is a fairly recent invention — a protected and disciplined category to which not everyone has access. Special protection and particular parental and social investment have not always, across cultures and time, been accorded to children. Rather, the notion that children warranted concerted attention, protection and discipline became popular in the European west in the Romantic period, in the 18th and 19th centuries. (Archer) Thus, the social category of child, and widely understood assumptions about what constitutes normalcy for children can be located in history and in more specifically in particular configures of social relations circulating in the 18th century in Europe that include racial as well as overlapping gender hierarchies.

The social category of child is not only located in history but also in particular configurations of social relations. "Normally," the social category of child is configured as "one who does not belong in prison" in opposition to the implicit spectre of someone who does deserve to be incarcerated, a proper inmate. While the figure of Normal Child Ashley in some ways brings her closer to being understood as belonging to a particular white middle class community, it does not render imaginable her existence as a social participant, an intentional, political actor or a maker of meanings. To the contrary, Normal Child Ashley has less agency than does Inmate Smith: Inmate Smith can choose one pole on a binary disciplinary set of oppositions. She can obey or disobey by making "good" and "bad" choices. However, the Normal Child Ashley figure invites media consumers presumed to be middle class, white, aging to pity and care for Child Ashley precisely because she cannot *help* what she does. Child Ashley has no meaningful agency.

The social category of child can be historicized in a politics of rescue. The "Child Savers" movement of the early twentieth century coincides with what has been called the "first wave" of feminism. Speaking *for* children is integral to the encroachment of middle-class white women into participation in rationality, as advocates in the juridical field and in political space. (Myers) There are continuities of rescue politics woven in with construction of the category of normal child in the age of risk. Discourses of the child victim figure very prominently in the current neoconservative agenda of governing through crime. (Best) The current Canadian Federal government's "tough-on-crime" approach to criminal legislation is justified frequently in terms of protecting children and saving child victims.[6]

Not all historical configurations of the child as a social category have been particularly benign. Treatment justified in the language of protection towards such childlike near-persons has often been limiting: the designation of childhood or child-like-ness has been used as a metaphor to signify groups of persons who are not fully persons under the law, who are not citizen-subjects. (Hamilton, 2009) Further, childlike persons who are unable to fully attain the status have a prominent place in the constellation of different abnormal monsters on which the norm is created. The status of child has been one to which colonized peoples have been relegated and slaves were consigned. The Canadian residential school system for aboriginal people was justified on the basis that the native people were "like children" and needed guidance on how to become civilized.

The perpetually-adolescent terminology of "girl" was historically used disparagingly to refer to women. The childlike nature of women is bound up closely with the construction of childhood as a social category in Romantic thought. Rousseau, despite advocating for education for girls, felt that women are always childlike. (Kelly and Grace) Further, it is not just women but all of the social groups who were disenfranchised in North American colonial history including aboriginals, African-American slaves, and women have simultaneously been referred to as "like children" where paternalism is a metaphor for the husband-wife and owner-slave relationships. (Springer, 2006)

In the Normal Child Ashley figure, Ashley Smith is understood as, not just a child, but a little girl who cried out for help. The social category of child intersects with gender to produce "girl" as a social category that is itself historically contingent, enmeshed in existing social relations and always already classed, sexualized and raced. Across cultures and time, and even messily overlapping at any particular place and time, there circulate numerous discourses of the girl. Discourses of the girl are always in flux as technologies of government deployed as technologies of the self. As configurations of social relations and processes of construction of gender, power and sexuality shift over time, so too do understandings of what girls are and have to be. Catherine Driscoll's attempt at a genealogy of girlhood is particularly useful in illustrating the historical contingency of the boundaries of the category girl. She tracks the category of girl in western societies through the twentieth century as a signifier of "malleable identity" and as "a publicly pre-eminent image of desirability." (Driscoll) Anita Harris, in her book *All About the Girl,* looks at ways in which the category of "girl" is "slippery and problematic" (2004) and at the diversity of the experiences of those identified as girls. She writes that "there is no universal, one-dimensional girl about whom we can know." (Driscoll, xxiv)

As discussed in Chapter 2, writing in the field of girls studies has theorized relations between girlhood, power, agency and resistance and has contributed to an understanding that agency is articulated and evidenced within the context of "the logic of the production of gender, the body and sexual, racial and cultural (etc.) differences." (Gonick) Girls Studies theorists provide insight into contemporary late modern "truths" that circulate widely about those identified as girls. Discourses of girl also reflect cultural anxieties because girls, like other children and youth, but even more so because of their potential to become now not only mothers but also capitalist workers, are persons on whom cultural reproduction and capitalist production — *the future* — depends.

Girls studies theorists have analyzed how the formerly widely accepted construct of the good and proper virtuous girl has been largely supplanted in late modern western democracies by new tropes of "girl power" and victimhood, by mandatory sexiness and assertiveness alongside vulnerability that produces a double-bind. (McRobbie; Gonick) These discourses are not politically neutral. As Gonick and her co-authors have written, "discourses of agency and resistance are continually commodified by the capitalist machine." (Gonick, 4) According to Olivia Koffman and Rosalind Gill, "technologies of sexiness" have largely replaced "virtue" and "purity" as what girls are required to display in the heterosexual marketplace. (2013) Angela McRobbie has critically unpacked how a contemporary era of commodified acceptance of 'girl power' produces a dominant narrative of girls' "successes" that renders continuing inequalities largely invisible and relies on a neoliberal logic of individualized responsibilization and the notion of rational "choice" as being the explanation for girls' negative experiences. (2008) Where the prevalent stereotypical representation of the neoliberal girl subject is as powerful and sexy, as in the discourse of girl power, the "unsuccessful" girl is unthinkable, or at least exceptional. Inequalities she faces are made invisible. This discourse contributes to marginalization, exception and exclusion of "failed" girls, failure that is in turn attributed to their own individual negative choices.

Late modern discourses of girl power and their promise to those identified as girls that "you can be and do anything" are particularly problematic for working class girls whose socioeconomic circumstances limits their educational and career opportunities. The discourse of girl power obfuscates this inequality. Further, widely assumed and accepted discourses of girl power and vulnerability implicitly rely on taken-for-granted assumptions about which girls *count* as future bearers. Racialized and otherwise marginalized girls, as Jiwani has argued in her study of the Reena Virk case and elsewhere, do not. (Jiwani)

Considering this theorization from girls studies of the construct of "girl power" relying on totalizing risk logic provides insight into how, in life, Ashley Smith was responsibilized by correctional and legal bureaucracies for "bad choices" and received as a risky and failed girl whose failures were produced by "bad choices," although these are not the same "bad choices" involving defiance of correctional authorities that are explored in Chapter 4. Rather, Ashley Smith fails in the discourse of girl power by failing to adjust to her adolescent development by navigating her teen years successfully. She fails by (being fed and) eating unhealthy foods that have too many calories for her to be mandatorily sufficiently thin. She fails (or refuses) to perform her sexuality as heteronormatively "sexy" to males. She fails (or refuses) to do well in school and succeed socially by becoming popular with peers and teachers. These failures are understood as her fault in a reasoning process that serves to remove empathy from the way she is received by community members, educational professionals and psy-experts. Similarly, Gonick's theorization also provides insight into how the Child Ashley figure intersects with pre-existing broadly accepted truths prevalent at the time of the Ashley Smith case in that it tries to situate Ashley Smith as a middle class noble victim, an Ophelia in need of rescue. This Child Ashley victim figure re-inscribes passivity as normative. In the Child Ashley configuration, Ashley Smith is *unagentic*, stripped of "girl power" as much as she is divested of an Inmate's ability to make "bad choices."

DISCURSIVE WORK – FITTING ASHLEY SMITH IN

Inevitably, the configuration of a being into a particular discursive figure involves the production of representations that foreground certain aspects of that being while they de-emphasize, obscure and make invisible others. A great deal of discursive work is required, by means of framing by selective description and omissions, to fit Ashley Smith into the taken-for-granted dimensions of the social category of the properly constituted normal little girl. At the time of her death, 19-year-old Ashley Smith was not chronologically a child under any commonly accepted definition of the term. Further, as discussed below, she was not self-evidently middle class in socioeconomic status, her home was not obviously paradigmatically normative, she is adopted, and her racialization is slippery and problematic. The backstory of Ashley Smith's childhood is framed in texts where Normal Child Ashley is constructed with obvious omissions that evidence a significant effort being made to make Ashley Smith seem as normal, average and middle class as possible. Child Ashley, a normal middle class white child, reveals how significant socioeconomic status and race are to attainment of the social category of normal child. It fits well with paradigmatic narratives about good victims and positions the public and the inquest jury as essentially patriarchal rescuers.

The "normalcy" of Ashley Smith's childhood is an assertion that it takes specific discursive work to maintain. The emphasis placed on the "niceness" of her house and normalcy (middle class socioeconomic status) of her family are based on a selective treatment of that facts that is difficult to maintain. The index offence for which she was incarcerated was, as noted, throwing apples at a postal worker. She claimed to do so because she was angry at delays her neighbours were experiencing while waiting for welfare cheques. (CBC Timeline) Looked at closely, this is a story that establishes both that she had welfare recipients as neighbours and was aware of the details of social assistance payments. "Middle class" children of the suburbs do not generally have an awareness of these matters nor do they live next to people on welfare. In fact Ashley Smith did not live in the suburbs. The family home was "downtown."(Vincent and Zlomistic, 19 December 2013)

Ashley Smith's family history is not the paradigmatically normal North American - two-parent, suburban, heteronormative, middle class ideal. There are very different ways available to tell the story of her early life than to say it was "normal." There were several disruptions in her early childhood including moves and changes to her parents' marital statuses. Ashley was adopted at three days of age by Coralee and her then-husband. This husband was not the father of Coralee's older biological daughter but rather a man to whom Coralee had been married for two years at the time of the adoption. Ashley Smith then experienced her adoptive parents' divorce at an early age. A "broken home" narrative would also be available to someone seeking to tell her backstory. After their divorce, she experienced her childhood as an adopted child of a single mother a generation older than most mothers.[7] While her experiences in a disrupted and complex home environment may not be statistically unusual for Canada's young people — Ashley Smith was one of 22% of Canada's children who live in a single parent household[8] — they do not reflect the prevailing social norm. In "A Rush To Judgment," the CSC union stated "some officers who dealt with her extensively at GVI feel that Ashley Smith had suffered emotional trauma in her home life that led her to act out, though this is unclear. The report indicates that she alluded to uncertainty regarding the real identity of her biological parents." (Rush to Judgment, 7) This claim suggests the possibility of blaming her family, and most significantly, her adoptive mother, for Ashley Smith's problems. Additionally, or perhaps alternatively, this might mean that officials had access to information from Ashley Smith that complicated an understanding of her "normal" home life.

Ashley Smith's family tree is complicated and may be overlapping. Coralee also had a 19-year-old daughter at the time of the adoption, whose father was also not the adoptive father of Ashley. The adoptive father, Harold, never maintained contact with Ashley after he and her adoptive mother Coralee split up. Ashley Smith's mother began a relationship with self-described "family friend" Herb Gorber at some point during Ashley's childhood. While he was her mother's partner at the time of the Smith case, Herb Gorber was never the adoptive father of Ashley. Gorber had what appears to have been a generally warm relationship with Ashley but did not stand in the place of a parent to her.[9] Ashley Smith's older adoptive sister was a pregnant teen during Ashley Smith's childhood. One of Ashley Smith's sister's children was two years older than Ashley and "had his own troubles with the law," spending time at NBYC himself. (*The Canadian Press,* 15 April 2013) Instead of being snugly nestled in a pleasant Norman Rockwell-painted home, Ashley was in and out of foster care, faced criminal charges for failing to return home at night (running away) in breach of probation and was living in at least three foster homes before being finally incarcerated.[10] She had a slightly older cousin (who she suspected was her brother) in prison. She was experiencing a great deal of conflict with her adoptive mother and other family members as of at least 2003. (CBC Timeline)

Conflict between adolescent Ashley Smith and her adoptive mother is made invisible in the prevalent narratives supported by the Normal Child Ashley figure. However, intergenerational conflict would have been entirely predictable and expected in the context of Canadian society as a child emerged into adolescence. Family conflict appears not only to have been likely, but even to have been more pronounced than usual, in her case. Ashley Smith, throughout her adolescence, experienced high levels of conflict with her mother. Coralee has said that the conflict was due in large part to Ashley's accumulation of huge bills for surfing "inappropriate" websites. The content of these websites has never been made public. They were websites that cost money. Some have speculated there was pornography involved; others have suggested these were chat rooms. According to Richard, "She would also spend a lot of time on the internet, chatting with others or accessing inappropriate and highly questionable material." (Richard, 2008) During this period, Ashley Smith was also in conflict with her mother for running up the phone bill, making what Coralee Smith contended at the inquest were "crank" calls. (Mandel, 20 February 2013)

At the time of the second inquest and after, and in the wrongful death suit, Ashley Smith's interests are seen as the same as those of Coralee Smith. There is no space imagined to differentiate her individual voice or agency from the views of her mother in the reporting of these proceedings. Ashley Smith's agency is generally unthinkable in the "normal child" figuration. This configuration obfuscates ways in which Ashley Smith was a world-creating, agentic, rights-bearing, political actor who held opinions, who spoke, who acted out, and who made complaints. Ironically, Ashley Smith's agency is erased more profoundly in the "benevolent" texts that purport to speak for her than in those texts that are intended to defend those considered at fault for her death.

When Coralee Smith testified at the second inquest, very few questions were asked of her. Multiple lawyers simply rose to offer her condolences; a "consensus had been reached amongst counsel" that questions about Ashley Smith's family life, including her biological family, weren't relevant. (Blatchford, 12 February 2013) This consensus to make Ashley Smith's biological parentage illegible to the legal gaze did not stop the social gaze from looking into it, however.

No one, not even perhaps Coralee Smith, knows who Ashley Smith's biological parents were. Coralee Smith claimed during the inquest that Ashley had been the subject of a public adoption. Confronted by a question about who Ashley's biological mother was, Coralee contended she did not hide her daughter's biological parentage and that it was unknown.[11] Other commentators have suggested however, that the identity of the birth parents of Ashley Smith is something sinister Coralee Smith knows and is keeping secret.[12] These suggestions are bound up with narratives that seek to responsibilize Ashley Smith's family for her incarceration and death and are a means to make Ashley Smith's death in custody into a personal, rather than a social, problem.

According to her psychologist at the Saskatoon Regional Psychiatric Centre, Cindy Press: "Smith believed her sister — 19 years older than her — was really her biological mother, and Coralee Smith was in fact her grandmother. She also believed her sister's son — two years older than Smith and with his own troubles with the law — was really her brother." (*The Canadian Press,* 15 April 2013) According to testimony of two front line guards who dealt with Ashley Smith in the days before her death, Ashley Smith claimed that "she had a brother who was in jail" and that "her brother taught her how to tie up." (Blatchford, 21 February 2013) The existence of an older cousin/ brother to Ashley Smith who got into trouble with, and was "known to" the same authorities, who apparently bore a striking resemblance to her and who served time at the same youth custodial facilities, was apparently in jail at the time of the 2013 inquest, but has not *died* in prison is a fascinating, little explored, detail in the case. One wonders in what situations this older brother/ cousin, with whom she was " very close" (Vincent) was present and in what ways their relationship contributed to Ashley Smith's growing problems as a youth. The presence of this cousin raises questions about to what extent the two relatives were engaged in similar activities and in criminal activity together, or to what extent this boy's presence in Ashley Smith's life may have been helpful to her. Perhaps his incarceration precipitated her feelings of alienation and contributed to her resistant behaviours. One wonders also to what extent each received similar or different treatment for the same sorts of conduct.

It is also quite interesting that Coralee Smith, when interviewed about the apple-throwing incident said, "Ashley wasn't alone. There were other kids with her." (Out of Control) Ashley Smith has been portrayed as a pathologically resistant, solitary, even lonely, individual. The storyline of Ashley Smith's adolescence in the mainstream media and in the docudramas has implied a small family and a solitary childhood, not a large extended family living at close quarters with two adolescent family members simultaneously in and out of jail.

It is the configuration of Child Ashley as "normal" that makes all of this intrigue around Ashley Smith's birth family — and the commitment to non-disclosure of their identities by counsel and even by Dr. Carlisle — relevant to the media and public in the Smith case. While presiding over the inquest, Carlisle said to an inquiring juror who sought to ask about the identity of Ashley Smith's birth parents "we must not ask Coralee what the fact of that matter is" (Blatchford, *ibid*) Queries by media commentators about Ashley Smith's birth family hint at a parentage quite abnormal, something *risky*, something that could derail the normal family storyline and responsibilize something other than CSC, imply that Ashley Smith belonged in the geographical space of the excluded, and destabilize the Child Ashley figure. The biological parentage of Ashley Smith was deemed not relevant in the formal legal context of the inquest proceedings and is not relevant to narratives that fit with the Inmate Smith construction discussed in the prior chapter. Rather, her birth is *made* relevant in the public square of the media coverage of the Smith Inquest by the insistence of progressive politics on the normal childhood storyline. Indeed, it is insistence on the Normal Child Ashley configuration that makes advocacy on behalf of Ashley Smith fragile and vulnerable: the notion that her treatment and death in prison were unjust is always potentially de-stabilized by suggestions that she was not the noble victim she is made out to be.

Despite the general acceptance of the truth that Ashley Smith was a "white kid," on the basis of the information presented in the texts that make up her case, there is a slippery and illusory quality to Ashley Smith's racialization as white. As noted, her biological parentage is unknown. She had relatively pale skin, dark eyes and dark hair. It would be reasonable to suggest that she may have had aboriginal heritage given statistics about children making up a high percentage of children in care across Canada, including children made available for adoptions[13] and on the basis of her physical genotypic presentation: the identity of Ashley Smith's birth parents has never been disclosed, and this was in fact a piece of information that caused her a great deal of difficulty not to know.[14] Indeed, as noted in Chapter 2, the 2008 article by Jena McGill acknowledges CAEFS executive director Kim Pate's assistance as supervisor of the project. This paper not only identifies Ashley Smith as an aboriginal woman but treats her death as an illustrative case of the discrimination against aboriginal women in Canada.[15]

My point here is that Ashley Smith could easily have "passed" for either aboriginal or white and that it was not inevitable that her case became constructed as one about a middle class white girl. I don't mean to suggest that there is an authenticity to "race" but rather that her "whiteness" is neither self-evident nor necessarily genetic and is not even a stable construction throughout the case. What is widely accepted as true at the end of the second inquest is that she had a passably middle class white adoptive mother, bore no obvious characteristics signifying she was obviously *not*-white and had no recognized aboriginal status. The pervasive insistence on her "middle class" background and the tenacious claims of her whiteness alongside the easy assumption about her aboriginality in an early academic intervention. This whiteness squarely places the discursive configuration of Ashley Smith as a child of "ours" in need of rescue.

Rescue politics can be seen as consistent with a good deal of feminist advocacy in favour of "saving" women and children over a long period of time. This underlying philosophical assertion on the part of women working as advocates for prisoners and also, in the context of the all-woman jury constituted in the second inquest represents likely at least in part conscious strategy to empower jurors not to be over-awed by the risk-based actuarial talk of CSC management. It is also not likely that it was accidental or unconscious that media and advocates for the Smith family framed the case in ways that fit Ashley Smith into the noble victim role in paradigmatic binary angels/demons scripts of the criminal law. (Irigaray)

Narratives that invoke the social category of child privilege the expertise of mothers, and not just any mothers: with the ideological construct of the good mother. Motherhood theorists like Andrea O'Reilly have tracked the figure of the "good mother" as a construct that celebrates only white, middle class mothers who stay at home as valuable. (O'Reilly) These narratives also invite the court to take on a patriarchal role, and invite the state to play the historical role it had under the JDA as having *parens patriae* jurisdiction. While the construction of the abnormal "tyrannical child" in expert discourse is deeply imbricated in mother-blaming and relies on an assumption of dysfunctional parenting, the discursive configuration of Normal Child Ashley relies heavily upon the presence of a middle class mother who is not drug addicted, not criminalized and sufficiently articulate as well as being appropriately socially positioned to participate in public debate. The question of the identity of Ashley Smith's birth parents is pushed aside in this construction, often quite deliberately. In other instances, some reference is made to the importance Ashley Smith apparently placed on wanting to know the identity of her birth mother. According to the Vincent and Zlomistic book: "It was a question that hung over the entire inquest: Ashley was deeply distressed, even resentful, that she didn't know the identities of her biological parents." (Vincent and Zlomistic)

For a variety of quite defensible stated reasons, questions about Ashley's biological parentage were not admissible at the inquest: they were determined to be irrelevant.[16] The legal gaze cast by the inquest decided to make the biological question of Ashley Smith's genetic parentage illegible. Ironically, it is the logic of the normal child construction that makes Ashley Smith's biological parentage relevant. It was strategically central to this configuration of Child Ashley as a noble victim that she had a "good" mother and that this parentage be unquestioned. Equally, in neoliberal logics of responsibilization, the foregrounding of Ashley Smith's (putatively middle class, white) family in the interests of legitimating her as a member of Canadian society to be included in political community, the family becomes another entity onto which CSC and public opinion on the case can shuffle blame for her biological death. Focus on exposing this family for its abnormalities, or on responsibilizing it for purportedly failing to get Ashley the "help" she needed is enabled by the emergence of the Normal Child Ashley configuration in its reliance on this family structure.

The positioning of Coralee Smith in a narrative where both she and Ashley Smith are cast as noble victims is made clear in the more emotionally manipulative, tabloid-style news media reports, for example, this Sun article:

> [It was] Coralee Smith's turn to speak of her beloved daughter as she bravely took the stand at the inquest into Ashley's senseless death.
>
> Despite battling serious heart disease, the 65-year-old grandmother had made this long-awaited trip from Moncton to pursue her long quest for answers: Why had her troubled child been bounced from prison to prison around the country like some serial murderer? (*Toronto Sun*, 20 February 2013)

In testimony at the inquest, Coralee Smith herself said she had "held off" telling Ashley Smith the identity of her birth parents because she felt the girl was "too young."(Perkel, 20 February 2013) Assuming the public adoption story to be correct, Ashley Smith, adopted in infancy, and back in foster care by age 13, could easily be made sense of not as a "normal" child but as a "system kid." If Ashley Smith is reconfigured as a child abandoned to state care from start to finish, she bears interesting similarity with Reena Virk, whose parents have been widely profiled but who was in state care along with almost all of her attackers on the night she was murdered. Insistence on the clean narrative of a normative upbringing and "good" middle class mother for Ashley Smith provides progressive politics useful tropes to manipulate public sympathies but also shields the state from investigation of its responsibility for this youth-in-care and of the connections between the child welfare and youth criminal justice systems. But for the reliance on configuration of Ashley Smith as a "normal" child from a "normal" home, the crisis for the little-girl-lost narrative presented by the allegations about her adoption would be easily addressed by what Coralee Smith said in a media interview in response to the adoption question "We are her family. We are not perfect. But we will never accept that Ashley should have been treated in this manner."(Perkel, 21 February 2013)

OBESITY AND SOCIAL EXCLUSION —
"ONE SIZE DOES NOT FIT ALL"

The report of the New Brunswick Ombudsman in the Ashley Smith case contains the following quote in reference to the imperative to change measures taken to deal with "challenging youth with complex needs," which is how the ombudsman characterizes pre-incarceration Ashley Smith: " one size does not fit all." (Richard, 2008) The Normal Child Ashley figure supports narratives that direct attention away from Ashley Smith's difficulties fitting in to the social categories of girl and child. Despite her ostensible "whiteness" in life, Ashley Smith could not socially accomplish a fit within the overlapping categories of "child" and "little girl." She could not attain performance of those roles as a properly constituted gendered and aged subject.

Although they work to accomplish this, the docudramas and media texts in which the figure of Child Ashley dominates do not (and perhaps cannot) completely reconfigure Child Ashley away from aspects of Ashley Smith's beingness that marked her for exclusion from the overlapping and interlocking categories "child" and "girl." In the construction of the figure of Child Ashley, aspects of her embodiment that rendered the identity of child difficult for her to access (her large size, her aggressiveness, her violence and her apparent sexuality) are de-emphasized. Images that depict her do not show her standing at full height; they zoom in on her face. They show her in pigtails. Early childhood photos of her are shown frequently instead of more recent photographs that present her as a full-grown adult, albeit a young one. Cropping is used in photos presented in mainstream media that cuts out much of the skin on her neck and chin, making her look slimmer and smaller than she would have presented to people who met her in person.

As discussed above, in the prevailing discourses of the girl circulating at the time of the Ashley Smith case, middle class girls are mandatorily successful, somehow simultaneously vulnerable and heteronormatively stereotypically sexually available in their interactions and body presentation. While this category presents impossible and conflicting requirements to subjects identified as adolescent females, it is accessible to some more than others. It was not attainable in life for Ashley Smith, who did not fit easily into the commonly accepted boundaries of the social category of the girl. As discussed, she was too tall; she was obese or overweight; she had acne; she was physically aggressive on occasion; to all indications she appears to have been an avid consumer of pornographic materials; she was a *failed* girl and an unsympathetic accused in a neoliberal context where either success or victimhood is necessary for attainment of adolescent girlhood. In the neoliberal risk logic of responsibilization, her failure was her fault, produced by her bad choices: the boundaries of the social category of girl marked her for exclusion and social death. However, in dying, Ashley Smith becomes a victim and gains, through this victimization and the passivity effected by her inability to speak back and resist, access to the social category of "good" or "normal" girl at last.

The following discussion will explore how, in short, Ashley Smith's beingness is to a great extent unthinkable within the category of girl and child. At the time of her death, Ashley Smith was 19, meaning she was not legally a "child" under the formal discourses of international law, child protection or domestic criminal law. Understood officially as a young female adult, she was a problematic subject for legal discourse. Further, Ashley Smith does not fit easily within gendered stereotypes of the socially acceptable girl child: she was large in a society where fat is shameful and diminutive stature is prized in "little" girls; she was assertive and oppositional in a culture where girls have been traditionally understood as compliant; she racked up huge bills on "chat" lines and websites that may well have been pornographic in a culture where girls are stereotypically traditionally understood as without sexual desire. In the following discussion, I look at how her unthinkability within the social categories of girl and child marked her for this exclusion before and during her time as a carceral subject.

It is clear that Ashley Smith's large stature was an aspect of her embodiment that contributed to rendering her unmanageable within, invisible to, or unthinkable within, the discursive ideal type of white child or white girl. She was also tall, measuring at least 5'8" at age 15. In the "Rush to Judgment" report put forward by the Corrections Union, she is referred to at times as a "kid" or "child" but elsewhere as "the 245 pound woman." (Rush to Judgment, 2)

She was at least this large. In later reports, for example the Vincent and Zlomistic book *The Life and Death of Ashley Smith* discussed in more detail below, she is described as follows: "Ashley was five foot eight and weighed 260 pounds." (Vincent and Zlomistic, 16) Ashley Smith's size is never described in "feminine" terms as softness or plumpness. Her size certainly led front line CSC staff to admittedly perceive her differently from a smaller woman: they felt threatened by her. As one correctional officer said in "Rush to Judgment," "when I looked at all the incidents she had been involved in and her size — she weighed 245 pounds — I thought, 'That girl could do some damage to me." (Rush to Judgment, 8)

Fatness intersects with race, class and gender in socially locating people, especially adolescent girls. Obesity marks children and adolescent girls for stigma and exclusion. Cornell nutrition scientists Donna Maurer and Jeffrey Sobal, in their co-edited volume about social management of obesity and thinness look at how thinness is "widely valued and rewarded in contemporary postindustrial societies"(1999) and that the flip side of this social value placed on thinness is a stigmatization and medicalization of obesity. They argue that "weight-stigmatized individuals" face a variety of negative social responses. (*ibid*, 7) Other researchers in the volume further contend further that obesity is a "spoiled identity" through which " individuals suffer both externally from negative stereotypes and internally from negative self-concepts." (Dehrer and Hughes)

Erdman Farrell, in her book, *Fat Shame: Stigma and the Fat Body in American Culture* (2011) critically interrogates the cultural and economic apparatuses that support the social mandate for thinness, looking at historical fat denigration and contemporary fat stigma. Her analysis of historical and contemporary representations of thinness reveals connotations of fatness that are attributed not just to the excess weight but to the fat person. The fat person is perceived in a totalizing way to be corrupted by his or her fatness and seen as "lazy, gluttonous, immoral, greedy, stupid, uncontrolled and lacking in willpower." (2011, 4) Fat is a devalued and stigmatized identity that has been found to correlate with lower levels of college acceptance, lower levels of peer acceptance as well as depression. (*ibid*, 12) Others have theorized the female fat body as transgressive and abject in postindustrial societies, fat female bodies as invisible or stigmatized in the representations prevalent in mainstream culture.(Braziel and LeBesco) As Le'a Kent writes, "fat bodies, and women's fat bodies in particular, are represented as monstrous and a kind of abject: that which must be expelled to make all other representations and functions, even life itself, possible.... Abjection is characterized by revulsion, fear of contamination ... a repeated expulsion that marks the self's borders." (Kent) This is consistent with the disembodiment of Ashley Smith in the vast majority of photographic texts depicting her alongside texts that present the Child Ashley construction: Smith had to be disembodied to be recuperated as the Normal Child.

According to Statistics Canada (2012), eating disorders such as anorexia and bulimia affect adolescent girls ten times as often as they affect boys and produce disordered eating in tens of thousands of young girls every year. Adolescents diagnosed with eating disorders have an "intense fear of becoming obese." (*ibid*) Eating disorders are individually pathologized in the mainstream as mental disorders, but, seen in this context, eating disorders on the part of adolescent girls are not *just* individual pathologies but also reflect a rational response within a neoliberal logic of exclusion whereby these girls are in jeopardy of not just social but also, as is suggested by the Ashley Smith case, perhaps penal consequences should they fail to achieve the socially sanctioned level of thinness. The prevalence of eating disorders amongst adolescent girls in postindustrial societies is pathologized as mental illness on their part but it is also evidence of the power of the compulsory social requirement that girls be thin to be socially valued. Whether or not Ashley Smith had an eating disorder, her "fatness" made her not fit easily within the category of girl and marked her for exclusion from community.

Obesity is prevalent in women's prisons. However, while fatness on the part of woman prisoners is often understood as their individualized failure, recent research into the body size of woman prisoners shows that obesity exists as a social relation in a loop of confirming logic in carceral settings of the late modern west, especially where women are concerned. Correlating especially with an inability to exercise, obesity rates for incarcerated women are significantly higher than those rates for the general population on average. According to a 2014 Oxford University health study of prisoners across 15 countries, female prisoners were more likely to be obese than the general female population.[17] These findings associate a high prevalence of obesity with provision of female prisoners with a diet designed to suit the caloric needs of males. (Herbert) Significantly here, one of the requests Ashley Smith formally made to CSC management was that healthier snacks should be provided to inmates. She wanted fresh fruit and vegetables to replace muffins. The request was denied. (Vincent and Zlomistic) Fatness on the part of Ashley Smith and other woman prisoners increases in a vicious circle. There is a double bind process by which the abjection, shaming and cultural construction of the fat body as uncivilized is exacerbated by a high calorie prison diet and lack of exercise making female inmates unthinkable subjects to be excluded from political community. It is unlikely that obesity was irrelevant to social and juridical necropolitical actions taken against Ashley Smith. One of the concerns raised about Ashley Smith's treatment in CSC custody by Coralee Smith was that she was undergoing rapid changes to her weight, both through gain and, finally, rapid weight loss. (Perkel, 21 February 2013)

Because gender differences and subjectivity are made and remade in the family, the school, the media, popular culture and formal legal discourses, in the recuperative discursive reconfiguration of Ashley Smith into Normal Child Ashley, the boundaries of the (white, middle class, successful, heteronormatively sexy) normal girl are reinscribed, as is the assumed truth of the unagentic passivity of subjects identified as adolescent females. Configuration and articulation of Ashley Smith as a child relies upon and even bolsters the same logic that produces her monstrosity and even likely her criminalization. This logic makes the large, strong, occasionally violent youth Ashley Smith *unthinkable*. It effaces her sexuality. It contributes to her exception from political community and from a stable, socially-endorsed identity. In consequence, she is pathologized for her size and other perceived failures, which are judged as failures of femininity without an appreciation for how contextual factors limit her available "choices."

CHILD ASHLEY AND THE LOGIC OF EXCLUSION

The prior discussion has shown the abundance of creative discursive work necessary to normalize Ashley Smith posthumously in the Normal Child Ashley configuration. I have unpacked ways in which she was, in life, configured by experts, CSC and other corrections officials and bureaucrats in the educational and child protection systems as a monstrous girl not thinkable within the category of child. I turn now to a discussion that locates the discursive normalization of Ashley Smith in the construction of the Normal Child Ashley figure in systems of macropower.

The social problem defined by the discourse of Normal Child Ashley is mistreatment and maltreatment of Coralee Smith's child, a child who could be "our" child, a cherubic, and feminine, white child: it is the mislocation of white, middle class girl in the correctional milieu that presents a problem to be solved in the "Out of Control" docudrama. This figure is located historically and economically in capitalist and post-colonial discourses of class and race. The effort expended upon the assertion that Ashley Smith was *normal* implicitly relies on racialized logics and colonial settler geographies of exclusion. It is a logic that builds on colonial understandings of aboriginal and racialized individuals as abnormal Others who are not full participants in the nation's statehood and accepts the correctional system unmodified as a place for those abnormals.

Razack looks critically at how a Canadian city and court's "capacity to dehumanize" murdered aboriginal woman Pamela George "came from their understanding of her as the gendered racial Other whose degradation confirmed their own identities as white … entitled to the land and to the full benefits of citizenship." (Razakc, 2002) The Normal Child Ashley figure has a spatiality. It is discursively constructed as situated and belonging within what Razack has called the "racial/spatial economies of the colonial city" from which aboriginal people (and racialized others) are excluded. (*ibid*) This configuration of Child Ashley locates her as a figure belonging in the (white, clean, middle class) suburbs. In so doing, the figure of Normal Child Ashley takes Ashley Smith out of the category of persons implicitly assumed to belong in prison, the space of the carceral other, and into a place of belonging in the white middle class communities of agents. Also, as Razack, Smith and Thobani have argued, neoliberalism's attachment to an imagined individualism devoid of a racial, ethnic or gendered self and the collective produces imaginaries that "make clear that 'outsider groups' and the 'barbarians' are always shaped by racial and gendered markers." (Razack, Smith and Thobani, 2010) These authors contend that the raced, classed and gendered division between insiders and outsiders shapes the governance of individual freedom for those considered properly constituted subjects and the "social death," through exclusion, or as Razack terms it "waste disposal" of the outsider others. (Razack, 2014) Further, Razack has also contended that, in mainstream Canadian society in general and the juridical field in particular, the aboriginal body is "seen as already dead," which makes the deaths of aboriginal people in prison rather than events worth investigating, to be expected: "the only thing we can expect of a disappearing race."(Razack, 2013)

As Jiwani (2006) and others have pointed out, there is a statistically demonstrable disproportionate vulnerability of racialized women and girls in Canada to violence while mainstream portrayals of Canadian society, largely make race invisible. Looking at the deployment of the figure of Child Ashley in negotiations with systems of macro-power, it is clear that systems including colonialism and neoliberalism are engaged in what Hannah Arendt called race thinking. (Arendt, 1944) As discussed above, white normativity is implicitly referenced in the use of the child Ashley figure to contend that Ashley Smith is one of *us*, not one of *those people* who are properly to be excluded as inmates. Arendt theorized that ideas about race, notions of racial and cultural superiority, and the right of 'superior races' to territorial expansion were themes that unified members of communities in white settler colonies [like Canada] in much the same way that they galvanized the fascist ideologies of early twentieth century Europe. (Arendt)

The problematic racist logic behind the Child Ashley construction can be articulated simply as follows: Ashley Smith was *not* the most dangerous inmate in the correctional system. Ashley Smith was a little girl. This line of reasoning is problematic because it accepts unquestioned assumptions about the category "girls," about "inmates" and about the correctional system, all of which are need to be troubled. In the Child Ashley figuration much of her attributes are personalized where they could be understood politically. The Normal Child Ashley figure acquires value relationally: she becomes worthy of consideration in reflection of her relationship to others who *count*. In doing so, it invokes discourses of normalcy and childhood built on heteronormativity/colonialism/ white supremacy.

Razack critically unpacks structures of mainstream thinking endemic to Canada as a white settler society transforming into a neoliberal empire. Razack looks at racialized power in its classed and gendered dimensions. (Razack and Smith) She critically explores violent, racist, colonial processes and structures that undermine liberal Canadian national mythology of law as dispassionate, fair and just. Razack argues that " colonialism "turns the native into a thing" violence against which and the exploitation of which is legitimate (Razack, 38) Thobani (2007) has set out similarly valuable analyses looking at the Canadian context.

Race thinking as introduced as a concept by Arendt and explored by Razack, is not the outsider logic of a few "bad apple" bigots but is a mainstream view. Its logic can be:

> captured in the phrase: they are not like us and also necessarily in the idea that "they" must be killed so that 'we' can live, race thinking becomes embedded in law and bureaucracy so that the suspension of rights appears not as a violence but as the law itself. Violence against the racialized Other comes to be understood as necessary in order for civilization to flourish, something the state must do to preserve itself. (Razack, 2008)

In the logic of race thinking, Others, like aboriginal and racialized people, are the proper subjects of incarceration in correctional contexts as well as immigration detention and other camp settings. To quote Razack, race thinking exists in the " the denial of a common bond of humanity between people of European descent and those who are not" is not a relic of a settler past but "remains a defining feature of the world order ... this "colour-lined" world is increasingly one governed by the logic of exception and the camps of abandoned or "rightless" people it creates. The camp, created as a state of exception, is a place where, paradoxically, the law has determined that the rule of law does not apply. Since there is no common bond of humanity between the camp's *inmates* and those outside, there is no common law. For those marked as outside humanity, law reserves the space of exception." (Razack, 2008, 6) Referencing Étienne Balibar, Razack looks at the logic of exclusion with reference to gender and the camp contends that those who are "other" including by reason of sexual difference can be excluded under the racism of empire if they are perceived as a threat to the nation. (Razakc, *ibid*, 16)

When the Normal Child Ashley figure is considered critically in the context of Razack, Thobani as well as Jiwani's analyses of racism in Canada and Hannah Arendt's concept of race thinking it becomes clear that part of the governmental work done by the discursive figure of Normal Child Ashley, a white, middle class girl, is in re-inscribing and amplifying the legitimacy of the "colour line" and affirming settler geographies in which white people belong in protected spaces while aboriginal and racialized others are excepted, "waste" to be disposed of, denizens of camps to be excluded: socially dead. By invoking the logic that disproportionately values white, middle class children to provide for Ashley Smith a sacrificial aura and re-cast Ashley Smith as a legitimate participant in political community who is not properly excluded, it re-inscribes the logic that some subjects *are* properly subject to the logic of exception. Further, Razack suggests that, "some Western feminists participate in empire through the politics of rescue." (Razack, *ibid*, 17) She, in this instance, is referring to the politics of the veil/ unveiling, taking the position that "gender operates as a kind of technology of empire enabling the West to make the case for its own modernity" (*ibid*, 18) and that "men claim the universal for themselves through confining women outside of it as non-rational subjects, so the Western woman requires the culturally different body to make her own claim of universality." (*ibid*, 86) I would argue that this contention applies to "child saving" politics woven in to the construction of the linked and overlapping social categories of the saveable "girl victim" and "child victim." Like the "veiled woman," girl child victims, of which generalizable type Normal Child Ashley is a case, are re-inscribed by these politics of rescue and victimhood as voiceless, apolitical, unagentic subjects.

ENDNOTES

[1] I use the term Risky girl with reference back to Christie Barron's *Rehabilitation in the Age of Risk* as discussed in Chapter 2.

[2] The UN Beijing Conference in 1995, and many UN texts since, have referred to the "girl child" as a particular social category of individuals needing protection. See, e.g., UN Report of the Foruth World Conference on Women, 1995 http://beijing20.unwomen.org/~/media/Field%20Office%20Beijing%20Plus/Attachments/BeijingDeclarationAndPlatformForAction-en.pdf#page=114.

[3] Family Services Act, SNB 1980, c F-2.2, s. 1.

[4] *Youth Criminal Justice Act* SC 2002 c.1, s. 2.

[5] To view the video, follow the following link: http://www.thestar.com/news/2013/12/19/ashley_smith_s_candid_conversation_with_guards.html.

[6] For example, *The Protecting Children From Online Predators Act*, Bill C-30, was originally entitled the Lawful Access Act and, under the guise of "protecting child victims," would have granted the Federal government sweeping powers to surveil the electronic communications of Canadians without a warrant. Public Safety Minister Vic Toews said in Hansard that Canadians could either "either stand with us or with the child pornographers" during a 2013 debate. The Bill was withdrawn by the Prime Minister, who cited widespread opposition to the proposed legislation, but a subsequent Bill, C-13, which came into force in March of 2015, brought in many of C-30's proposals. For the full text of the Bill see http://www.parl.gc.ca/HousePublications/Publication.aspx?Language=E&Mode=1&DocId=5380965&File=4.

[7] Forty at the time of the adoption.

[8] http://www.statcan.gc.ca/daily-quotidien/140429/dq140429c-eng.htm

[9] All According to Coralee Smith's testimony at the second Smith inquest, see, e.g., Perkel, Colin, "Ashley Smith's Mother Talks About Happy Childhood, Troubled Teens," *The Canadian Press* (20 February 2013).

[10] In 2003, Ashley Smith was placed in three different foster homes,

which, according to reports, were all unsuccessful due to Smith's unruly behaviour (Richard, 2008).

[11]By her account, Coralee told Ashley "when you're a bit older we'll go to a registry in PEI and we'll find out stuff for you." Vincent, Donovan. "Ashley Smith Inquest: Coralee Smith Says Adult Jail Changed Her Daughter," *Toronto Star*, 20 February 2013).

[12]See testimony of Cindy Presse.

[13]As of 2011, almost half (48.1%) of children in Canada aged 14 and under in foster care were Aboriginal children. Almost 4% of Aboriginal children were foster children compared to 0.3% of non-Aboriginal children. Statistics Canada National Household Survey 2011 Aboriginal peoples and language, Catalogue no. 99-011-X2011003.

[14]According to inquest testimony of Saskatoon Regional Psychiatric Centre psychologist, Dr. Cindy Presse.

[15]McGill, Jena, "An Institutional Suicide Machine: Discrimination Against Federally Sentenced Aboriginal Women in Canada," *Race/ Ethnicity: Global Contexts* 2.1 (Autumn 2008) http://muse.jhu.edu/journals/rac/summary/v002/2.1.mcgill.html. This paper is strange given that Pate has subsequently been such an active participant in the construction of the Child Ashley figure, and even in defining the Patient Smith figure with her first-hand testimony and claims to "know" Ashley Smith. Could it be that, in 2008, Pate couldn't recollect enough about Ashley Smith to remember whether or not she was aboriginal? Could it be that she WAS aboriginal and this is somehow being deliberately hidden to sustain the narrative of Child Ashley as a middle-class white "good girl"? Or could it be that this is an illustrative example of how progressive advocates, in constructing figures of Ashley in the Smith case, are not very attentive to or interested in her particularity? It is not possible to know which of these is the case; perhaps some combination of these possibilities is reflective of what happened here.

[16]Although the importance of Ashley Smith's biological parentage to her sense of self was asserted by psychologist Cindy Presse in testimony. See Vincent, Donovan "Questions Resurface About Ashley Smith's Birth Mother" (*Toronto Star*, 15 April 2013).

[17]Around 18% with some jurisdictional variation and especially pronounced in high income countries).

5. Patient Smith

From Problem Inmate to Mental Patient: Pathologization, Assimilation, Domestication

There are things in that paper which nobody knows but me, or ever will. Behind that outside pattern the dim shapes get clearer every day. It is always the same shape, only very numerous. And it is like a woman stooping down and creeping about behind that pattern.

—Charlotte Perkins Gillman,
"The Yellow Wallpaper,"(1892)

The more sanely I talked and acted the crazier I was thought to be by all except one physician, whose kindness and gentle ways I shall not soon forget.

— Investigative Journalist Nellie Bly,
"Ten Days in a Mad-House," (1887)

INTRODUCTION

The story "The Yellow Wallpaper" is a first person narrative tale of a young woman's journey into madness. Gillman's protagonist is driven into desperation by a course of treatment that involves a prolonged period of solitary confinement in locked room enforced not by correctional apparatus but as remedy for a diagnosed crisis with her mental health. At the end of the story, the protagonist has a psychotic break. The story supports different readings but one that is particularly relevant here is that it is a tale of descent into self-harm: arguably, the yellow wallpaper she tears away is not on the walls but is the narrator's skin. This story has been taken as a feminist text that expresses the ways in which women's agencies have been made invisible, unthinkable and silenced by the discourses of mental health and which provides insight into relationships between oppression, communication, and self-harm. It is useful to consider in the context of my analysis of the discursive figure of Patient Smith that emerges in the Smith case because it problematizes a woman's descent into mental illness in the context of governance by mental health discourse within which her agency is illegible.

In this chapter I conduct a critical discourse analysis of a figure of Ashley Smith that, while present throughout the Smith case in a variety of texts, only becomes dominant at a later stage in the case. The figuration of Patient Smith is of course not one monolithic figure but a set of overlapping, multiple figures of her as a mentally ill woman or girl. I analyze them together because they are constructions of Ashley Smith that foreground mental illness as her primary defining feature, and, in so doing, direct attention in particular ways. I scrutinize configurations of Ashley Smith that emerge from texts as a figure of Patient Smith, where her mental health, and eventually, madness, is foregrounded as the most significant aspect of her identity, in which sense is made of her as properly understood as a mental patient. I look at three variations on the figuration of Patient Smith.

First, I analyze figures of Ashley Smith as a troublesome but cognitively normal teen with behavioural problems, which form the dominant understanding of her as a mental health subject from the beginning of her experiences with the juridical field in 2002 until well into her incarceration. In 2006, after Ashley Smith is transferred to CSC custody, some legitimacy is accorded the notion that she has mental health issues and the construction of the figure shifts: Ashley the Inmate-Patient figure appears in a growing number of discursive sites, especially in official texts. After Ashley Smith's death, sense is made of her using mental health discourses that produce a different configuration, that of Patient Smith. This becomes the figure of Ashley Smith that ultimately dominates the overwhelming weight of texts produce from late 2010 until the end of the Smith case in 2014 and has the effect of redirecting public and juridical attention away from the systems and procedures of CSC in general in favour of a narrow and specific focus on the treatment of what are characterized as a very few "complex" "high needs" "severely mentally ill" woman offenders.

Throughout the duration of the Smith case from the time of her first conflicts with actors and systems in the juridical field in 2002, differing figures of Ashley Smith have competed for dominance. In the first chronological period, spanning from the time of her first interactions with the juridical field until her transfer to adult corrections custody in 2006, Smith is regarded as an illegitimate patient. During her period in adult CSC custody, once she almost immediately becomes problematic as an inmate for CSC to manage, this figuration transforms into an understanding of her as Ashley the Inmate-Patient, a figure that is primarily defined by its status as a carceral subject and whose "behaviours" are individualized and pathologized. During this period, from 2006-2007, CSC enlists the assistance of mental health expertise and technologies in managing this carceral subject. It is only after Ashley Smith dies, and after the recuperative figuration of Child Ashley becomes the most frequently articulated, widely accepted and even assumed, representation of her in media texts about the Smith case that, in late 2010, with the release of the "Behind the Wall" documentary and the release of Margo Rivera's psychiatric report that this configuration transmutes and the recuperative figure of Patient Smith as a sympathetic victim becomes the dominant construction of her in the case, inviting in a slightly different apparatus of power and knowledge in the form of the mental health system instead of corrections.

As mentioned earlier, the conditions of possibility laying the groundwork for the figure Patient Smith figure are present throughout her case. As discussed in Chapter 3, Ashley Smith was placed in a mental health institution before she was ever incarcerated. Certain conditions of possibility appear to have been present that made her plausibly constructible as a mental patient throughout her contact with legal and correctional systems. For example, in the NB Ombudsman Report, Smith is at one point characterized as one instance of a type of "youth suffering from mental illness and severe behaviour disorders." (Richard, 2008)

By the end of 2010, the Child Ashley figure lost its dominance to a new configuration of Ashley Smith that was not contradictory to, but mutually supportive of, and derived from, the Child Ashley figuration. The dominant representation of Ashley Smith transforms into a mental patient. This new configuration of Ashley Smith had stabilized in media portrayals by 2013 and the end of the second inquest in December of that year. Howard Sapers' 2013 "Risky Business" report (Sapers, 2013) played an important part in solidifying the figure of Patient Smith as the "final word" on Ashley Smith at the time of the inquest decision in December 2013. What appears to be the ultimate overriding understanding of Smith is as a case of a type of whom there are perhaps six to thirty, a case of a very seriously mentally ill woman offender in Canada. This is the figure of Ashley Smith presented equally in more progressive and more conservative media sources. In these sites, media reports invoke the language of angels and demons when describing Ashley Smith as a mentally ill woman and bestow on this figure of Patient Smith a sacral aura. For example, CTV's "Kevin Newman Live" special aired on December 19, 2013, the day the inquest verdict was rendered. In it, Ashley Smith is described by both the narrator Kevin Newman and *Toronto Star* and guest interviewee journalist, Diana Zlomistic, as mentally ill and infantile: "diagnosed with ADHD and a personality disorder... a child crying for help." (19 December 2013) In May of 2013, *National Post* columnist Christie Blatchford described Ashley Smith as suffering " from a severe antisocial personality disorder with florid borderline features... it was a hellish mental illness." (Blatchford, 9 May 2013) Also, in December 2013, after the inquest verdict was rendered, Blatchford articulated the figure of Patient Smith as not just a case but the *ultimate* case of a mentally ill girl victim mislocated in prison as follows:

> Generally, the mentally ill in this country, but specifically the mentally ill who are in prison, and in particular young, severely mentally ill women behind bars, have suffered for too long. Poor Ashley, with her sweet smile and clever charm, and that unrelenting sickness that had her strangling herself multiple times a day, was the penultimate

[sic] embodiment of all that can go wrong. (Blatchford, 19 December 2013)

As is the case with the other figurations discussed in this book, there is not one tidily bounded and universally acknowledged figure of Patient Smith. Messy and overlapping figures collide, conflict to some degree, and collect together in the form of a set of representations similar enough to one another to be treated as a singular discursive formulation. All of the configurations of Ashley Smith discussed in this chapter foreground mental illness as the primary social problem identified by the Smith case and the primary social problem defining her.

On the whole, Patient Smith is defined as one of a very small subset of a particular type of exceptionally high risk inmates. Specific words deployed to define Patient Smith include a "mentally ill inmate," "one of a very few seriously self-harming female inmates," a "troubled teen with mental health issues" one of a "handful of mentally disordered women offenders," (Sapers, 2013) and one of "about 20 to 40 women in prison on any given day who cut or bite themselves, head bang, ingest objects or self-asphyxiate." (Vincent, 19 December 2013) Similarly, Patient Smith is also defined as "a mentally troubled teen who had a history of acting out, and who, her inquest has heard, had a compulsive habit of self-harming." (Vincent, 21 April 2013)

While there is an official and doctrinal separation between the correctional and mental health systems of governance for both adolescent and adult subjects in Canada, there are ways in which the two systems overlap. While, as will be discussed below, many articulations of Patient Smith in mainstream media sites uncritically portray the mental health system as separate from the correctional system, a review of the discursive figure of Ashley the Inmate-Patient shows that this is not accurate. The CCRA sets forth at sections 86 and 87 an obligation on the part of CSC and youth corrections to provide health, including mental health, treatment. Human rights legislation, such as the *Canadian Human Rights Act*. 1976-77, c. 33, s. 1. as well as the *Charter of Rights and Freedoms* further reinforce the rights of prisoners to health treatment, including mental health treatment. There is a large institutional machinery in the CSC system where psy-experts work either as employees or contractors for CSC, provincial or youth corrections. (Service) The bureaucracy of CSC's mental health machinery is itself complex: under it psychologists and psychiatrists have split but overlapping jurisdiction to address the mental health needs of inmates and are administered by different managers. Significant percentages of inmates regularly receive mental health treatment, including psychotherapy as well as psychotropic medications. (Brink, Doherty and Boer)

NUISANCE

During most of her life, Ashley Smith was not widely regarded by officials in justice, mental health, child protection or educational systems as a subject legitimately in need of mental health treatment. Rather, she was represented as a nuisance to mental health professionals and institutions. She was understood as a troublesome, badly behaved and vexing but mentally *healthy* adolescent subject. The paradigmatic statement of the quite consistent way in which her capacity was regarded by mental health professionals throughout her case is summed up in the following quote from a psychiatrist at Restigouche hospital in 2003: "Ms Smith clearly understands her responsibilities and their consequences and can control her actions when she chooses to." (CBC Timeline) The prevailing construction of Ashley Smith in texts produced by mental health officials (psychiatrists etc.) before she died is as a carceral subject: these texts provide mental health modifiers to a subject primarily identified as an inmate. This construction is consistent with a narrative that Ashley Smith made choices motivated by rebelliousness and demonstrated in doing so a type of unruly agency. Smith did not attract the incapacitating mental health diagnoses now assigned to her until a late stage and even when the diagnoses were applied, priorities in response were security, not treatment. Indeed, ironically, more attention appears to have been paid to Ashley Smith's mental health in prison than in the mental health system.

As discussed in Chapter 4, before she was incarcerated, Ashley Smith was determined by psy-experts to have behavioural problems, but not "real" mental illness. Mental health professionals on numerous occasions simply did not see her behaviours as evidencing legitimate mental health issues. According to her mother's testimony at the Smith inquest, Ashley Smith was understood by psy-experts prior to her incarceration as an immature, but not a mentally ill teenager. Coralee Smith told the inquest jury that Ashley saw a psychiatrist who decided Ashley was "just a normal teenager … I'm too fat and I have acne," is what Ashley Smith said about the session. (Perkel, 20 February 2013) In 2002, an unnamed psychologist is reported to have found that Ashley Smith had "non-learning verbal difficulties" (CBC Timeline) that might be connected to "neurological deficits." In 2003, at the Pierre Caissie Centre, she is found to have "a learning disorder, ADHD, and borderline personality disorder and narcissistic personality traits." At sentencing in Miramachi Youth Court, she is determined to have "anger management problems." (Richard, 2008) Recall also that, once in prison, Ashley Smith is constituted by psy-experts as a "child." Psychiatrist Dr. Jeffrey Penn's notes that were brought forward in testimony in the second inquest in the Smith case stated: "This young woman is essentially a large tyrannical child who can't tolerate limits, feels estranged and isolated from peers, unloved, unliked, and often hopeless." This label of Smith as a "large, tyrannical child" also appears in testimony from psychologist Dr. Allister Webster, as discussed in Chapter 4, who referenced Penn's notes and adopted the label. As previously explored, this is a diagnosis relating to disordered behaviour, not to treatable mental illness.

While a mental health diagnosis suggests a logic of care, it was a risk logic that governed treatment decisions about Ashley Smith in the mental health system. Notably, mental health facilities refused to accept Ashley Smith as a patient repeatedly over the course of her life, whether by rejecting her or discharging her early, not on the basis of a logic of caring for what might be her interests but on the basis of calculations made in a logic of risk as to what might cost money for or expose facilities to disruption. Recall from Chapter 3 that, before she was ever incarcerated, on March 30, 2003, 15 year old Ashley Smith was discharged from a mental institution (New Brunswick's Pierre Caissie Treatment Centre) after having only completed 27 days of her recommended 34-day assessment. Her stay was discontinued when it was determined by management that Smith posed a security risk to the handling of the rest of the population at the centre. Smith was discharged because she was a nuisance "since she was seriously disrupting the assessments of the other youths."(Richard, 2008, 16) During her stay, Smith received "psychological, psychiatric and educational assessments" (*ibid*, 17) Smith was recommended to have individualized counseling in the community by a psychological expert (although this was not specifically arranged by the institution) and to take "follow-up" medication.

The discharge of Ashley Smith from the Caissie Centre was not an aberrant event but rather only one in a series of early releases and rejections of her as a patient by several mental health institutions over the course of her case. As discussed in Chapter 3, she was removed from Saskatoon's Psychiatric centre "for her safety" after being assaulted by staff there. She was subsequently discharged from Pinel Institute in Montreal before an assessment could be completed. In June 2007, Ashley Smith was then sent to, and discharged rapidly from, St. Thomas Psychiatric Hospital in Ontario, before an assessment of her was completed.(Sapers, 2008) The administration at the St. Thomas hospital found her too ill to treat. Further, CBC's "The Fifth Estate" makes an unattributed claim that "three days before her death Ashley asked to go to a psychiatric hospital. She told correctional staff that she would take medication and stop choking herself. There were no beds available at the hospital." (CBC Timeline) These rejections have been framed in many texts where Patient Smith dominates as a reflection of a need for more infrastructure and resources in the mental health system. However, these rejections are also comprehensible as necropolitical actions excluding Ashley Smith from treatment on the basis of risk logic. Seen this way, the mental health system can be understood as excluding Inmate Smith because of the risks she poses to their general populations and burdens she would place on their resources, and suggests the complicity of decision-makers within those institutions in decisions that produced Inmate Smith as an inhabitant of a death world, a *homo sacer*.

It is evident from this pattern of exclusions, rejections and early discharges from mental health treatment that the general security and smooth functioning of the mental institutions was prioritized over the mental health needs of Ashley Smith. Energy was not expended on treatment of Ashley Smith during her life. To the contrary, what appears evident is the operation of risk logic and exception in a series of exclusions of her from mental health treatment opportunities. Security and risk logics were mobilized even when alternative care-based approaches were evidently recognized as suggesting other potential courses of action. Ashley Smith was represented as the bringer of disruption; as a nuisance. Indeed, I would argue that the pattern of actions taken to exclude Ashley Smith from mental health systems mirrors and interlocks with the series of transfers, abuses and segregation as necropolitical actions undertaken against Inmate Smith by the legal and correctional systems. This is consistent with the theorization now widely put forward in critical criminological literature. As criminologists Kilty and Hannah-Moffatt have argued, when risk discourse emerged into dominance in late modern western societies, it did not replace the psy-discourses. (Hannah-Moffatt, Kelly and Shaw; Kilty) As discussed in Chapter 2, Christie Barron has applied this analysis to the specific context of governing adolescent girls in correctional facilities. (Barron) It is argued by these scholars that psy-discourses are deployed in conjunction with risk discourses to pathologize resistant behavior or responses to inequalities as individual dysfunction. Arguably, the psy-discourses and risk logic have fused and risk logic is now pervasive not just in correctional settings but also in mental health institutions.

In light of this fusion of the discourses of exclusion, security, mental health and risk, had Inmate Smith been understood as a psychiatric patient from the beginning of her interactions with the interlocking governmental apparati of the neoliberal state, it is not clear that she would have ended up in conditions materially different from those she faced in CSC custody. Like prison inmates, subjects held in secure psychiatric facilities are often held in solitary confinement (albeit by a different names including "seclusion" and "therapeutic quiet") and are found to have committed suicide at high rates. (Gordon, 2002) Mental illness is characterized by the

Canadian Mental Health Association as "the second leading cause of premature death in Canada." (CMHA)

INMATE – PATIENT

Early in 2006, the Ashley the Inmate-Patient figures starts to emerge in official texts; the notion that Inmate Smith has some sort of mental health abnormality starts creeping into the official story about Ashley Smith once she is transferred to CSC custody. Once Inmate Smith is transferred to adult custody, she does attract a wide-ranging series of mental health diagnoses. Even so, mental health experts consulted to deal with Ashley Smith during her life generally continued to produce documents in which the dominant construction of her is as an inmate.[1] Expressing uncertainty as to how to manage the risks presented by Inmate Smith, CSC management moves her twice to mental health facilities. In January 2007, Inmate Smith is transferred to the CSC Prairie Regional Centre in Saskatoon in order "to obtain a clear diagnosis, and to develop and implement a specialized treatment plan." (Sapers, 2008) However, the treatment to which Inmate Smith is subject in this mental health facility that doubles as a jail is at least as problematic as that she faced in prior CSC placements. When technically housed in psychiatric facilities, Inmate-Patient Smith was frequently kept in "seclusion," the institutional term for solitary confinement.[2] While in mental health care in March 2007, Inmate Smith is assaulted by correctional Staff at the CSC Prairie Regional Centre. (Richard, 2008) In April 2007, following assaults by correctional staff, Smith is voluntarily transferred out of CSC Prairie Regional Centre "for her own personal safety" (Sapers, 2008) and into Institut Phillippe-Pinel de Montreal for treatment. However, this new placement is discontinued after only two weeks, on May 10, 2007. (Richard, 2008)

Assessments were ordered and made, but Inmate-Patient Smith was assessed for how best to be coded in the institutions' bureaucratic languages of risk and security. These assessments were conducted in accordance with an institutional logic to which care is not comprehensible and risk and security are the paramount considerations. Dr. Penn based his influential "large, tyrannical child" diagnosis on 35 minutes he had spent interviewing Ashley Smith through the food slot of her segregation cell while she was in Nova Institution. Four days later, he met with her again, communicating once more through the food slot. It is notable that, on this analysis, "craves stimulation" is defined as her pathology. There is no reference made to the *lack* of stimulation with which Inmate Smith was contending at the time of the diagnosis. Similarly, Penn noted that Inmate Smith "is hopeless" without any reference to the fact that her situation, to an outside observer, *was* pretty hopeless. This is one example of a pattern of pathologization and decontexualization prevalent in texts generated by mental health professionals who met with Ashley Smith during her period of incarceration. Also significant, and apparently typical of many reports about Ashley Smith authored by psy-experts during her incarceration, is the confident certainty with which Penn asserts the correctness of his diagnosis notwithstanding the difficult and limited circumstances under which the information on which it was based was derived.

When the diagnoses were made, priorities in response were overwhelmingly security-focused. It is a much-repeated statement in the Smith case that Ashley Smith "never received a comprehensive psychological assessment." However, Inmate-Patient Smith was psychologically and psychiatrically "assessed" multiple times. Inmate-Patient Smith was assessed at St. Thomas psychiatric hospital by Dr. Sam Swaminath, a forensic psychiatrist, who gave testimony at the inquest that the priority was not treatment of her diagnosed mental illness but security and containment: "First and foremost, the issue was to keep her safe and try to contain her." (Blatchford, 6 May 2013) Similarly, in the days leading up to her death, according to testimony at the inquest, Inmate Smith was "assessed" several times by SCS psychologist Cynthia Lanigan: on October 9, 10, 12 and 16, Inmate Smith was given psychological assessments.(Vincent, 24 June 2013) These assessments were security-based calculations of risk: evaluations of the likelihood that Inmate Smith would seek to commit suicide, not of what might help her. It is widely understood that Canada's mental health and correctional systems are separate and discrete entities. The formal criminal law sets up a binary split between what are understood as two separate systems.³ Definitions of mental disorder and capacity and frame inquiries in criminal proceedings that responsibilize actors with capacity and consign them to corrections custody while they completely de-responsibilize actors found not to be "criminally responsible by means of mental disorder"⁴ or not "fit to stand trial."⁵ There is no "middle ground" in these determinations: the inquiry is binary and results in an either/or determination as to sanity, or capacity for criminal fault (*mens rea*). (Eaves and Roesch)

Under earlier formal regimes set up to deal with problematic behaviour by adolescents in Canada, an exception was made to this binary mental health/criminal law split. The *Juvenile Delinquents' Act*, in force until 1984, dealt with adolescents in a hybrid system where adolescents found to have committed criminal or quasi-criminal acts could be labeled with a "status" of delinquent and incarcerated in "training schools" for indeterminate periods. As discussed in Chapter 2, abuses of, and problems with, this "benevolent" approach to government of adolescents were sought to be remedied when new rights-based legislation was ushered in. It is out of recognition for problems with the past approach that the YOA eliminates status offences and then the YCJA specifically prohibits the use of carceral sanctions (custody) for reasons in the "best interests" of the child such as mental health treatment.⁶

It is not only in the youth system that custodial mental health treatments have been seen to be problematic. Where a finding of guilt in the criminal system results in a determinate sentence, a committal to mental health custody is much more open-ended, could be permanent, does not have to be proportionate or even referential to the relative seriousness of the offence, and is subject only to periodic reviews. Indeed, a committal to mental health custody does not require a preliminary court order or hearing.⁷ In short, many have argued that the mental health system has more Draconian power, exercisable in less transparent ways, to exclude subjects from political community than does the criminal/correctional one. (Morrow)

An important formal legal text that sets out conditions of possibility shaping the Smith case is Ontario's provincial *Mental Health Act* (MHA) RSO 1990 c. M. 7. This is the provincial law that applies to the mental health assessment and treatment Inmate Smith underwent while at Grand Valley. The mental health legislation of other provinces applies in respect of her time held in other jurisdictions (e.g. Saskatchewan and Nova Scotia.) The MHA defines the jurisdiction for interventions to be undertaken that affect adolescents on the basis of mental health. The MHA also authorizes detentions for reasons of risk and provides jurisdiction for strip and body cavity searches such as those to which Inmate Smith was subject.[8] Significantly, also, s. 25 of the MHA authorizes the use of restraints against mental patients, including chemical restraints (such as psychotropic drugs).

There is significant overlap between subjects identified as criminal and those labeled as having a mental illness, particularly where women inmates are concerned. Large percentages of prison inmates have received diagnoses of mental illness, either before or after being incarcerated. (CSC, 2009) This overlap is especially pronounced when the inmates considered are gendered female. More than twice as high a percentage of female than male inmates (30% / 11%) have mental illness diagnoses when admitted to CSC custody.(Brink, Doherty and Boer) The percentage of inmates receiving mental health diagnoses and treatment has changed over time. Mental illness is now generally sought to be treated in the community; this has resulted since the 1960s in a de-institutionalization of people diagnosed with mental illness by the mental health system. However, there is a corresponding increase in numbers of people with mental illness being admitted to prison.(Wasylenki) A growing body of research shows that the same population being de-institutionalized by the mental health system is being *re*-institutionalized in the prison system. A 2013 report referring to U.S. statistics put forward by *Mother Jones* provides a schematic that shows how, where numbers of prison inmates have gone up over the past 20 years or so, numbers of persons held in mental institutions have decreased by roughly the same percentages. ("Locked Up But Where?")

A connection between de-institutionalization of the mentally ill in the mid-twentieth century and disproportionate homelessness and incarceration of the same populations of mentally ill individuals has also been demonstrated in Canada. A recent study by the Mental Health Commission of Canada tracks negative consequences to populations diagnosed as mentally ill of the closure of over 80% of mental health beds across Canada since the 1970s. What the study argues has followed is increased homelessness, a decreased life expectancy and the emergence of "jails and prisons" as "the new institutional setting" for those identified as mentally ill. ("Turning the Key") At the macro-level, de-funding of mental health institutional care and "tough on crime" agendas in contemporary neoliberal nation states and especially Canada under the Harper government are increasing numbers of prison populations; counter-discourses are being deployed to seek to intervene in these general trends. (Davis) Indeed, the de-institutionalization of Ashley Smith as a mental patient through her release from the Pierre Caissie Centre and her re-incarceration as a carceral subject in the correctional system mirror in microcosm these broad social trends.

At the same time, organizationally, different discrete bureaucratic apparati exist: while there are mental health experts at work in the Federal correctional system, there is also an overlapping mental health system administered at the provincial level. Between these two systems, at a different level of power, corrections and mental health authorities are trying to shift responsibility and blame for mental health issues of inmates on to one another. It was not just tactical decisions by CSC counsel at the inquest or media attention that contributed to the demise of the dominance of the Inmate Smith figure. Aspects of meso-level formal legal apparati that shaped the conditions of possibility in which the case came to prominence also contributed to the dominant reconfiguration of Ashley Smith from an Inmate into a Patient. Once the Smith case became infamous, it became in the interests of Federal politicians to characterize it as a case not of a problem with (Federal) corrections but with (Provincial) mental health. The division of powers set forth under Canada's *Constitution Act*, 1867 divides various powers between levels of government, a division that politically incentivizes a shell game where actors from different levels of governments recast problems as in each other's jurisdiction. Health, including mental health, falls in provincial jurisdiction (under s. 92) while the criminal justice power is Federal (under s. 91). The first Canadian assertion of Federal jurisdiction over penitentiaries took place with the *Penitentiary Act*, 1868. As a result, the Federal government is responsible for inmates in penitentiaries (serving adult sentences of two years or more) and provincial and territorial governments are responsible for dealing with inmates serving shorter sentences as well as youth in custody.

Patient Smith is configured during her life as pathological and exceptional and her mental health is framed generally as a cause of her problems in the juridical field and not as an effect of her treatment there. An illustrative example of this is presented by the core psychopathic element of Borderline Personality Disorder that a patient "lacks a sense of self." (Winston)

It is unclear why treating mental health professionals assumed Smith could have consolidated and maintained a "sense of self" under the circumstances and did not read negotiations of subjectivity into the resistances she was "doing." Indeed, this interpretation completely ignores the complicity of CSC's bureaucracy in her alleged lack or loss of a sense of self, makes invisible the burden placed on Ashley Smith's sense of self by CSC management's unrelenting disciplinary actions against her. While the resistant behaviours of Patient Smith are read under this diagnosis as reflecting a lack of a sense of self, quite the same sorts of resistant behaviours by men in prison have been read in other contexts as negotiations of subjectivity men engage in to *retain* their masculinity and *foster* a sense of self when they are incarcerated and their freedom is limited to less than that accorded a young child. (Ugelvik) Further, adolescent girls are held widely in popular psychology to be in the process of developing a sense of themselves, and literature about developmental psychology and gender now largely contends that developing a "healthy" sense of self is particularly difficult for "normal" adolescent girls. (Sandler) Given that Ashley Smith was a longterm inmate in solitary confinement since age 15 and had been subjected to social and juridical necropolitical actions which in effect *eliminated* her social and political selves from existence in human community before she reached adulthood and received this diagnosis. Further, traumatic experiences are being increasingly linked with the diagnosis of "borderline personality disorder" (BPD) by cultural studies theorists, as well as psychologists and psychiatrists. (Sandler; DSM-IV) The traumatic experiences of abuse Ashley Smith experienced while an inmate appear strikingly absent from the testimony and texts of all but one mental health professional who treated Inmate-Patient Smith.[9] The contention that Patient Smith lacks a "sense of self" obscures the institutional course of action not altogether unlike what Primo Levi describes in Auschwitz as a logic of the camp calculated to bring about "the demolition of a man." (Levi) It is remarkably unreflexive on the part of those labeling Ashley Smith with the BPD disorder not to comment on this context.

Reframing by government of the Smith case as not one of an Inmate but properly a Patient is analogous at the meso level to the microprocesses that took place in the seventeen transfers she underwent while in CSC custody: passing the case along to be someone else's problem. At the inquest, St. Joseph's Health Care, operator of St. Thomas psychiatric hospital, where Ashley Smith spent nine days shortly before her death, was represented by counsel. Counsel for the hospital, after the inquest verdict, is quoted as saying: "The hospital ... foresaw that there would be an issue in this inquest over whether responsibility for women inmates suffering with complex mental disorders should be the responsibility of the federal corrections system or the provincial mental health sector." (*St. Thomas Times-Journal* 21 December 2013)

The Federal government is able to protect its own practices from scrutiny by casting the issues raised as mental health problems. When, on October 25, 2012, in the House of Commons Hansard, Vic Toews, then Minister of Public Safety and Corrections was questioned by the MP Judy Foote of Opposition Liberals as to why the Ashley Smith inquest was being "obstructed" (Hansard) Toews responded that the Smith case was about the "need for mental health care to be dealt with by our provinces." This can be seen as an evasion of responsibility for the Smith case by the Federal government not dissimilar to the series of transfers between institutions she underwent while in CSC custody. This statement functioned both to pass blame for her death from the Federal to the Provincial government and to bolster the structures and systems of the prison industrial complex by sidestepping criticism. Similarly, when Prime Minister Stephen Harper, also in 2012, told media he was "horrified" by the CSC surveillance tapes and decried the conduct of CSC in the Smith case, (CTV News, 12 November 2013) this statement drew focus onto the problematic aspects of CSC management and away from from any links that might be drawn between the treatment of inmates and his government's "tough on crime" agenda and its characteristically exclusionary regime of governance through crime.

However, while there are different bureaucracies in the federal and provincial mental health and correctional systems, the mental health treatment Ashley Smith received while incarcerated reveals, rather than the operation of two separate systems of power and knowledge in mental health and incarceration, an enmeshment of the two. Certainly, the systems use different technical languages and invoke different formal legal texts, and are at times mutually unintelligible. However, the overlapping processes of the mental health and correctional systems in the Smith case present as a messy, tense, intertwining with the two discursive systems functioning together.

Ashley Smith was transferred not just between CSC facilities but was rather shuttled between mental health and correctional placements. She was placed in mental health facilities managed by various provinces (Quebec, New Brunswick and Ontario) as well as in mental health facilities administrated by CSC in addition to CSC prisons and New Brunswick youth correctional facilities. Management of her in mental health facilities and at the direction of certain mental health experts appears to have been at least as problematic as her treatment by CSC management.

Just as critical discourse analysis of the figure of Inmate Smith reveals messiness and the radical contingencies of guards' agencies so does analyzing the figure of Patient Smith reveal resistances, messiness and muddiness in the mental health field. There is not one monolithic or unitary mental health diagnosis or approach taken to Patient Smith. In contrast to the high degree of certainty of Dr. Penn evidently felt in his diagnosis given the given context of his brief session with Inmate-Patient Smith, psychologist Dr. Gordana Eldjupovic, who treated Ashley Smith briefly at Grand Valley Institution stands out. Dr. Eldjupovic's testimony at the inquest evidences resistance on her part against the v regime: "I don't think I ever received training to provide therapy through a food slot." Eldjupovic's characterization of Smith is less confident and less simplistic than that of many other treating professionals. Anomalously, in inquest testimony, she contextualized Smith's behaviours in her experiences while incarcerated. Eldjupovic said Smith sometimes "showed tremendous joy and happiness … anyone having to spend so much time in segregation would not do well. It's important to find things the person likes to do." Eldjupovic's testimony stands out as resistant and, in the face of a CSC regime that employed her and also sought to silence the inquest inquiries, brave. (CBC News 18 June 2013)

The figuration of Ashley the Inmate-Patient intersects with pre-existing discourses of mental illness when she is assigned various mental health diagnoses. Ashley Smith was never, at any point during her experience within the juridical field and mental health systems, determined to be psychotic, or out of touch with reality. Rather, she was diagnosed with a variety of personality disorders. Ashley the Inmate-Patient is diagnosed with "antisocial personality disorder with borderline traits" while at the Institute Philippe-Pinel in 2007. (Beaudry) As Saskatoon Regional Psychiatric Centre, she is diagnosed with "borderline personality disorder." (*ibid*) Personality disorders are diagnosed based on divergences from the norm. (Nervenarzt) The term "personality disorder" in mental health discourse stands in the place of longstanding behavioural abnormality.[10] What would be described in the official discourse of CSC as persistent "bad choices" would be characterized in mental health discourse as the persistent "maladaptive behaviours" signaling a personality disorder. People with personality disorders are not defined as incapacitated: they are able to make plans and take action purposefully. They are not confused nor have they had a "psychotic break" from reality (unless they have a simultaneous disorder additional to a personality disorder). Rather, they have persistent habitual behaviours not generally found to be socially acceptable. (DSM-IV, 646-649)

The Ashley Inmate-Patient figure, as it emerges from official expert mental health discourse in texts and inquest testimony, is not unagentic. Rather, the agency of this figure is constructed in a very similar way to that of Inmate Smith, albeit using different terms. Where Inmate Smith is capable of compliance or non-compliance and can make good or bad choices, in expert discourse, Ashley the

Inmate-Patient has the capacity to comply with therapeutic direc-
tions and choose to "adapt" her persistent maladaptive behaviours
to conform to societal expectations and be more pro-social. While
Inmate-Patient Smith's agency is de-politicized, understood as
having no *meaning*, and hindered by the external constraint of her
habitual maladaptive functioning, it is she and she alone who is
understood as capable of overcoming those habits, and it is only
once she starts to co-operate with treatment that mental health
professionals may be able to support her in changing.[11]

However, during her time in corrections custody, Ashley Smith
actively resisted being characterized as a patient. She persistently
refused medical and mental health assessments and treatment.
(Sapers, 2008, paragraph 20) Because she refused treatment, she
was "certified" four times under Ontario's Mental Health Act
and four times under Saskatchewan's legislation in the same year,
2006. (*ibid*) This certification gave mental health authorities the
power to give her medication by force. She maintained claims
that she was not mentally ill; indeed her repeated assertion of
this claim is referenced in several instances as *evidence* of her
mental illness.[12] With mental health authorities' authorization,
although not in accordance with formal regulations as to how
this authorization should be procured, Ashley Smith was, while
in restraints, administered forced injections of psychotropic drugs
on July 22, 23 and 26, 2007 at Joliette Institution. (Beaudry)
The rationale given for the use of these restraints was security
of staff and other inmates: mental health "treatment" was thus
invoked for security reasons.

One of the mental health labels put on Ashley the Inmate-Patient
that seems to stick better than some others is that of "borderline
personality disorder." Indeed, towards the end of her life in prison,
diagnoses coalesce around BPD. This is not unproblematic. BPD
is a thoroughly unscientific, historically gendered and stigmatizing diagnosis. (Zlotnick et al.) A diagnosis of BPD seems to, but
doesn't *really*, distinguish Ashley the Inmate-Patient from other
carceral subjects. Many, if not most, prisoners are diagnosed or
diagnosable with BPD. According to a report by 57 independent
monitoring boards of prisons in the United Kingdom (UK), 90
percent of inmates have at least one diagnosable mental disorder.

25-50% of prisoners studied were diagnosed as having BPD with women more likely to be so diagnosed. (Zlotnick et al.)

As Foucault has theorized and as research by feminist scholars has previously shown, mental health discourses serve as technologies of government that depoliticize and decontextualize the acts and other responses of actors, and in particular women. (Ussher) Feminist criminologists have critically scrutinized ways in which mental health diagnoses are consistently assigned to women who resist authority in carceral settings. (Smart) More specifically, personality disorder diagnoses are slippery and problematic labels of abnormality. (Bosworth) Borderline Personality disorder in particular has been the subject of a great deal of feminist critique. (Wirth-Cauchon) At least 75% of those diagnosed BPD are female. (DSM-IV) BPD has been criticized by feminist researchers as pathologizing technologies that depoliticize certain behaviours and remove them from, or make invisible, the oppressive context in which they emerge. (Rosenfield) Indeed, there are prevalence studies that indicate, contrary to patterns in diagnosis, the symptoms underlying a BPD diagnosis are comparably present at roughly equal rates amongst women and men. (Grant et al.) A diagnosis of BPD has been criticized for making invisible experiences by girls and women of trauma and sexual abuse. (Proctor) Gillian Proctor calls BPD "the latest example of a historical tendency to explain away as "madness" the strategies some women use to survive oppression and abuse."(*ibid*, 115) BPD is diagnosed based on a patient's observed behavioral pathologies and not with reference to the context in which these behaviours have arisen. Acts often associated with BPD could alternatively be understood to reflect adaptations to experiences of powerlessness. Proctor contends that the diagnosis of BPD "pathologises and stigmatises women who struggle to survive experiences of abuse and oppression" (*ibid*, 1) Similarly, Clare Shaw, among others, has argued that BPD is diagnosed relative to an assumed normal that is based on stereotypes of feminine behaviour as passive and non-resistant. (Shaw) Proctor writes:

> The diagnosis of BPD is located within gendered structures
> of power and processes of understanding. This can be un-

derstood simplistically in terms of a dual approach.

Labeled mad: Women are labeled 'mad' when they don't conform to society's norms.

This approach argues that the concept of 'madness' — rather than describing disease entities—is an idea which has been created by society to exclude and stigmatize people who refuse to behave as society expects they should.

Driven mad: Women are driven mad by their lot in this society. This approach looks at how women cope with life in a society in which they are less likely than men to have access to money, status, power and other resources, and are more likely to experience sexual abuse and violence. (Proctor, 112)

In addition to being problematic as a diagnosis, much like the Correctional "maximum security" designation, the mental health diagnosis of BPD does not mean what it is widely taken-for-granted that it means. A diagnosis of BPD may sound to a person without psy-expertise like it has a nuanced and specific meaning. However, Proctor disparages BPD as a "catch-all label applied to 'difficult patients." (Proctor, 117) BPD may simply stand in for saying a subject has committed acts of self- harm. Acts of self-harm, are, according to Proctor, often definitively diagnostic of BPD; seen in this light, the diagnosis adds nothing to what is said in official CSC sites that Inmate Smith is a carceral subject who has committed self-harm while in prison. It is not at all conclusively proven on a scientific basis that the BPD diagnosis is clinically valid, or is based on, or reveals more than, the uncontested fact that Ashley Smith, especially after long periods in segregation, self-harmed.

BPD and other personality disorders with which Ashley the In-mate-Patient was diagnosed such as Oppositional-Defiant disorder are discourses that psy-experts claim an expertise in defining and diagnosing but not really in treating or curing. Psy-experts have developed few treatment resources to match these labels, and the treatment that does seem to have efficacy, dialectical behaviour therapy, involves longterm interaction between patient and treating expert in an environment that fosters trust. (Proctor, 116)

Analysis of the Ashley the Inmate-Patient figure reveals the entanglement of the criminal, correctional and mental health systems as overlapping and often unified governmental apparati. The commonly assumed understanding of mental health system as separate from corrections obscures the connections between different forms of governance and the ways in which mental health powers and treatments are used in necropolitical exclusions and punishment. Further, it sheds light on the messiness of the diagnostic apparatus to which Ashley the Inmate-Patient was subject and the problematic nature of the certainty of many mental health experts who dealt with her as to particular diagnoses. Close scrutiny of the Ashley the Inmate-Patient figure raises questions about the enmeshment of Canada's correctional and mental health systems in mutually supportive systems of governmentality as well as about the legitimacy of mental health expertise. So, Ashley the Inmate-Patient figure has potential to be articulated as a technology of resistance against uncritical, simplistic retrenchments of the governmental apparatus of mental health discourses and systems.

PATIENT SMITH – A SYMPATHETIC VICTIM

Immediately after the death of Ashley Smith, the configuration of her as a mental patient and victim of both her disease and the correctional system is present in a number of progressive and liberal texts and in political debate. The Patient Smith figure dominates from early on in the Smith case in texts produced by feminist and other progressive advocates in the Smith case. For example, Kitchener-area Liberal MP Karen Redman, raising Smith's death in question period, refers, without referencing any specifics of her condition or any authority to back up the assertion of her mental illness, to Smith as a "mentally unstable teenager." (Link, 24 November 2007) In a local New Brunswick paper, Smith is referred to as a "mentally ill Moncton Teenager." (*ibid*) Executive Director of the Canadian Association of Elizabeth Fry Society, Kim Pate, has frequently articulated the Patient Smith construction since well before it became dominant in the case. Pate is quoted as referencing "inmates like Smith who are dealing with mental health issues."(CBC News, 16 November 2007) As early as 2007, Pate is quoted as defining Smith as one of many "women in the justice system who have severe mental health issues." (CBC News, 29 October 2007) The configuration remains stable in mainstream media texts until at least the time of the inquest decision. For example, during the inquest Pate in 2013 is quoted as character-izing Smith as one instance of a type of "the mentally ill." (MSN News, 14 January 2013) It is not clear on what basis Pate makes this assertion, although she elsewhere references her first person experiences meeting with Ashley Smith as evidence of the validity of her views on what Smith was like. Further, the assertion fits with a pre-existing agenda of the CAEFS, an advocacy organization of which she is executive director, articulated to the United Nations and elsewhere at least as early as 2005, to establish more and better mental health services for women across Canada.[13]

It is also, at a minimum, perplexing that the paper by McGill previously discussed in Chapter 4, which was a project supervised by Kim Pate, identifies Ashley Smith in 2008 as an aboriginal wom-an when Pate was, at least since 2009, one of the chief engineers of the narrative that Ashley Smith was a middle class white girl. (McGill) This is not helpful to the credibility of this advocacy, or to the general cause of reducing aboriginal over-incarceration, and, in light of the multimillion dollar settlement yielded in the civil settlement of the Smith family's suit with CSC, and the donation of a significant chunk of those monies to CAEFS, it is troubling indeed. However, perhaps CAEFS advocates can be most fairly understood not as misrepresenting Ashley Smith but as colonizing her expe-riences in the service of predefined social agendas. Configuration of Patient Smith has its roots as a counter-discourse articulated by reformers speaking back against the official story about Inmate Smith and apparently seizing upon a selective telling of Ashley Smith's story to advance their pre-existing agendas, agendas which closely match those of the nineteenth century "child savers"; it is not until three years after her death that Patient Smith becomes the dominant configuration of Ashley Smith more generally. According to Jessica Ring's quantitative analysis of mental health labels in mainstream media reporting of the Smith case:

> liberal and centrist news articles on Ashley Smith dispute her
> 'prisoner' label by maintaining a dichotomous relationship

between Ashley and 'other' prisoners. In this dichotomy, 'offender first' language is considered acceptable for incarcerated individuals who are not mentally ill. Offender first language emphasizes the 'offender' label over any other characteristic of the individual—the primary identity ascribed to the person is that of 'offender'. (Ring, 87)

By late 2010, the dominant configuration of Ashley Smith in the Smith case is no longer as an inmate or child but as a mislocated mental patient. A discussed by Jessica Ring in use of "topic models" of mainstream media depictions of Ashley Smith, (*ibid*) by 2010, "Smith is typically presented as mentally ill" in mainstream media sites. Two texts appear to have been critical in effecting the metamorphosis of the configuration and the emergence of Patient Smith as the dominant configuration in the Smith case: the "Behind the Walls" documentary portrayed Smith's time at Saskatoon's Regional Psychiatric Centre and the release by *Globe and Mail* reporter Kirk Makin among others of excerpts from psychologist Dr. Margo Rivera's internal CSC report together appear to have brought the discursive pattern to a tipping point. Dr. Rivera found that: "I consider it highly likely that Ashley Smith's death was not a suicide, but rather an accident, and that no one intended Ashley Smith to die — least of all Ashley Smith herself." (Makin, 29 October 2010)

By 2012, the Patient Smith figure has clearly eclipsed other figurations of Ashley Smith in mainstream media sites. A significant text that assures this is the November 12, 2012 episode of CBC's *The Current* entitled "Ashley Smith and Mental Health in Canada's Prisons." (CBC) This episode airs the day before the second inquest in the Smith case commences. In this episode, Ashley Smith is described by narrator Anna Maria Tremonte as "a troubled 19 year old." Prisoner advocates Lee Chapelle and Kim Pate are interviewed, as is Candice Bergen, parliamentary secretary to the Minister of Public Health. In the segment, the question explored is: "whether the mentally ill get the support they need in Canada's prisons- and whether prison is really the best place for them." An assumed starting premise of the question at issue is that Ashley Smith is an instance of the type Patient whose mental health issues have been dealt with erroneously by authorities and who has been mislocated in prison rather than in a mental institution.

With the 2013 release of Sapers' "Risky Business" report, the "caseness" of Patient Smith is further solidified with her being a representative case of a type of which there are very few. (Berlant) The "Risky Business" report, and the preponderance of subsequent texts in media sites about the Smith case, focused on "chronic self-injury among federally sentenced women" of whom Sapers estimates there are 37 at the time the report is released, and of whom there is a further subset of 8 "most high risk and chronic self-injurious women in the federally sentenced women population." (Sapers, 2013) Reconfiguring the "caseness" of Ashley Smith away from being one of 40,000 inmates and into being one of 8 to 12, or perhaps 32 to 37 seriously mentally ill self-harming female inmates re-frames her from being an ordinary inmate to being an extraordinary one. The figure of Patient Smith turns Smith into a case to be mobilized within specific pre-existing change discourses, specifically in relation to increased funding for mental health treatment.

Patient Smith is a "chronic self-injury case." (Sapers) This construction is convenient for CSC because it makes Ashley Smith, not their bureaucracy, the problem. Because she has come to be understood as so aberrant and monstrous, on this understanding, conclusions to be drawn about, and actions called for by, the Smith case, are no longer broadly relevant in the public square to debates about CSC policy, the administration of justice in relation to youths and neoliberal governance through crime.

The verdict in the inquest released on December 19, 2013, is detailed, nuanced and complex; it sets forth 104 recommendations. However, overwhelmingly, the public has not made sense of the Smith case through the full text of that decision. Rather, it is the construction of the case in media and political sites that is definitive of how popular meanings are made of the Smith case. The overwhelming preponderance of texts about the verdict in these sites simplify it into single theme, a narrative structure that centres around the correctional system's failure to treat the mental illness of Patient Smith.

Representations of Patient Smith are not, by and large, stigmatizing or disparaging: the configuration is framed benevolently in the preponderance of sources. Certain visual texts in embedded in the docudramas about Ashley Smith and also in the videos shown at the second inquest then disseminated in mainstream media sources have become pivotal in coalescing the Patient Smith figure. One key visual text in this respect is the video, released after CSC was ordered to unseal it in 2012, of an RCMP officer using duct tape to restrain Ashley Smith while she was being flown away from Saskatchewan Regional Psychiatric Centre to Pinel Psychiatric Centre in Quebec on April 19, 2007. After Smith began to visibly "fidget" and disobeyed an order to keep both of her hands on the armrests of her airplane seat, the video depicts CSC guards shackling Smith, and covering her with "spit hoods." The plane's co-pilot, RCMP Cpl. Stephane Pilon then secures her hands with duct tape. In an oft-reported exchange that has become a moment in which the figure as victim of mental illness and mislocation in prison is rendered coherent and crystallized, Pilon and Smith speak briefly as follows:

> "Don't bite me," he says.
> "I'm not," Smith responds.
> "It'll get worse if you do."
> "How can it get worse?"
> "I'll duct-tape your face."[14]

Pilon testified at the inquest that Smith had undone her seatbelt, but this is not readily verifiable by the video footage. This videotaped visual text is excerpted in hundreds of media sources, generally embedded in written text in print media or, on video news, with a voice over that, as counsel for the Smith family did at the inquest, defines Ashley Smith as mentally ill and refers to the footage as a reflection of Corrections' lack of appropriate mental health tools to deal with her. Falconer's summing up of the video in the inquest testimony has been powerfully influential over interpretations of the film: "This is how CSC does business in transferring a victim." (Perkel, 31 October 2012)

Another important visual text in the Smith case in forging the Patient Smith figure and lending it a coherence is image of her being forcibly injected with psychotropic drugs on July 22, 2007. In this visual text, also released in 2012, in a dimly lit cell, Ashley Smith is surrounded by CSC guards in riot gear and medical personnel (apparently nurses) in haz-mat suits. The image is particularly invasive in that her legs are visible underneath a prison-issue smock and various media outlets have obscured or censored this portion of the representation. (CBC, 31 October 2012) The glaring visibility of Smith's most intimate physicality is jarring. Her sexed and sexualized body is both invasively revealed and crudely effaced by the image, both invaded and covered up. While this image has become paradigmatic as a visual used in mainstream news media sites where Smith is represented as mentally ill, this is in some respects counter-intuitive: a re-reading of the text as an image of a lucid, sexed and sexual, agentic adult being mandatorily forced to receive mental health treatment, or even sexually assaulted, is also plausible.

By the time of the release of the inquest verdict in December 2013, the victimized figure of Patient Smith dominates official as well as media sites. The inquest verdict in its opening paragraph characterizes Ashley Smith as "an identified mentally ill, high risk, high needs inmate." An opinion piece by Christie Blatchford puts forward a particularly effusive version of this configuration, one that demonstrates the mutual support offered by the Child and Patient figures to one another as follows:

> Young, severely mentally ill women behind bars have suffered for too long.... Poor Ashley, with her sweet smile and clever charm, and that unrelenting sickness that had her strangling herself several times a day was the penultimate embodiment of all that can go wrong ... [with] someone so ill and vulnerable. (19 December 2013)

Significantly, counsel and witnesses engaged in defending the conduct of CSC in the Smith case also accept the figure of Patient Smith at least by the time of the start of the second inquest. Don Head, commissioner of Correctional Service of Canada, in testimony at the inquest, conceded both that CSC has "gaps" in meeting mental health needs, indicated that CSC would be agreeable to surrendering all prisoners with serious mental illness to provincial mental health systems, and agreed that the Smith inquest was about "how the criminal justice system as a whole deals with mental health issues." (Perkel, 16 October 2013) This testimony was made at the same time that Head contended the system had already corrected problems with staff training and management made evident by Inmate Smith's death and that the jury should "not bother to make expensive recommendations." (*ibid*)

By the legal closing of the Smith case, the dominant figure of Ashley Smith has shifted from being someone who — it was *obvious* to mental health professionals — did not have mental illness to someone who is understood to *obviously* have stable, identifiable, perhaps genetic, mental illness before she was incarcerated. Oddly, although Ashley Smith entered the juridical field as someone understood as "normal" and died in CSC custody as someone determined to be problematically mentally ill, in the recuperative discourse of Patient Smith, mental illness is seen not as produced by her treatment in CSC custody but rather as a pre-existing, stable feature of her essential being. Claims about how Smith was understood at various points are rewritten by this diagnostic paradigm to a point where the public is unlikely to remember earlier figures of Ashley Smith. A clearer figure of Patient Smith is in a process of being written in to more ambiguous earlier narratives about the Smith case. Interlocutors are actively working to produce a historical narrative that consistently portrays the Smith case as from start to finish an instance of mental health as a social problem. For example, sometime in early 2014, a line was added to the CBC *Fifth Estate* timeline about Ashley Smith as follows:

October 16, 2009. *The Fifth Estate* has learned that three days before her death Ashley asked to go to a psychiatric hospital. She told correctional staff that she would take medication and stop choking herself. There were no beds available at the hospital.[15]

This claim is not attributed or referenced to any document. Further, it was evidently added in haste — there is a clerical error as to the year, which should read 2007, not 2009. This addition to the timeline text exemplifies the retrospective reinterpretation of history involved in the transformation of the influential figure of Ashley in the Smith case into Patient Smith.

While psy-experts who actually met Ashley Smith during her life repeatedly declined to label her as mentally ill, or excluded her from the social category of patient, after 2010, a myriad of texts are produced in which her mental illness is a taken-for-granted received truth. It is only from a distance and after her death that she becomes definitively understood as primarily defined by mental illness. An interesting editorial published in 2014, authored by a psy-expert who neither treated nor ever met her, claims confidently that Ashley Smith's behaviour derived from Fetal Alcohol Spectrum Disorder (FASD). The opinion piece comments on how no one at any point during Smith's life appears to have considered this possibility. The opinion piece contends that: "Smith presented as a fairly classic case of the [FASD] disorder in a young girl."(Cunningham) It is of course unknowable whether and to what extent Ashley Smith had mental health issues that pre-existed her incarceration. However, it is fascinating that the documents I reviewed do not provide examples of anyone who actually met Ashley Smith who thought she was severely mentally ill, at least until a very late stage in her period of incarceration. What is significant and knowable on this analysis is the rupture between how systems made sense of her during her life and how, at the end of the Smith case, experts and systems now define and understand her.

The figuration of Patient Smith arises at least in part as a strategic trope constructed and invoked for social justice aims. The patient figure is used as a "case" in support of three main social "causes." First, it is invoked in support of increased mental health funding. Second, it is invoked by advocates seeking to reduce CSC's reliance on solitary confinement as a management measure. Third, it is deployed by liberal feminist advocates in support of the general de-carceration of woman subjects. These deployments of Patient Ashley as a strategic trope raise questions about when and in what ways it is helpful, and in what ways it might be problematic, to mobilize a narrative known to be simplistic in order to advance what is understood to be a broader good.

Reducing or eliminating the reliance on solitary confinement in prison systems in Canada and internationally is a social cause with global popularity.[16] There are numerous texts that instrumentalize figures of Inmate- Patient Smith or Inmate Smith in service of this political cause, criticizing longterm use of segregation in prisons. For instance, according to Sapers, "[t]here is reason to believe that Ms. Smith would be alive today if she had not remained on segregation status and if she had received appropriate care." (Sapers, 2008) Another example of this is presented by a September 2013 CBC Radio *Ideas* docudrama discussion instrumentalized Patient Smith as a case study to initiate a broader discussion about "the longterm effects of administrative segregation." (Story and Desson, 8 December 2013) While it does not delve into Ashley Smith's mental health, and in fact makes no conclusions as to whether she had an "illness," legal academic Alexandra Campbell's 2012 LL.M. thesis "A Place Apart: The Harm of Solitary Confinement" (Campbell) similarly instrumentalizes Ashley Smith's case towards progressive politics seeking a decreased reliance by corrections on solitary confinement. "

Overwhelmingly, the portrayal of Ashley Smith's mental illness is as a pre-existing condition precedent to her treatment in corrections' custody, as a stable reality that CSC had to manage and deal with, and health officials were tasked to treat. Sapers' 2013 "Risky Business" report, a key text in solidifying the discursive figuration of Patient Smith, studies only women who were diagnosed with a mental disorder prior to their incarceration. Ashley Smith was not.

Particularly in light of feminist critiques of the diagnoses with which she was labeled as well as the shaky basis for the diagnoses, it is plausible to view Ashley Smith's behaviours not as reflections of individual pathology but as predictable responses to abuse, powerlessness and protracted periods of solitary confinement experienced by a subject. Very little has been said that explores the possibility that Patient Smith was produced by the necropolitical juridical exclusions of Ashley Smith. Expert reports and testimony in the inquest reasonably and plausibly support either a contention that Ashley Smith was not diagnosed with a mental disorder before going in to prison because she didn't have one, *or* that her condition was under-diagnosed, *or* treatment was underfunded, *or* some combination of all of these things. The information available is inconclusive at best. In consequence, the persist articulations of Patient Smith by progressive advocates reveal more about the modality of persuasion regularly employed by agents of civil society in the contemporary political moment in Canada. In the context of governance through crime, progressive advocates are incentivized, however perversely, to cast those on whose behalf they purport to speak, as passive "victims." The tactical decision to do so reflects dominant discursive patterns in political rhetoric about protecting victims and victims' rights, but it is not clear that it addresses the potential on the part of a highly educated Canadian political community to understand appreciate complexities and nuances in situations they are tasked with understanding.

While the figure of Ashley the Inmate-Patient as constructed in expert discourse has a particular kind of agency, the recuperative figure of Patient Smith has none. The implicit assumptions about Ashley Smith's mental health in this recuperative construction are not consistent with the details of the personality disorders with which she was diagnosed. As discussed previously, these disorders are not understood in expert discourse to render a subject incapacitated, confused or infantile. However, it is precisely through a popular understanding of mental illness that assumes it brings about the conditions for her lack of agency, her *incapacity*, that "poor, vulnerable Ashley" gains entry into the status of a properly constituted "good victim." For example, in the Donovan and Zlomistic book, Ashley's mental illness is opposed in a binary way to "purposeful" in an all or nothing construction, with mental illness configured as an absolute refutation of the contention that Smith acted with intentionality:

> A key question that arose during the inquest was whether Ashley was mentally ill or whether her behaviour was "purposeful." Breese Davies, a lawyer at the inquest who acted on behalf of the Canadian Association of Elizabeth Fry Societies ... argued that Ashley was clearly mentally unwell and needed therapeutic treatment. (Vincent and Zlomistic)

The figure of Patient Smith thus configured completely forecloses the idea that Ashley Smith acted with some level of (albeit imperfect and not sovereign) purposefulness, intentionality, political subjectivity and agency. It shifts public focus away from the practical impossibility of Ashley Smith's attempts to articulate and perform agency, from her attainment of adult personhood and coalescence of a self.

Representations of Patient Smith are configured with implicit reference to, and in the context of pre-existing discursive figures. Looking at these figures, feminist scholars since the 1970s have developed a literature that criticizes mainstream western cultural associations between the concepts of femininity and madness. (Ballou and Brown) Notable among these literary figures is Shakespeare's Ophelia. The character of Ophelia is perhaps the most influential figure in the neoliberal west of an adolescent young woman descending into madness. As discussed in the literature review, Ophelia figures prominently in popular psychological literature about adolescent girls. (Pipher) The discursive figure of Ophelia is an archetype of noble victimhood while it is also, in contemporary literary theory, understood to signify the illegibility of women's and girls' agencies in patriarchal discourse. In Shakespeare's *Hamlet*, Ophelia is found dead by drowning, from either an accident or suicide. According to contemporary literary theorists and popular psychology about adolescent girls, dead Ophelia is an archetype of innocent victimhood and female madness, and of how we conflate accident and "suicide."

Literary theorists have argued the Ophelia signals the illegibility of the agencies of women and girls in the public discourses of politics and law. As Elaine Showalter (1985) has argued, in dominant patriarchal discourses in literature and mental health, madness is *equated* with femininity. David Leverenz (1978) argues that Ophelia's madness and suicide represent the unknowability of woman in male discourses about rationality: "in [Ophelia's] madness, she has no voice of her own." (*ibid,* 301) Thus, Ophelia's madness and suicide in contemporary literary theory confirm the banishment of the female and the illegibility of women's agencies as other than madness. Relatedly, Gilbert and Gubar have argued that "the madwoman" is textual archetype in literature produced by men of woman as madness or madness as woman. These authors track the association of creative and sexual expression by women with madness. (Gilbert and Gubar) Similarly, feminist theorist Luce Irigaray has theorized masculinist narratives in literature as well as psy- and legal discourse as confining women's realities in imprisoning male narrative structures. (Irigaray, 1991)

I would argue that the discursive reconfiguration of Inmate Smith into the Patient Smith (made possible by the Child Ashley figure) is a governmental technology that, together with the Child Ashley figure, fits Ashley Smith into the pre-existing discourse of the noble, innocent girl victim. In doing so, the now-dominant recuperative Patient Smith figure intersects with pre-existing meso-level discursive structures in which deviance, agency in women and girls is unreadable as resistance and pathologized as madness. This is highly troubling in the context of a history of the exclusion and containment of women through institutionalization that has never begun and ended with prisons. Thinking back to Gillman's "Yellow Wallpaper" story, read intertextually with Ashley Smith's case, Gillman's "Creeping women" can be understood as embodied agents subject to governance and the paper as the official discourse of the mental health field. Similarly, on a feminist reading, Ophelia represents adolescent young women's illegibility to the law: Ophelia has nothing to say in the public discourse of the law. These subjects identified as female are pathologized as insane until the treatment for that pathology — in both the "Yellow Wallpaper" story and in the Smith case, among other things, longterm solitary confinement — actually does drive them mad. Significantly, in Gillman's story solitary confinement is imposed on the narrator not in name as a carceral measure but as a mental health treatment but is, in effect, a carceral sentence.

These longstanding literary theory and feminist social science critiques of social constructions of mental illness in general and BPD in particular call into question the uncritical adoption by purportedly feminist advocates of the received expert diagnosis that Ashley Smith was mentally ill in a way that was stable, static and independent of her context. Phyllis Chesler has made significant contribution to problematizing the imaginations of mental illness as masculinist. (Chesler) In the context of these theorizations from literary and feminist theoretical literatures about the close association between woman and madness in western cultural discourse, the diagnosis of BPD assigned to Inmate- Patient Smith takes on a political aspect.

Dr. Renée Fugère of the Philippe-Pinel Institute gave testimony at the inquest to the effect that Ashley Smith's BPD was not likely to be permanent, but rather would most likely resolve once she ceased to be a young woman: "Personality disorders tend to become less florid with age, and by the time a woman is 40, she may be relatively mellow." (Blatchford, 2 May 2013) Seen in the light of feminist and Foucauldian criticism of governmentality through the discourses of mental health, (Foucault, *A History of Insanity in the Age of Reason*) the prognosis that Ashley Smith's condition is likely to improve once she reaches middle age becomes nothing short of darkly comic. Considered in the light of theorizations of discursive equivalencies between young woman and madness, the assertion that Ashley Smith's condition would have likely resolved by the time she hit menopause are troubling indeed: under a critical feminist reading, with the BPD diagnosis, in effect, Ashley Smith has been diagnosed with being a young woman who has been abused and disempowered, or, even more simply, on a critical literary reading, with nothing more than being a young woman.

The figure of Patient Smith fits well with narratives about mislocation of a mental patient in correctional space: the implicit assertion is that "if only" Ashley Smith had received mental health treatment she could have been "helped." It is not correct to say that the mental health system had no involvement with Ashley Smith. Critical discourse analysis of the figure of Ashley the Inmate-Patient shows the messy enmeshment of the mental health, correctional and criminal systems with one another. Barron (2007) has provided insight into this enmeshment. It is also not obvious that the mental health system is equipped to "help" people diagnosed with BPD.

The Patient Smith figure does not just make Ashley Smith legible but also has the governmental function of assigning accountability and blame. The work of this figure is primarily in the responsibilization it effects. Mental health as a social problem is foregrounded by the Patient Smith figuration while other concerns are obscured. When the critical gaze of investigative journalism and the public eye is focused on how a small, defined subset of very mentally ill female offenders is dealt with, the systematic apparatus of the correctional system eludes scrutiny. The Patient Smith figure is fueled in large part by its power to shift blame. It reframes the social problem identified by the Smith case to fit available solutions and exculpate political leaders and correctional institutions as well as their bureaucracies from responsibility for her death.

With the rise to pre-eminence of the Patient Smith configuration, certain aspects of Ashley Smith's life, behaviour and experiences are made visible while others are not. The manifold instances in which Ashley Smith acted purposefully and legibly (including her scores of quite coherent grievances filed with CSC management) are ignored. Her agency is de-legitimized: the benevolent construction incapacitates her agency. The detailed and nuanced set of 104 recommendations made by the inquest verdict, most of which do not specifically refer to mental illness, is simplified into a public understanding that the social problem defined by the Smith case was *simply* failure to fund mental health.

The dominance of the Patient Smith figuration is convenient for, and welcomed by, CSC management in that it shifts attention away from what the CSC Guards' Union in the "A Rush To Judgment" Report call a "catastrophically dysfunctional management culture." (at 5) Indeed, with the reconfiguration of Inmate Smith into Child Ashley and then into Patient Smith, focus of criticisms referencing the Smith case in texts produced in institutional, political and media sites has shifted away from systemic change to the prison industrial complex and the logics of macropower. Notably, CSC management has adopted and even embraced the discursive reconfiguration of Ashley Smith as a mental patient and not an ordinary inmate. Upon the release of the verdict of homicide in the second inquest, a spokesperson for Public Safety Canada, on behalf of CSC released the following statement:

> We will carefully review the recommendations to determine what further actions should be taken to meet the mental health needs of offenders so that tragedies such as this one does not happen again.... Since Ashley's death, several actions have already been taken to improve the way offenders with mental health needs are managed. (Carlson, 19 December 2013)

Notably, in this statement, CSC both accepts the figuration of Patient Smith and simultaneously claims that the issues raised by this figure have already been addressed. The acceptance of Patient Smith is with her configured in a way that supports the infrastructures of the prison industrial complex: such patients are incredibly hard to handle according to the narratives that fit well with this figure, and it is the expertise of CSC management working in tandem with mental health professionals that is supported by this claim while the existence of proper facilities for their housing and care is legitimated. Of particular note, the most concrete measure taken to date by government to address the recommendations of the Smith inquest is a provincial Ontario "pilot project" where two new mental "health beds" reserved for women have been opened at a facility in Brockville, Ontario. (*ibid*)

Like the name "therapeutic quiet" for solitary confinement in the youth system previously discussed, the figure of the "bed" in the mental health context is euphemistic. Although these proposed facilities are termed "beds" as they will be small, secure rooms for solitary confinement of prisoners, possessing a geography quite similar to solitary confinement cells or existing mental health "quiet rooms." Advocates for the Smith family have disparaged this project as "insulting" (*ibid*) and insufficient to address the recommendations of the Smith inquest. However, those advocates are complicit in producing this result by enabling the distraction made available by actively promoting the dominance of the figure of Patient Smith. Thus, the figuration of Ashley the Patient has been absorbed by the systems of politics and legal power in the juridical field as an aberration that has already been solved by small scale tinkering around the edges of CSC systems and an undisclosed amount of compensation to her family.

The figure of Ashley Smith as properly configured as a Patient fits well with progressive politics that seek to ameliorate the conditions of increasing use of solitary confinement in prisons, increasing rates of incarceration in lieu of mental health treatment and general growth of the prison industrial complex. It is unsurprising, therefore, that this figure has been mobilized by several communities of activists in their change discourses. In addition to the advocates for woman prisoners discussed in Chapter 4, left-leaning politicians and mental health experts have articulated the figure to criticize under-funding of mental health treatment and to draw attention to problems faced by mentally ill women in prison.

Liberal politicians have articulated and deployed Patient Smith in their critiques of the current government for governing through crime. The NB Ombudsman was quoted as saying in the "Behind the Wall" docudrama, "we are using the prison system as a de facto mental health facility." As leader of the official opposition in parliament, Interim Liberal Leader Bob Rae in 2012 called for a public inquiry into the Ashley Smith case as an instance of "the general inability of the prison system to cope with mentally ill offenders," a call which was also supported by the NDP. (CBC, 8 November 2012) Similarly, in a 2012 press release, Senator Bob Runciman articulates the Patient Smith figure as a "worst case scenario" instance of a mentally ill person being inappropriately placed in prison and as evidence for "the need for action" so that "outside mental health treatment can be sought for mentally ill offenders." (14 December 2012) However, as articulated by CSC officials, government actors and even Prime Minister Stephen Harper, the figure of Patient Smith has been deployed as a govern-mental technology that bolsters the integrity of the status quo in the correctional and criminal justice systems: these political defenders of the status quo have been able to rely on her exceptionally acute mental illness to differentiate her from prisoners in general and to refute the notion that her case reveals problems with the correc-tional system in overall. It is discomfiting how tidily configurations of Patient Smith as an innocent victim of her mental disorder in liberal and progressive sites, including texts put forward by those purporting to be her advocates, coincide with configurations of Patient Smith as a "poor girl" in more right-wing publications and acceptance by CSC of the figure.

Mental health experts have eagerly deployed Patient Smith to advance pre-existing (and self-interested) arguments about the need for more health funding. For example, the recuperative Patient Smith figuration is invoked by psychiatrist Dr. Sandy Simpson, chief of forensic psychiatry at Toronto's Centre for Addiction and Mental Health to support the construction of her case as social problem relating to inadequate mental health funding and inadequate attention to mental health in formal policy making. Simpson states:

> The distressing images of the last moments of Ashley Smith's life convey a stark message about the struggles that correctional officers have in caring for people with serious mental illness. This much-needed inquest will undoubtedly provide the public, politicians and the health and correc- tions sectors with much to reflect on, and much that must be improved...
>
> There is a small group of inmates who are more seriously unwell and not manageable by health and correctional staff in prison. Some of these persons need to be in a psychiatric hospital bed. Such access is very limited.... It follows from this that we need sophisticated mental health services in prisons... here is much work occurring to address these shortcomings and start filling the gaps in mental health provision to prison inmates. (Simpson, 26 January 2013)

Canadian Mental Health Association Executive Director, Steve Lurie, writes in a December 19, 2013 letter to the *Toronto Star* that the Ashley Smith case reveals "treatment gaps in the commu- nity that led to her incarceration for throwing crab apples. Only one in three adults and one in six children with serious mental health problems are able to access appropriate prevention and treatment services in the community. Mental health spending has been declining as a share of health care spending for over thirty years. Unless we address this deficit, Ashley Smith's death will be the canary in the coal mine that we continue to ignore." (Lurie, 19 December 2014) In a 2012 publication from the University of Toronto, Elizabeth Bingham and Rebecca Sutton of the Faculty of Law similarly refer to the Smith "case as an example of how Canada needs to change the way it deals 'federally sentenced women with mental health issues.'" (Bingham and Sutton)

The seriously-mentally-ill-self-harming-woman-in-prison is treated on this analysis as what Foucault would describe as a particular, unusual, genre of abnormal. On Andrew Sharpe's analysis of the logics of "monsterization" which determine 'who is legible as a human?', and 'who counts as a human?', (2010) the figuration of Patient Smith functions as a governmental technology in re-inscribing discursive structures in which woman inmates, and women, do not count. These are structures in which women's voices are not credible in judicial proceedings, not believed by police when they make reports of domestic violence or sexual assaults and not heard around the boardroom table or in political debates. The Patient Smith figure is outstandingly virulent in no small part because it fits into spaces made by pre-existing critiques of the treatment of the mentally ill and into facile interpretations of women's agencies as madness that have a great deal of historical depth. Further, the figure of Patient Smith invites into action, and empowers, the pre-existing apparati of systems of power and knowledge and bureaucratic apparatus of the mental health system. Thus, in re-inscribing the Patient Smith figure through their advocacy, I would argue, progressive reformers are also complicit in the re-inscription of the illegibility of the agencies of girls and women in the juridical field and in public discourse and the retrenchment of the figure of the monstrous madwoman.

From the perspective of a governmentality analysis, the putative opposition of the discourses of justice and mental health is problematic: mental health apparati are deployed in similar manners to govern the conduct of subjects that also involve reliance on risk logic and the logic of exception. An implicit and problematic "solution" to the defined social problem of mislocation of mentally ill persons in correctional facilities would be retrenchment and re-establishment of the prior regime of increased institutionalization of subjects on the basis of mental health diagnoses; institutionalization and exclusion of subjects diagnosed as mentally ill has a troubling history cite. Further, in the context of adolescents in particular, the history of subjects identified as adolescent females being institutionalized for benevolent/ treatment-related reasons is problematic indeed. A great deal of effort towards law reform and social change was undertaken since the mid-twentieth century (Carrigan) to formalize and make visible the grounds for institutionalization of adolescents, and adolescent girls in particular. Uncritical acceptance of mental health diagnoses of woman prisoners on the part of feminist advocates is problematic because it fits well with older patriarchal narratives about women lacking capacity and rationality and needing to be cared for by the benevolent ministrations of mental health services.

The mobilization of Patient Smith in furtherance of better funding for mental health relies on unexamined implicit problematic binary logics: it implies an acceptance that the criminal justice and mental health systems are separate, accept as a condition of possibility that a noncompliant subject should be dealt with either in the criminal justice system or in the (opposed) mental health system; it assumes that, if the correctional system is bad, the opposed mental health system is the alternative, and therefore good. This logic misses ways in which the criminal and mental health systems were very much enmeshed and operating in linked and duplicative risk and exclusion frameworks in the Smith case and it also assumes fallaciously that a criticism of the correctional system is or should be implicitly an endorsement of the mental health system. (Porter)

Critical scrutiny of the Patient Smith figure allows readers to diagnose problems with interlocking legal, mental health and social systems. Through mutually supportive discursive constructions of Child Ashley and Patient Smith those purporting to be her advocates gain legitimacy; it is in removing her distinct voice and agencies that her behaviour can be explained completely and Ashley Smith can be tidily "spoken for." Additionally, it is in reconfiguration as a noble victim that the death of one of a wildly unpopular type of subject- carceral subjects or prisoners — that progressive advocates no doubt think Ashley Smith can become more sympathetic to a neoconservative regime that fixates on the rights of "victims" to justify governance through crime. In mobilizing Patient Smith as a technology, advocates are invoking a modality of representations ("victims") that is efficacious in the contemporary political moment. However, they are trafficking in a genre of representations with a highly problematic impact. The strategic decision to present Ashley Smith as a vulnerable, noble, child-like victim has an ironic result: Ashley Smith's agency is erased more profoundly in the "benevolent" texts that purport to speak her interests on her behalf than in those texts intended to defend those individuals, institutions and structures accused of being at fault for her death. While the figure of Patient Smith has been instrumentalized as a governmental technology militating towards ameliorating the conditions of female carceral subjects held in prisons (by making their *criminality* unthinkable), it is also a technology that simultaneously insists upon her inability to make decisions, such as the choices to comply with rules or end her life, which remove the possibility of her participation in political community had she not died, and thereby her role as an equal citizen (by making her *agencies* unthinkable).

ENDNOTES

---

[1] See e.g. testimony of Dr. Allister Webster, Nova Institution psychologist at Ashley Smith inquest: "We needed to consider her behaviour as a result of choice *as opposed to* mental illness" As reported in Vincent, Donovan "Ashley Smith not psychotic, psychologist testifies at inquest" *Toronto Star* (4 March 2013).

[2] For example, Smith spent her entire time at St. Thomas psychiatric hospital in "seclusion" according to testimony of forensic psychiatrist Dr. Sam Swaminath. As quoted in Blatchford, Christie, "Prison system forced to pick up the pieces with the mentally ill," *National Post* (6 May 2013).

[3] To see the operation of this binary test see the leading case *Winko v British Columbia (Forensic Psychiatric Institute)*, [1999] 2 SCR 625, 1999 CanLII 694 (S.C.C.) at para 31.

[4] Pursuant to the test set out in s. 16 of the *Criminal Code*.

[5] Pursuant to the test set out in s. 2 of the *Criminal Code*.

[6] YCJA s. 39.

[7] Section 17 of Ontario's MHA provides police with authority to take a person to for examination by a physician, where it would be "dangerous" to proceed to obtain a Form 2. In other words, police may apprehend a person and take him or her to a mental health facility for committal at a psychiatrist's order, without prior Form or order, if the circumstances set out in section 17 are met. Other provinces and territories in Canada have analogous provisions.

[8] Form 1 of the *Ontario Mental Health Act* RSO 1990 c. M.7 allows for psychiatric assessments to include body cavity searches: http://www.forms.ssb.

gov.on.ca/mbs/ssb/forms/ssbforms.nsf/GetAttachDocs/014-6427-41~1/$-File/6427-41_.pdf.

[9]The exception is Dr. Eljdupovic, see below.

[10]As defined in the DSM-IV, a personality disorder is an enduring pattern of behaviour that deviates markedly from cultural expectations, is pervasive, has its onset in adolescence or early adulthood, is stable over time, and leads to distress or impaired functioning.

[11]See e.g. inquest testimony of Dr. Renée Fugère, psychiatrist at Institut Philippe-Pinel de Montréal.

[12]Dr. Renée Fugère, psychiatrist at the Institut Philippe-Pinel de Montréal, referenced Ashley Smith's refusal of treatment as evidence of her "antisocial personality disorder" in her inquest testimony.

[13]CAEFS' 2005 submission to the United Nations is available at the following link: http://www.caefs.ca/wp-content/uploads/2013/04/april05.pdf

[14]This video has been referenced in scores of mainstream media articles and, for example, is quoted by CTV news: http://www.ctvnews.ca/canada/i-ll-duct-tape-your-face-rcmp-pilot-defends-actions-at-ashley-smith-inquest-1.1242964#ixzz3FOPesIP1. Another segment of the video is posted online by CBC at: http://www.cbc.ca/news/canada/videos-show-dehumanizing-treatment-of-teen-ashley-smith-1.1203668.

[15]CBC *Fifth Estate* Blog http://www.cbc.ca/fifth/blog/the-life-and-death-of-ashley-smith Web. Accessed 2 October 2014.

[16]E.g. On October 8, 2011, UN Special Rapporteur on torture Juan E. Méndez told the General Assembly's third committee that the use of longterm solitary confinement should be eliminated from the world's prisons.

6. Conclusion

Multiple Agencies

They don't know what goes on in my head.
—September 2006 journal entry of Ashley Smith
(Richard, 2008, 23)

...You see us as you want to see us ... in the simplest terms, in the most convenient definitions. But what we found out is that each one of us is a brain ... an athlete ... a basket case ... a princess ... and a criminal. Sincerely yours, the Breakfast Club.
—*The Breakfast Club* (1985)

SUMMARY: PRODUCING ASHLEYS

Ashley Smith's mother, Coralee Smith, is quoted in many sources on December 19, 2013, as saying, after the verdict was rendered in the second inquest: "now the whole story has been told." Starting from theoretical foundations in social constructivist feminist analysis, I have conducted this research from an epistemological position that telling the "whole story" about Ashley Smith is not possible: all narratives are selective, incomplete and necessarily partial. (Butler, 1990) In consequence, this book has not sought to tell a different, singular, "truer," story of the Smith case. Rather, I have conducted a critical discourse analysis to deconstruct the different ways Ashley Smith's case has been told, the ways in which meanings have been made, and governmental technologies have been crafted, articulated and deployed, out of Ashley Smith's life and death. Much as I wish it could provide a venue for Ashley Smith to speak, this book can reveal nothing certain about what she wanted, thought or felt. However, the analysis presented has revealed patterns in discourse present in, and re-inscribed by the Smith case.

I have presented a critical discourse analysis of three types of which Ashley Smith has been represented as a case: inmate, child and patient. These figures are understood as outcomes of microprocesses of governance in relation to micro-and macro power. The analytical questions addressed in this analysis touch on how these figures work as technologies of power. The dominant interpretation of the Smith case is, as stated in paragraph 1 of the inquest decision, a "system failure." I offer quite a different interpretation. My analysis has shown that dissonance with and inability to fit within the categories of child and girl contributed to Ashley Smith's social death while the correctional and mental health systems together ensured her juridical and biological deaths. My theoretical assertion is that the Smith case is read most accurately not as a case of system failure but one of necropolitical success, a story about how Canada's prison industrial complex successfully rid itself of a resource-drain in the spectre of an incredibly troublesome inmate. The critical discourse analysis conducted in this book has revealed that the domestication of the inquest verdict by the dominant configuration of Ashley Smith as properly understood as a tragically victimized mental patient leaves intact, and even reinforces, dominant logics and systems of gender, risk, race thinking and exclusion in power and knowledge that make it predictable that similar deaths in prison will recur.

This book has examined the conspicuous absence of discourses of Ashley Smith's agencies as well as examining figurations of her and of the girl in that make up the corpus of the Smith case. It has tracked how the very idea of Ashley Smith as an agent becomes increasingly impossible with each figuration of her that becomes widely accepted in the Smith case, with the final, most sympathetic rendering of her relying completely on her passivity. Even a hint of agency on her part would crumble the widely accepted figure of Patient Smith. The removal of agency from Ashley Smith is thus intimately bound up in necropolitical logic and action. This research has shown how the logics of risk, mental health and legal discourses in the juridical field intersected with discourses of the girl in ways that made alternative plausible readings and Ashley Smith's own writing of her story unintelligible and unwritable. In this book, I have worked to puncture the sacral aura given to Ashley Smith by liberal reform advocacy and to show the death of Ashley Smith not to be an exceptional or aberrant event but an instance of the day to day brutal bureaucratic logics acting as usual. My hope for this project is that it can intervene in those logics to help make alternative endings possible and to make steps towards supporting the agencies of adolescent girls in having active roles in shaping and living their lives.

As Coralee Smith said in a December 14 press conference where she protested the inaction and lack of response to the Smith inquest by CSC:

> This is not just an Ashley story. This is the story about how our prisoners are being treated — mistreated I should say. The dire conditions that they're living under. Something has to take place. We have to do something. (Stone, 10 December 2014)

Understanding Ashley Smith as a case of a the general type "inmate" through analysis of the figure of Inmate Smith that coalesces from a variety of texts in the Smith case opens up potential for her example to be deployed in public debates about the interlocking utilitarian rationalities of risk and the logic of exception. These logics are specifically evident in the enactment and amendment of the YCJA, which in "reserv[ing] its most serious interventions for the most serious offenders," (Department of Justice Canada) struck what, in LeGuin's terms, could be understood as an Omelan bargain to allow harsh punishment for a few adolescents in order to reduce Canada's much maligned over-reliance on incarcerating adolescents under its precursor, the YOA. Again, for the good of the many, to reduce risks calculated to be faced by the population, "protection of the public" was in 2012 amendments made into the single top priority of the YCJA, at the expense of principles in the legislation that showed concern about accused and convicted adolescents. In this analysis, Smith can be seen as *homo sacer* and thus as an exemplar of totalitarian logics of exclusion and exception that, as Agamben argues, are pervasive below the surface in western democracies. (Agamben) An analysis of Ashley Smith as an inmate also offers a haunting reply to Ashley Smith's mother Coralee at the end of "Behind the Wall" when she asks, "who gave that order, Hana?" in reference to the non-intervention order that absolved the front line CSC staff from criminal charges in Ashley Smith's death. As I have shown here, there was not one single order that killed Ashley Smith but rather, over a period of several years, a series of actions, inactions, decisions and orders by a large number of people that led to Ashley Smith's social, legal and biological deaths. In the Omelas, all who know of the flawed exclusionary, carceral foundation of the society, all who know of the locked room and the child, are responsible for them. As a technology of governance, the discursive figure of Inmate Smith has powerful potential to implicate — and ideally incite action by — us all.

Through this critical discourse analysis, the figure of Inmate Smith has raised questions about the necropolitical operations of interlocking logics of exclusion and risk in the juridical field in their production of the juridical exclusions and legal deaths of inmates. These questions are broadly relevant to public policy about criminal law, administration of correctional systems and youth criminal justice systems in Canada. Concerns about Ashley Smith's treatment echo longstanding criticisms about treatment of prisoners, especially woman prisoners, in this country. Events giving rise to the inquiry into 1994 incidents at Kingston's Prison for Women are similar to details of the Smith case.

Further, aspects of Ashley Smith's death bear similarities to persistent patterns in prisons. Deaths of prisoners in Corrections custody are not unexpected; suicide and failures to respond to medical emergencies have, since the opening of Canada's first prisons, been leading causes of prisoner death. A study of deaths in CSC custody that occurred between 2001–2005 found that the majority of these were ruled suicides by CSC and also found that inmates commit suicide at eight times the rate of people in the general population. Failures to administer CPR are found to regularly recur along with persistent delays in seeking and obtaining health care support. (Gabor) These patterns predate the Smith case and continue, unaltered, after it. Illustratively, between the time that Ashley Smith died and the first inquest into her death commenced, between 2007 and 2010, another 130 inmates died in Federal Custody. (CSC, 2014, 4)

Analysis of the figure of Child Ashley has revealed how race thinking and mandatory gender performativity set up the conditions of possibility for social exclusion of certain persons who do not "fit" within pre-existing social categories of "girl" and "child." More specifically, critical discourse analysis of the Child Ashley figure has revealed the great extent to which the pre-existing over-lapping categories of the "normal," "saveable," and "good" girl are defined with reference to middle class socioeconomic status, smiling agreeability, a socially acceptable mother, white racial purity, diminutive size and performances of gender signaling cul-turally-condoned levels of heteronormative sexual availability. The exclusion of certain subjects by the boundaries of these categories lays the foundation for the disproportionate legal exclusion and juridical deaths of certain types of embodied subjects as carceral inmates. Subjects like Ashley Smith, who do not "fit" the normal child category by virtue of being obese, resistant, tall, working-class or poor, racialized, ambiguously raced or aboriginal, refuse or fail to fit within culturally accepted tropes of the saveable girl and are in consequence vulnerable to being excluded from citizenship and political community in ways that make their incarceration and even biological death readily possible.

Finally, analysis of the figure of Ashley the Patient has shown how the Smith case is engaged in the bolstering and re-inscription of the illegibility of girls and women in the narratives of the juridical field. In the Patient Smith configuration, the diverse instances in which Ashley Smith acted purposefully and legibly (including her scores of quite coherent grievances filed with CSC management) are ignored. Her agency is de-legitimized and incapacitated.

Critical scrutiny of the construction of Smith as a mental patient has revealed the potency and uses of the Patient Smith figure in service of the governmental function of assigning accountability and blame. I have looked at how the work of this figure is in responsibilization and blame shifting. Mental health as a social problem is foregrounded by the Patient Smith figuration while other concerns are obscured. Most significantly, in narratives supported by the Patient Smith figure, the systematic apparatus of the correctional systems (both youth and adult) escape criticism. It shifts attention away from political leaders, bureaucratic managers and correctional institutions as well as their bureaucracies as having responsibility for her death.

I conclude that, in several interlocking ways, the Smith case is not an aberration but reflective of broad systems of thought endemic to patriarchal neoliberalism, and, in its resolution, representations of Ashley Smith as a Child and as a Patient are implicated and complicit in processes that are producing and will produce the same conditions of possibility that lead to Ashley Smith's social, juridical and biological deaths.

This book has explored what has been gained and what has been lost in discursive processes in which Ashley Smith is turned into an inmate, social problem, a celebritized victim and a "cause." I have looked at three dominant configurations of Ashley Smith over the progression of the Smith case: the official configuration of her as Inmate Smith, the celebritization of her as Child Ashley and the recuperation of her in official discourses as Ashley the patient. The three dominant constructions of Ashley Smith in the Smith case: as inmate, child and mentally ill person, allow for the opening up of certain understandings of her case while, as discussed in the foregoing chapters, they distract from, foreclose and make unthinkable others. The preceding chapters have looked at three figures of Ashley Smith that emerge as dominant constructions at various sites and temporal points in her case. I have looked critically at how, in none of these constructions does Ashley's voice get heard nor does her political agency get taken seriously.

I have also looked at how progressive politics has been implicated in the necropolitical processes that successfully effected Ashley Smith's social, juridical and biological deaths. Configuration of Ashley Smith in ways that make her fit within widely accepted discourses of who can be a noble and therefore noticeable victim has been embraced by progressive politics but I contend this only serves to bolster and reinforce the narrow confines of those discourses and confirm her monstrosity. As Margaret Atwood wrote in her essay: "If You Can't Say Something Nice, Don't Say Anything At All":

> Women are not Woman. They come in all shapes, sizes, colours, classes, ages and degrees of moral rectitude. They don't all behave, think or feel the same way any more than they all take size eight. All of them are real. Some of them are awful. To deny them this is to deny them their humanity and to restrict their area of moral choice to the size of a teacup. To define women as by nature better than men is to ape the Victorians.... There are many strong voices; there are many kinds of strong voices ... does it make sense to silence women in the name of Woman?" (Shields and Anderson, 144-145, 148)

In the preceding chapters, I have looked at how Ashley Smith has been configured in different ways in the Smith Case that compete with the construction of her as an Inmate. It is not my argument that those other constructions are irrelevant, but rather that they are problematic, that they have dangerous potential to act as distractions from critiques of our carceral configuration of political community, and that they are potentially relevant to understanding the particular circumstances and life histories of *all* inmates. Put another way, all inmates have particularities; in losing the figure of Inmate Ashley, texts that are generated later in her case may also lose their potency as social critiques with broad relevance.

The figure of Inmate Smith is a powerful tool that has been deployed in public debates about the exercise of macro-power. Considering the "caseness" of Inmate Smith is significant to contemplating the deployment of the representation of Inmate Smith and its possible uses in relation to macro-power. While, on the one hand, representing Ashley Smith as one case of a type of which there are many in Canada can diminish her significance in de-emphasizing her particularity in her lifetime and the construction of her as an inmate contributed to the individual and system failures identified by the Correctional Investigator that led to her death, this construction is double-edged. As a case of a common type, Inmate

Smith can be taken as representative of a large class or group of people: this makes rulings about the death of this inmate potentially powerful as governmental tools that are relevant to and can be referenced in arguments/ initiatives to effect broad, system-wide change in Corrections practice in Canada. Further, this analysis, it is politically disempowering that the inmate construction of Ashley Smith has to a large extent been eclipsed in dominance — or at least diluted — by the mental health-linked construction of Ashley Smith as one of a much smaller subset that I study in Chapter 5. It is therefore unsurprising that critiques of Canada's criminal justice and correctional systems, such as that proffered by CBC's October 2014 docudrama "State of Incarceration" make no mention of the Smith case in reference to problems with neoliberal governance through crime. (October 9, 2014)

Ironically, in the texts studied, the figure of Ashley Smith that emerges in articulations of her by those who purportedly speak *for* her – notably her family's lawyer Julian Falconer and representatives of the Elizabeth Fry Society, is the least agentic. This is consistent with Irigaray and Foucault's concern that an uncritical, singular attempt to resist oppressive systems on behalf of an oppressed group – and in particular as Irigaray considers it, to simplistically liberate women, reconstructs and reconstitutes the conditions of possibility that re-entrench their muteness in formal discourses like law. Consider, as Irigaray wrote in *This Sex Which is Not One*:

> But if their [i.e. feminist movements] aim were simply to reverse the order of things, even supposing this to be pos-
> sible, history would repeat itself in the long run, would revert to sameness: to phallocratism. It would leave room neither for women's sexuality, nor for women's imaginary, nor for women's language to take (their) place. (Irigaray 33)

The critical discourse analysis presented in this book bears upon the broader theoretical questions of whether, to what extent and in what ways the agencies of diversely situated subjects, and in particular the agencies of subjects identified as women and girls, speakable and knowable in formal legal texts and proceedings as well as other public discourses. On this analysis, I have argued that commonly assumed constructions of Ashley in the Smith case re-inscribe confining conditions of possibility for adolescent young women that render subjects identified as members of that category marginalized, silenced and likely to receive the same sanctions, and be excluded in substantially the same manner as Ashley Smith. Further, linked constructions of Coralee Smith as a "good" mother similarly reinforce problematic, racist, classist, confining boundaries imposed on mothers' subjectivities and assumptions about which mothers count.

Recalling Foucault's notion of the "great carceral continuum," it becomes obvious that government of women, including compulsory enforcement of gender performativity through confinement, incarceration and exclusion has never been just about prison. This book has explored how the ultimate acceptance in the Smith case of Ashley Smith as "one of a very few mentally ill women in prison" leaves certain taken-for-granted assumptions unquestioned: prison structures, management and existence are unquestioned and mental illness is accepted as defined in mental health discourse. Further, the boundaries of problematically defined categories of girl, mother, and woman are untroubled. This book has looked at how all of those categories: prisons, mental illness, mother, and woman become problematic on a critical discourse analysis of figures of Ashley Smith that emerge in the Smith case. The analytical chapters in this book have looked at how certain configurations of Ashley Smith in the Smith case open up certain possibilities while they foreclose others.

This critical discourse analysis has revealed a temporal trajectory in the Smith case in the dominance of discursive figures of Ashley Smith from abnormal/risky girl through to inmate to properly constituted/good girl-child-victim to mental patient. It is only after the child construction becomes dominant through the recuperative reconstitution of Ashley Smith in media and advocacy sites into a properly constituted girl subject that her non-compliance is re-read as madness. This raises broad theoretical questions about how the resistances and agencies of particularly situated subjects are made legible. The critical discourse analysis undertaken in this book suggests it is necessarily *through* the reconstitution of Ashley Smith as a "normal" child that she can be understood as a patient. From this trajectory, it appears that the noncompliance/ deviance/ agentic resistance of an *abnormal/* risky girl subject is in the dominant logic of the thought system dominant in neoliberal Canada read as criminality while the resistances/ noncompliances/ agencies of properly constituted girls are by default too often read as madness. This discursive logic also goes a long way towards suggesting an explanation for why it is the most marginal girls and women who are criminalized: in this logic, by *definition* those girls who are claimed and located under the protection of patriarchal structures as daughters and sisters, will not be easily understood as criminal. This is consistent with theoretical predictions from Luce Irigaray and David Leverenz.

Looked at in the context of the historical pathologization of women for madness discussed in this book, the discursive journey from Inmate Smith to Child Ashley to Ashley the Patient and the malleability of her case into being definitive of social problems relating to corrections and mental health, while unusual in becoming taken up as a social "cause," does not seem unique in other aspects. The logic that predetermines the labeling of properly constituted adolescent girls' noncompliance as madness disproportionately to labeling adolescent boys' noncompliance as criminality calls into question the statistical discrepancy between criminal charge rates for adolescent boys and girls. As feminist criminologists have identified, the disproportionately low number of girls criminalized relative to boys is a fact calling for explanation. Interestingly, there are disproportionately *more* girls treated through mental health means than boys. The discourse analysis undertaken in this book reveals gendered logic as to how resistance is labeled in the Smith case that suggests those numbers might actually roughly *match*. It would be logical to predict that the behaviours of subjects identified as adolescents girls and boys are far less different than generally assumed. Rather, the difference between female and male offending rates may be explainable in large part by differently situated subjects being understood, approached and *labeled* differently. This contention would be powerfully explanatory of the discrepancies between girls' and boys' roughly comparable self-reporting rates in respect of committing crimes and official crime statistics. (Savoie) It may be that the apparent gender difference in offending rates are not reflections of essential sex differences or actual gender performativity but rather explainable, in whole or in part, by prevailing logics in discourse. This suggestion is potentially powerfully explanatory of the gender differential in charge and incarceration rates and would warrant more study. Useful future research could be undertaken to inquire further into specific acts for which adolescent girls and boys are criminalized or diagnosed with mental illness.

LOOKING FOR ASHLEY'S AGENCIES: ALTERNATIVE IMAGININGS

I can understand how you'd be so confused
I don't envy you
I'm a little bit of everything
All rolled into one
I'm a bitch, I'm a lover, I'm a child, I'm a mother
I'm a sinner, I'm a saint, I do not feel ashamed
I'm your hell, I'm your dream, I'm nothing in between
You know you wouldn't want it any other way
So take me as I am.
　　—Meredith Brooks, "I'm A Bitch I'm A Lover" (1997)

At the beginning of the second inquest into the death of Ashley Smith, presiding coroner Dr. John Carlisle opened with the following statement:

We cannot now reverse the course of history as it unfolded, but we can learn from the circumstances of this death, and try ... to implement measures to prevent future tragedies.... What matters now is the sincerity and success of our efforts to make from [the past] something that can benefit the future.

I have argued that the death of Ashley Smith and the domestication of the incident into a narrative about mental illness can be read not as a system failure but a necropolitical success story that reinforces the strength of patriarchal social categories and the prison industrial complex. I have looked at how all of the dominant configurations of Ashley Smith — as a child, a mental patient and an inmate — foreclose the "world making possibilities" of her acts of resistance.

But is the illegibility of Ashley Smith's agency *inevitable*? Are there only three things women can be: compliant subjects (ideally "good" mothers), children or madwomen? Is there no space for agentic, complex constructions of women in public debate? Is the angels-and-demons, masculinist narrative of the law inescapable? I refuse to accept that. I believe re-reading Ashley Smith's acts as moments of agency can produce different stories. In the following discussion, instead of starting from a predefined construction of Ashley Smith, I suggest how sense could be made of the Smith case if Ashley Smith was permitted to be unknowable and complicated and could be simultaneously a victim and an agent.

While I accept that Ashley Smith's agency is read as madness in the current dominant construction of the case, I refuse to accept the illegibility of Ashley Smith's subjectivity to legal and more generally public discourse as *inevitable*. Like Sandra Gilbert and Susan Gubar when they suggest that the fact that the preponderance of the English literary canon is masculinist does not prevent the existence of other narrative perspectives alternative to the dominant hetero-male narrative structure, I think that the public discourses of the law and politics have been, to a great extent still are, but need not necessarily *remain*, masculinist. As Ewick and Silbey wrote "individual acts of resistance become consequential as they are transformed into stories." (Ewick and Silbey)

As discussed in Chapter 2, narratives matter a great deal to how legality is constructed and to how people are governed. Telling stories about Ashley Smith that recognize or even celebrate reversals and exposures of power has implications for power; different stories can change not just how we see the world but the socially constituted world itself. Certainly the inquest finding of "homicide" could be characterized as such a reversal. The unprecedented homicide verdict constitutes a refusal on the part of the jurors to do what is generally done. Rather than resolving the inquiry into of the cause of Ashley Smith's death, this verdict raises questions. A finding of "not determined" would have concluded for all time that the mysteries of Ashley Smith's life and death were unsolvable and unknowable but this verdict provides for the possibility that it could be know, that more questions should be asked.

By way of conclusion, in the following discussion, I take up Dr. Carlisle's challenge and suggest several ways that the Ashley Smith case could be re-imagined that challenge her assumed passivity. I do not adopt any particular imagining, but instead invite readers to consider how these alternative formulations might produce conditions of possibility that would make prison deaths like hers less likely to recur in the future. The necropolitical actions that assured her social, juridical and biological deaths would be made less predictable by making space in the public imaginary for the world-making potential of the voices and agencies of girls in general, and of incarcerated subjects in particular, in especially those identified as female. Removing the sacral aura accorded Ashley Smith by framings of her as a noble victim, rather than doing violence to her beingness, instead of brutalizing her humanity and flattening her complexity by rendering her into new figures, in the following discussion I look at moments of agency by Ashley Smith discernable throughout the case that reveal possibilities for the complexities of her agencies to be legible, for her existence as a social participant and as an agentic actor whose world-creating potential renders her a maker of meanings, and opens up possibilities for those meanings to be read and understood.

Ashley Smith, in the Child and Patient figurations, which are mutually supportive, has been discursively configured fit into angels and demons narratives as a *noble victim*. The following is a discussion of agentic moments in the Ashley Smith case that might, instead of fitting Ashley Smith into their paradigmatic structures, be reinterpreted in ways that disrupt the structures of these victim/ villain narratives and open up a space for her life and death to be re-read in stories with that provide opportunities for effecting social change at the micro level. It is hoped that this book will contribute to opening up new possibilities for adolescent young women to be understood as meaning makers and participants in the agentic world-creating subjectivity in the juridical field of politics and law.

Pieces of what has been said about Ashley Smith can be re-read in ways that interrupt the flow of prevailing narratives of the

Smith case. Instances in which Ashley Smith acts in ways that can be read as expressive, creative, rebellious, heroic, political or athletic, show ways in which she was, in the limiting context of how agency exists as always already partial, limited and complicated in multiple and overlapping forms of oppression, involved in the authoring of her own life story. These incidents emerge and disappear in the texts that make up the Smith case like flashes on the landscape, almost never making it into the popular and official narratives told in various sites about her life. The weight of the oppressive situation in which she was enmeshed is not easily unburdened by these moments of possibility, but moments in which agentic openings are revealed do emerge from a variety of texts. For example, a glimpse of alternative possibilities for making sense of Ashley Smith is offered by the segment of video of her in flight transfer to Pinel institution from Saskatoon Regional Mental Health Centre in 2007[1] in which she laughs and jokes with the guards, and inquires about whether their seating positions are comfortable without a hint of sarcasm or facetiousness as well as stating that her incarceration was for stealing the CD of "Who Let the Dogs Out." In this video, Smith converses congenially, and from it at least one piece of new information about her is gleaned: we at least know about a song she liked, we at least are invited into consideration of the notion that she liked some things and disliked others, in short, that she held opinions. This is the same flight on which Inmate Smith is later duct taped to her chair by the RCMP co-pilot, and it is the video of her subsequent abuse by CSC guards that has figured prominently in the inquest.

None of the dominant discursive constructions or prominent figures of Ashley Smith in the Smith case invite the interpreting subject into identification *with* her — these alternative possible figures of Ashley open up the possibilities of readers and interpreters more readily asking themselves not "what if I were Ashley's mother, sister, brother or father" but rather the more urgent question: what if *I* were Ashley Smith? Identification with her subjectivity could lead readers and interpreters to the inference: what happened to Ashley Smith could happen to *me*. Looking at the Smith case for agentic openings within oppressive structures has the potential in turn to reveal ways in which Ashley Smith, never free, was not unagentic but rather had moments where she expressed rebellious, political and expressive agencies.

Study of agentic openings in the Smith case allows for development towards theorization of a less naïve notion of how actors experience agencies, including carceral agencies and feminine agencies, operating always already in oppression, while being consumed by oppression and dissolved by oppressive processes. (Shotwell) This conclusion will, I hope, open up the possibility of interrogating her case as a "case study" not in the governance to which a subhuman enemy population of inmates are subject, the lack of treatment, abuse and neglect to which a small sub-group of the "worst of the worst" mentally ill offenders are subject or even to which our children, current or putative, could be subject, but a case study that reveals logics and arts of governance to which we are *all* subjected.

Rebellious Agency

Numerous incidents in the Smith case can be re-read in ways that see her actions as volitional and agentic by deliberately flouting the will of a variety of official agents of various systems. There is a broad consensus in social science research that youthful rebellion is a "normal" and necessary, even desirable, developmental stage on an adolescent's journey to adulthood.(Caissy) I think it is facile and oversimplistic to suggest that Ashley Smith could be properly categorized within the emerging figure in psy-discourses of the "spirited child,"[2] but I do think it might be appropriate to suggest that she could be understood as less ill than *willful*. Widely held assumptions about adolescent rebellion have been critiqued by feminist scholars as masculinist (Reynolds and Press), a theorization which raises questions about how much of Ashley Smith's challenging behaviour would have been received and understood as rebellious and thereby "normal" and not pathological had she been identified as male. Psychologists have contended that rebellion has a positive side in adolescent identity formation, and should be *channeled* instead of contained.(Nowinski) Indeed, mainstream popular psychology takes a consensus position that attempts to contain rebellion in adolescence are likely to be counter-productive to fostering pro-social behaviours in teens. (*ibid*)

There are many actions and statements attributed to Ashley Smith that could be easily re-read as rebellious. Although the Wikipedia page about Ashley Smith's case and the dominant narrative of her case is that the long series of incarcerations which ultimately led to her death was that it was started by the incident where she threw apples at a postal worker, this narrative presents the apples incident as a single event and downplays the series of incidents and charges for which Ashley Smith was coming into conflict with authorities in education and legal systems starting in 2001, and leading up to her incarceration in 2003. (Richard, 2008) For instance, she was placed on probation in 2002 for making harassing phone calls, assaulting passersby on Moncton streets, haranguing fellow bus passengers and hassling municipal bus drivers. Further, there is another incident, on December 29, 2003, where on the CBC timeline it is indicated that Ashley Smith "waived a knife on main street" (sic) and refused to give it to police." (CBC Timeline) Once she was incarcerated, as has been discussed, Ashley Smith disobeyed guards in at least 800 incidents while at the New Brunswick Youth Centre, and over 160 while in CSC custody. As noted in Chapter 2, in several instances she did plead not guilty and even appealed guilty findings against her. In the Patient Smith configuration of Smith, this conduct is seen as compulsive: an alternative formulation is that these actions were, while not coldly calculated, understandably volitional and agentic behaviour, while unusually persistent in its repetitiveness, in the context of her age "normal" and expectable from a rebellious teen. Consider Smith's remark to guards in 2006: "If that was the taser, I'm going to do everything I can to get it every day." (CBC Timeline) It is very plausible to re-read this as defiance.

Ashley Smith herself in journal entries claimed to be "messing" with guards while in prison. For example, she wrote: "When I use to try to hang myself I was just messing around trying to make them care and pay attention. Now it's different. I want them to fuck off and leave me alone." (Ashley Smith Journal Entry September 4, 2006, as cited in CBC Timeline) What guards in the "Rush to Judgment" report characterized as a "game" (Rush to Judgment) is easily reframed as the sort of challenge to their authority and an assertion of agency by Smith frequently referenced in popular psychology texts as to be expected from rebellious youths. Indeed, the constancy and stamina of Ashley Smith's micro-movements to "mess with" various systems can be seen as itself a modality of her rebellious agency.

Male adolescents perceived as rebellious are often culture heroes, and figure prominently in popular music as well as films.[3] However, recently, popular texts produced in fictional and cinematic sites have represented rebellious girls who commit violent acts as heroic. Notable among these are girl heroes in recent youth novels made into Hollywood films such as Katniss Everdeen in "The Hunger Games"(Collins) and Tris (Beatrice) in "Divergent." (Roth) Similarly, the runaway success of the book and film "The Girl With the Dragon Tattoo" provides Lisbeth Salandar, an example of a rebellious, at times violent young woman who is ultimately heroic, albeit not a teen.(Larsson) Thus, contemporary western neoliberal mainstream culture provides discourses of agentic, rebellious, meaningfully violent, sympathetic actions by girls. The prevalence of girl heroes in popular culture may also signal an openness that was not previously present in the cultural mainstream to reading girls' agencies as something other than madness.

Readings of Ashley Smith's actions as rebellious are very occasionally present in texts produced in the Smith case. For example, one 2009 *Toronto Star* article directly challenges the commonly accepted label of Ashley Smith as mentally ill. In the article, journalist Rosie DiManno describes Ashley Smith as being not mentally ill but "incorrigible while incarcerated" and argues that it was because Inmate Smith's resistant attitude was judged by authorities to be one that "needed crushing" that she was met with punitive responses in prison. DiManno describes Ashley Smith not as a victim but as a complex woman, a violent, combative, challenging "iconoclast " who "never did surrender." (9 March 2009)

Admittedly, with the benefit of hindsight, I would argue that progressive advocates for prisoners' rights, and for the Smith family, radically underestimated the complexities of agency that the inquest jury and the Canadian public were able to understand. In contemporary late modern North America, notwithstanding the victim/ villain rhetoric of neoconservative government through crime agendas, where there is an African American U.S. President, the Premier of Ontario is a lesbian, and the fictional girl-hero characters discussed above enjoy great popularity, there does seem to be discursive space for advocates to suggest that prisoners who die, including women, as women in general, are complex. The stakes in the strategic wager played by advocates for Smith to present her as a simplistic and ostensibly sympathetic noble victim are high indeed: not just Ashley Smith but all adolescent girls who express rebellious agencies on their developmental paths to adulthood are re-inscribed as madwomen by the naïve assumptions about "normal" girls strengthened by the Child Ashley figure. In order for women to participate in the processes of law and government, whether in their own cases or as advocates in cases relating to others, their voices must be heard and trusted. Simplistic re-inscription of victim narratives about Ashley Smith contributes to girls' and women's ongoing illegibility and inaudibility of their voices, in the public square and to the law.

Political Agency

Further afield of "innocent victimhood " than the popular psychological notion of "adolescent rebellion" lies another way to re-read Ashley Smith's actions as meaningful. There are a number of incidents and statements made by Ashley Smith in the texts that make up the Smith case that provide material where her conduct and speech acts can be re-interpreted as political statements. As discussed, the offence of assault for which Ashley Smith is often understood to have been originally incarcerated in the series of escalating incidents that ultimately led to her death was throwing apples at a postal worker: in the CBC timeline, the allegation is made that Ashley Smith did so for political reasons: "She was told that the postal worker deliberately delivered the welfare cheques late." (CBC Timeline) If this assertion is accepted, then Smith can be re-read to have been resisting not individuals but systems and configurations of power. Read this way, Smith can be seen to have acted, from beginning to end, not simply to resist or flout the will of particular adults, but in a programmatic and consistent way to quite deliberately throw a monkey-wrench into *systems* of power. This would have been both creatively agentic and political behaviour.

Ashley Smith engaged in public debate to an extent unusual for a teenager, and especially unusual for someone held in youth custody. On November 2, 2005, a letter to the editor authored by her was published in the Moncton *Times and Transcript*. Ashley Smith's letter read as follows:

> Dear Editor: I'm writing this letter because I believe the community should know. I'm currently at the New Brunswick Youth Centre serving a rather long sentence for petty crimes. When the judge sentenced me, the community went way to go! One less troublemaker on the streets. Do they not realize this place makes youth worse not better? Since I have been here, I've become a more angry person. I have learned way more about how to commit crimes and not get caught.... (*Hamilton Spectator*, 26 January 2013)

Of course, Smith's own narrative of her incarceration is limited, selected, partial, and properly the subject of analysis like any other text, not to be simplistically taken as a monolithic truth. What is significant, however, is that her own words open different possibilities for understanding her and alternative potential framings of her case. Further, as I have noted, Ashley Smith filed many grievances while in CSC custody. Notably, these grievances were not just about her own conditions but were often about treatment of offenders in general, such as the distribution of healthy foods, such as fruits instead of muffins for snacks. (Sapers, 2008)

Some psychological researchers have offered a perspective on adolescent aggression and rebelliousness that it is not just an indicator of a "normal" trajectory in emotional development towards adulthood but also a signal that an adolescent has potential to be a leader, whether socially or politically. As has been suggested by certain researchers: "bullying is power."(Vaillancourt et al.) This suggestion certainly accords with Foucauldian notions of power in relationships and interactions: Ashley Smith's resistances to authority are capable of being read as political. Read as intentional, political action, Ashley Smith's unmanageability in prison can be understood as itself a success story: it could be seen as a triumph of will.

While I of course cannot argue that this is conclusively provable, it is alternatively plausible that even Ashley Smith's death could be read not as compulsive, irrational behaviour symptomatic of severe mental illness but rather as a communicative act, a meaningful act, a political act. While, since about 2010, as discussed, psy-expert opinion (from Dr. Margo Rivera) that Ashley Smith's death was not intentional has controlled the narrative of how she died, her death was initially understood to be a suicide. Rather than acting impulsively or without volition in self-harming, it is arguable that Ashley Smith quite deliberately did end her life. It is alternatively plausible that, faced with silence and non-response to her grievances, Ashley Smith knew that her predicament of endlessly escalating charges was attracting no outside attention, and that her prison term was likely to be endless. Her death could be read as a communicative act of political resistance, a suicide calculated to bring down the institutional response in the form of an inquest and the public scrutiny in the form of media attention that it in fact did. Read this way, her death could have been a suicide that was *also* simultaneously a homicide that was *also* simultaneously a political statement. Looked at in the theoretical framework of necropolitics, this could be understood as a series of deaths: social and juridical homicides that were completed by means of biological suicide. The "cause of death" question asked at an inquest require jurors to decide *between* causes of death and therefore do not permit responses that understand complex, messy, interactions of agencies and institutions.

Expressive Agency

Even while on probation, in foster care and in prison, Ashley Smith expressed herself in a wide variety of creative ways. As has been discussed, by all accounts, Ashley Smith was a large person. There are references in texts to her enjoyment of physical activities such as canoeing and basketball; she had her own kayak. (Vincent and Zlomistic) These reports hint at the possibility that Ashley Smith had at least moderate athletic potential, or at least enjoyed her physicality. However, at no point is her physicality ever characterized in a positive light: at no point is her body characterized as powerful with a constructive connotation accorded to that term and there is no evidence that anyone sought to provide her with means by which she could channel her physical size and strength into something constructive. It is almost unimaginable that a large boy with significant physical strength and size hailing from a middle-class background wouldn't have been channeled into some sort of athleticism — football, hockey, something to work with his muscles and get his aggression out. Interestingly, the inquest verdict contains recommendations that suggest at least the jurors thought of this possibility: they suggested that former carceral subjects should be involved in the design of programming for inmates.

It is also evident from the Smith case that Ashley Smith enjoyed expressing herself artistically, through writing a journal, writing poetry and drawing pictures. Notice that, apparently, Ashley Smith complained about the writing paper and writing instruments after the concerns about force and before mentioning basic necessities like soap, toilet paper and even food.[4] Perhaps, as guards suspected, she wanted to use a pen to self-harm. However, it might be that she also or alternatively wanted to use the pen to write.

THE LOCKED ROOM

There are many possible ways to tell stories about Ashley Smith, and each narrative that could be told would, as Butler has theorized and this book has shown, involve selective processes in its telling and silences that make it into fiction. Rather than posit a "truer" story about the Smith case, or an alternative rendering of her as some other sort of figure than those now on offer, this discussion has tried to show how material exists in the texts that constitute the case that could allow for her agency to be understood as engaged in the narration of her life and construction of her case in a variety of ways. I have gone beyond the question of how she died in prison on October 19, 2007 to ask broader questions about how she came to die there. In the Smith case, as discussed above it is clear that progressive politics early on either consciously or unconsciously accepted the starting premise that complex, agentic young women are unthinkable subjects. In fact it is those who purport to be Ashley Smith's advocates who are most deeply implicated in foreclosing the possibility of her being understood as an agentic, world-creating, meaning-making subject.

Progressive politics have instrumentalized the figure of Inmate Smith in opposition to prolonged use of solitary confinement in prisons. Advocates have also instrumentalized the Patient Smith figure in service of causes in relation to increasing the funding for mental health services. However, violences and wrongs done to Ashley Smith by social institutions, educational institutions, mental health facilities and prisons do not start and end with solitary confinement: she was tasered; she was pepper sprayed; she was beaten; she was tortured by confinement for long periods of time in "restraints" resembling medieval torture devices found in dungeons; she was given forced injections; she was drugged against her will and in ways not supported by any diagnosis; her human rights and needs for basic necessities were ignored; she was touched, beaten, confined and denied clothing in ways that would have, anywhere but her in her carceral context, been understood as sexual assaults; her sexual agency and autonomy were effaced; her agency was enlisted against her to bring about her own death. Further, accepting uncritically that Ashley Smith was self-evidently, stably, "mentally ill" depoliticizes the highly problematic pathologization of women's agencies that is endemic to our culture and retrenches psy-discourses that have historically been implicated in rendering women's agencies illegible to the law and in the public square. Prevalent instrumentalizations of Ashley Smith are not as powerful as they could be: a different appreciation of the complexities of Ashley Smith's agency has potential to cut even closer to the heart of the prison industrial complex by providing a case that illustrates the dangerousness of its risk and security logic and the evils that are routinely perpetrated by a rationalized bureaucracy.

The Smith case is a revealing instance illustrating several neoliberal tensions and discomforts: with mandatory gender norms, race thinking, the gendered social construction of mental illness, and the intersecting logics of necropolitics and exclusion endemic to Corrections. Working with instances of agentic action by Ashley Smith, perhaps the inquest verdict of homicide in the Ashley Smith case might provide technology that could be deployed in efforts to seek another possible course of action alternative to accepting the conditions of possibility understood by Omelans in LeGuin's story: of complicity in the logic of exception through membership in the society of or of walking away from the Omelas.

While the Smith case has become uniquely celebritized, in Canada's carceral systems, there is not just one child in a locked room. Ashley Smith's incarceration was, in many respects, not unusual. When she was a living carceral subject, Smith was a "case" of one amongst a type ("inmate") of which there are many. According to Statistics Canada, in 2012-2013 there were 41,049 offenders, both adults and youth, in custody on an average day. Per capita, this number translates into a rate of 118 persons in custody per 100,000 people in Canada's general population. (CSC 2012-2013) With recent changes to criminal legislation in Canada, such as the growth in mandatory minimum sentences, and the overall inclination of the current government to get "tough on crime," incarceration rates[5] (although not crime rates) are at an all-time high in Canada; predictions generally indicate that these numbers will at least remain stable for the foreseeable future and may, according to the June 2013 Report of the Correctional Investigator as Tabled in the House of Commons in fact be in the process of increasing. (Sapers, 2013)

When Agamben's concept of *homo sacer* and Ong's understanding of the carceral subject in solitary confinement as the archetypal neoliberal subject (Ong, 2006) are considered, the caseness of Inmate Smith opens up: maybe she is a case of a type of which *we* are part. The inquest verdict of homicide in the Smith Case, rendered even after CSC counsel contended a homicide verdict was unavailable and unthinkable, opens up questions about who is responsible for the lives of inmates. The verdict's assertion that inmates *can* be killed in Corrections custody in circumstances for which CSC is blameworthy can be considered broadly relevant if read as a rejection an Inmate's logic-of-exception status as juridically dead already. Politically, this inquest verdict could be construed as a rejection of the assumption that Smith was *homo sacer*, of the logic of exception, of governing through crime and camps and a condemnation of the monstrosity of CSC's rationalized bureaucratic logic. The figure of Inmate Smith might be effectively deployed to confront the operating logics of risk and exclusion; it may be used towards making it imaginable to write another ending to Le Guin's story where the mirrors of surveillance reflecting in on each other are shattered and the prisoner — the one in carceral solitary confinement and also the neoliberal subject in general — is (more) free.

DENOUEMENT

I had the dream again. Since moving here to this lovely red brick rented house far away from my homes and histories to start law school, I have been having the dream. I wake up thinking I hear a girl's voice calling for help; it seemed real. I actually went outside in the pre-dawn grey light this morning looking for her, for the girl I heard shouting. And I think maybe there wasn't anyone at all, that it was the dream, that although I am comfortable and warm in bed with my law school books spread out on the desk in front of my window, the girl desperately wandering out on the street calling for help is still also me.

— Rebecca Jaremko, Journal,
Kingston, Ontario, October, 2000

Doris Lessing, in *The Golden Notebook* wrote that "this is the way to deal with the problem of subjectivity ... there [is] no way of *not* being intensely subjective ... nothing is personal in the sense that it is uniquely one's own. Writing about oneself, one is writing about others, since your problems, pains, pleasure emotions — and your extraordinary, remarkable ideas, can't be yours alone." (Lessing, 13) The converse is also true: when we write about others we are also writing ourselves.

LeGuin's story about the Omelas referenced in Chapter 3 also bears a psychoanalytic reading that is relevant to my research. As discussed, the child in the locked room can be understood as the carceral subject of neoliberal exclusion and it can also be understood as much like Gilbert and Gubar's madwoman in the attic, the agentic potential of the selves we foreclose by living within certain dominant discursive frames. It is beyond the scope of this book to explore in detail but important to consider how technologies of the logic of exclusion imbricated in neoliberal governance impact our expressions, performances and understandings of ourselves.

Writing about Ashley Smith in this book has been peculiar for me. I empathize with her easily, and perhaps over-identify with her too readily; she was not me. I cannot know what went on in her mind and it would be misleading for me to assume I do based on my own subjectivity; like everyone else, I cannot speak for Ashley. However, from beginning to end, in no small part because of my life experiences in all sorts of trouble in the juridical field as an adolescent girl, I see Inmate Smith as a possible self in another, nearby and entirely plausible, possible world. A ghostly presence with whom I have been contending throughout my research and writing of this book is a figure of an imaginable alternative Ashley, 20 years down the road from her death: me.

This book emerges in no small part out of my own experiences as an adolescent girl who had to make difficult decisions and act in the moment. *Unlike* Ashley Smith, at certain critical junctures, I did not enact resistance; I complied in order to survive. I consciously shed strategic tears; I consciously performed femininity. I was not so physically excluded from the norm. In consequence, as do so many of us, I survived to be integrated into the broader society. It is analytically important for me to be reflexive; when I am speaking about Ashley, I am always already coming from a place where I am speaking about me, even if that is understood in the limited methodological sense that the analysis of the Smith case is the space through which I, as author of this book, speak. I like what Foucault said about writing, as follows:

> I don't feel that it is necessary to know exactly what I am. The main interest in life and work is to become someone else that you were not in the beginning. If you knew when you began a book what you would say at the end, do you think that you would have the courage to write it? What is true for writing and for a love relationship is true also for life. The game is worthwhile insofar as we don't know what will be the end. (Foucault, 1982)

Albeit not in a simplistic, tidy way, the experience of writing this book has been transformative. The underlying hope I have worked from in researching towards and writing this book stems from the empowering notion consistent with Foucauldian discourse analysis: a painting, a poem, even academic writing is a technology that can rupture the socially constructed world and it can change us in that process. Put another way, I have been working from a notion similar to that developed by Lefanu in her study of feminist science fiction *In the Chinks of the World Machine,* that the goals of creating a space for women and breaking down binaries between masculinity and femininity are not irreconcilable. Rather, like her, I am seeking to work towards a discursive moment when those "'ancient dualities' have been interrogated and revealed as 'specific, limited phenomena' [and] women can take responsibility as subjects, and as readers." (Lefanu, 182) It is in no small part my own agency I have been working to make legible in legal discourse; I have been working to use my creative agency to write myself, and other subjects like and unlike myself, arriving later in time, into a set of normativities that are more open and allow us to be more free.

Identification with the deceased subject of the case has advantages and pitfalls. There are major methodological problems with over-identification when what I am seeking to do is provide an emancipatory space for someone else's agency. I must be wary of the violence I would do to a subject by turning her life and death into a narcissistic project. In particular, in writing this book I have had to struggle to be aware of the dangers in *over* identifying with Ashley Smith and doing injustice to her life and death by making it into a story about me. In writing this book, I am aware that I began by looking to redeem myself, to find peace, to narrate both my story and hers into a happy ending, and that I carried with me a preconceived figure of Ashley Smith. I am aware that the writing of this was fraught with danger of colonizing Ashley Smith with my own identity.

However, I am alive to, and always reconfiguring, my objectives: at the start of undertaking this research and writing, I did not know where I would be at this journey's end. As it turns out, there is a twist ending to this narrative that surprises the author; this is not my narrative of redemption. By way of literary analogy, in *Jane Eyre* (Bronte, 1861) it is the incendiary power of Charlotte Bronte's wandering madwoman that reconfigures the structure of Thornfield Hall and the gender relations between her and Mr. Rochester into a more livable formation. Ashley's mother Coralee Smith is often quoted for the statement, after the inquest verdict that "now Ashley is at peace." (Taber, 2013) This claim that a resolution has been reached, a sealed civil settlement and the opening of two new mental health beds present a tidy, and perhaps kind, Hollywood, happily-ever-after ending to the dominant narrative arc of the celebritized Smith case.

Interestingly, however, the opening of even these new beds and the response of Public Safety Canada to the inquest recommendations has been put "on hold" indefinitely and will take place "in due course" according to a statement made on behalf the Minister of Public Safety for Canada in September 2014. (Stone, 2014) Further, although Correctional Investigator Howard Sapers, an outspoken proponent of change in response to the Smith case, sought reappointment, he was effectively publicly terminated when his job was posted as vacant in May 2015. Rather than adopt the inquest recommendation to put in place new monitors over the correctional establishment, the Federal government elected to rid itself of an existing, troublesomely effective one.

The central argument in this book is that it is just too neat, too simple, to end the story with the promised opening of health "beds." Ashley Smith died in prison at age 19. She most emphatically did *not* live happily ever after. Nothing I can speak or write can change that. I have argued that it would be helpful for rendering girls' agencies legible and challenging logics in macropower in ways that could provide conditions of possibility that allow more freedom for "other Ashleys" that late modern Canada remains haunted in advocacy and public debate by the mystery of what Ashley Smith meant and what was lost by her death. I want this book to leave readers reflecting on the oppressive world of systems in which Ashley Smith was enmeshed and the world-creating potential of her micro moments of agency. Thinking of Judith Butler, I have argued that Ashley Smith's case can be re-read if the reader troubles the distinction between words and actions. (Butler, 2005) The speech act always has potential for a non-ordinary meaning: why not the physical act? It is my argument that we have much insight to gain into not just her death but also into the government of our own lives, as women, as girls, as mothers, as Canadians, and as members of late capitalist populations, from reading Ashley Smith's voice into her resistant actions, by seeing them as micro movements towards toppling the bureaucratic apparatus in which she was trapped, and towards wedging open the world machine.

ENDNOTES

---

[1]To view the video, follow the following link: http://www.thestar.com/news/2013/12/19/ashley_smith_s_candid_conversation_with_guards.html.

[2]It is beyond the scope of this book to really explore this contention, but I would suggest that the figure of the "Spirited Child" is problematic in many of the same ways as earlier figurations of the child (such as "delinquent" or "incorrigible" child). This figure reveals how discourses of the girl and of the child are always in flux, and that they adapt in response to critiques in ways that can be dangerously insidious. For an example of this figure, see Kurcinka, Mary Sheedy *Raising Your Spirited Child: A Guide for Parents Whose Child is More Intense, Pereptive, Sensitive, Persistent, Energetic*. New York: Harper Collins, 1991. Print.

[3]Examples are wide-ranging, from James Dean in *Rebel Without a Cause* to Eminem in *8 Mile*.

[4]For example, in July 2006, Ashley Smith filed grievances at Nova. She grieved that: "Excessive force was used against her. She wasn't permitted writing paper or writing instruments. She wasn't permitted sufficient toilet paper for hygiene purposes. She was not permitted soap in her cell, was only given finger foods, and was only given a small piece of deodorant on her finger at a time. While menstruating she was not permitted underwear or sufficient sanitary products to meet her hygiene needs." "Timeline: The Life and Death of Ashley Smith" http://www.cbc.ca/fifth/blog/the-life-and-death-of-ashley-smith.

[5]A growing number of incarcerated persons have not been convicted but are being held in "remand." They are waiting for sentencing on a variety of charges. While they have not been found guilty of an offence, persons

on remand are carceral subjects subject to the rules and regulations of the correctional facility in which they are held, the breach of which can result in further charges.

Bibliography

SECONDARY SOURCES

Adelberg, Ellen and Claudia Currie, eds. *Too Few to Count: Canadian Women in Conflict with the Law*. Vancouver: Press Gang, 1987. Print.

Agamben, Giorgio. *Homo Sacer: Sovereign Power and Bare Life*. Trans. Daniel Heller-Roazen: Stanford: Stanford University Press, 1998. Print.

American Psychiatric Association *Diagnostic and Statistical Manual of Mental Disorders*. 5th ed. Arlington, VA: American Psychiatric Publishing, 2013. Web. Accessed June 2, 2015.

Archer, D. "Social Deviance." *Handbook of Social Psychology*. 3rd edition, Vol. 2. Ed. G. Lindzey and E. Aronson. New York: Random House, 1985. 413-483. Print.

Arendt, Hannah, "Race Thinking Before Racism" *The Review of Politics* 6 (1944): 36-73. Print.

Backhouse, Constance. *Carnal Crimes: Sexual Assault and the Law in Canada 1900-1975*. Toronto: Osgoode Society, 2008. Print.

Bailey, M. E. "Foucauldian Feminism Contesting Bodies, Sexuality and Identity." *Up Against Foucault: Explorations of Some Tensions Between Foucault and Feminism*. Ed. Caroline Ramazanoglu London: Routledge, 1993. 99-122. Print.

Bailey, Jane and Steeves, Valerie, eds. *E-Girls, E-Citizens*. Ottawa: University of Ottawa Press, 2015. Print.

Bala, Nicholas. "The Development of Canada's Youth Criminal Justice Law." *Understanding Youth Justice in Canada*. Ed. In K.

Campbell. Toronto: Pearson Education Canada, 2005. Chapter 3. Print.

Ballou, Mary and Laura Brown. *Rethinking Mental Health and Disorder.* New York: Guildford Press, 2002. Print.

Balsamo, Anne-Marie. *Technologies of the Gendered Body: Reading Cyborg Women.* London: Duke University Press, 1996. Print.

Bamberg, Michael. "Narrative Discourse and Identities." *Narratology Beyond Literary Criticism.* New York: Walter de Gruyter, 2005. 213-237. Web. Accessed June 1, 2015.

Barcai, A. and M.K. Rosenthal. "Fears and Tyranny: Observations on the Tyrannical Child." *Archives of General Psychiatry* 30(3) (1974): 392-395. Print.

Barron, Christie. *Governing Girls: Rehabilitation in the Age of Risk.* Blackpoint, NS: Fernwood, 2011. Print.

Barron, Christie and Lacombe, Dany. "Moral Panic and the Nasty Girl." 42 *Canadian Review of Sociology* 1 (2008): 51-69. Print.

Barron, Christie. *Giving Youth A Voice.* Blackpoint, NS: Fernwood, 2000. Print.

Bartky, Sandra. "Foucault, Femininity, and the Modernization of Patriarchal Power." *Feminism and Foucault: Reflections of Resistance.* Ed. Irene Diamond and Lee Quinby. Northeastern University Press: Boston, 1988. 25-45. Print.

Beck, Ulrich. *Risk Society, Towards a New Modernity.* London: Sage Publications, 1992. Print.

Belzer, Hillary. "Words + Guitar: The Riot Grrrl Movement and Third-Wave Feminism." MA Thesis. Georgetown University, 2004. Print.

Berlant, Lauren. "On the Case." *Critical Inquiry* 33(4) (2007): 663-672. Print.

Bernstein, Robin. *Racial Innocence.* New York: New York University Press, 2011. Print.

Best, Joel. *Threatened Children: Rhetoric and Concern About Child Victims.* Chicago: University of Chicago Press, 1990. Print.

Bhabha, Homi, ed. *Nation and Narration.* London: Routledge, 1990. Print.

Bingham, Elizabeth and Rebecca Sutton. *Cruel, Inhuman and Degrading? Canada's Treatment of Federally-Sentenced Women with Mental Health Issues.* University of Toronto, Faculty of

Law, International Human Rights Program, 2012. Print.

Bond and A. Gilliam, eds. *Social Construction of the Past: Representation as Power.* London: Routledge, 1994. Print.

Bosworth, Mary. "Confining Femininity: A History of Gender, Power and Imprisonment." *Theoretical Criminology* 4(3) (2000): 265-284. Print.

Boyle, Christine et al. "The Criminalization of Young Women: An Editors' Forum." *Canadian Journal of Women and the Law* 14 (2) (2002): 389-428. Print.

Bridgeman, Jo and Monk, Daniel, eds. *Feminist Perspectives on Child Law* London: Routledge, 2000. Print.

Brink, J. H., D. Doherty, and A. Boer. "Mental Disorder in Federal Offenders: A Canadian Prevalence Study." *International Journal of Law and Psychiatry* 2 (2001): 330-356.

Burchell, Graham, Colin Gordon, and Peter Miller. *The Foucault Effect: Studies in Governmentality.* Chicago: University of Chicago Press, 1991. Print.

Busby, Karen. "The Protective Confinement of Girls Involved in Prostitution: Potential Problems of Current Regimes." *Being Heard: The Experiences of Young Women in Prostitution.* Ed. Kelly Gorkoff and Jane Runner. Blackpoint, NS: Fernwood, 2003. Print.

Buss, Doris, Joanne Lebert, Blair Rutherford, Donna Sharkey, and Obi Aginam, eds. *Sexual Violence in Conflict and Post-Conflict Societies: International Agendas and African Contexts.* London: Routledge, 2014. Print.

Butler, Judith. *Giving an Account of Myself.* Bronx, NY: Fordham, 2005. Print.

Butler, Judith. *Excitable Speech: A Politics of the Performative.* London: Routledge, 1997. Print.

Butler, Judith. *Gender Trouble: Feminism and the Subversion of Identity.* New York: Routledge, 1990.

Butler, Judith. "Variations on Sex and Gender: Beauvoir, Witting, and Foucault." *Praxis International.* 4 (January 5, 1986): 505-516. Print.

Byrnes, J. P., D. C. Miller, and W. D. Schafer. "Gender Differences in Risk Taking: A Meta-analysis." *Psychological Bulletin* 125 (1999): 367–383. Print.

Caissy, Gail.*Early Adolescence: Understanding the 10 – 15 Year Old*. Berkeley, CA: Perseus Publishing, 1994. Print.

Campbell, Alexandra. "A Place Apart: The Harm of Solitary Confinement." LL.M. Thesis, University of Toronto, 2012. Print.

Campbell, Sue, Meynell, Letitia and Sherwin, Susan. *Embodiment and Agency*. Pennsylvania: The Pennsylvania State University Press, 2009. Print.

Carrigan, Owen. *Juvenile Delinquency in Canada: a History*. Concord, Ontario: Irwin Publishing, 1998.

Castaneda, Claudia. *Figurations: Child, Bodies, Worlds*. Durham, NC: Duke University Press, 2002. Print.

Chatman, Seymour. *Story and Discourse*. Ithaca: Cornell University Press, 1978. Print.

Chesney-Lind, Meda. "Girls Crime and a Woman's Place: Toward a Feminist Model of Female Delinquency." *Crime and Delinquency* 35 (January 1, 1989): 5-29. Print.

Chesney-Lind, Meda and Martha Eliason. "From Invisible to Incorrigible: The Demonizationof Marginalized Women and Girls." *Crime Media Culture* 2(1) (2006): 29-48. Print.

Chesney-Lind, Meda and Katherine Irwin. *Beyond Bad Girls. Gender, Violence and Hype*. New York: Routledge, 2008. Print.

Chesney-Lind, Meda and Nikki Jones. *Fighting for Girls: New Perspectives on Gender and Violence*. Albany: SUNY Press, 2010. Print.

Chessler, Phyllis. *Women and Madness*. New York: Palgrave Macmillan, 2005. Print.

Cohen, Albert. *Delinquent Boys: The Culture of the Gang*. Glencoe, Illinois: Free Press,1955.Print.

Collins, Suzanne. *The Hunger Games*. New York: Scholastic, 2008. Print.

Conaghan, Joanne. "Gender Sexuality and the Law: The Making of a Field." *Feminist Legal Studies* (2009): 303-307. Print.

Coombe, Rosemary. "Room for Manoeuver: Towards a Theory of Practice in Critical Legal Studies." *Law and Social Inquiry* 14 (1) (1989): 69-121. Print.

Coombe, Rosemary. "Tenth Anniversary Symposium: New Direction: Critical Cultural Legal Studies." *Yale Journal of Law & the Humanities* 10 (1998): 463. Print.

Creed, Barbara. *The Monstrous-Feminine: Film, Feminism, Psychoanalysis*. New York: Routledge, 2007. Print.

Crenshaw, Kimberle. "Mapping the Margins: Intersectionality, Identity Politics and Violence Against Women of Colour." *Stanford Law Review* 43 (1993): 1241-1299. Print.

Crowley, Una and Kitchin, Rob. "Producing 'Decent Girls': Governmentality and the Moral Geographies of Sexual Conduct in Ireland (1922–1937)." *Gender, Place and Culture* 15(4) (2008): 355-372. Print.

Cunliffe, Emma. "(This is Not a) Story: Using Court Records to Explore Judicial Narratives in *R v. Kathleen Folbigg*." *Australian Feminist Law Journal* 27(1) (2007): 71-95. Print.

Daly, Kathleen and Maher, Lisa eds. *Criminology at the Crossroads: Feminist Readings in Crime and Justice*. New York: Oxford University Press, 1998. Print.

Daly, Kathleen and Meda Chesney-Lind. "Feminism and Criminology." *Justice Quarterly* 5 (1988): 497-538.Print.

Davis S. "Assessing the 'criminalization' of the mentally ill in Canada." *Canadian Journal of Psychiatry* 37 (1992): 532–38. Print.

Davis-Barron, Sherri. *Canadian Youth and the Criminal Law: One Hundred Years of Youth Justice Legislation in Canada*. Toronto: LexisNexis Canada, 2009. Print.

Dean, Amber Richelle. *Locking Them Up to Keep Them Safe*. Vancouver: Justice for Girls, 2005. Print.

Dean, Mitchell. *Governmentality: Power and Rule in Modern Society*. Thousand Oaks, CA: Sage, 1999. Print.

De Cillia, R. , M. Reisigl, and R. Wodak. "The Discursive Construction of National Identities." *Discourse and Society* 10(2) (1999): 149-173. Print.

De Lauretis, Teresa. *Figures of Resistance: Essays in Feminist Theory*. Champagne, IL: Teresa de Laurentis, 2007. Print.

Diagnostic and Statistical Manual of Mental Disorders, Fourth Edition, Text Revision (DSM-IV). Print.

Douard, John. "Sex Offender as Scapegoat: The Monstrous Other Within." *New York Law School Law Review* 31 (2009): 53. Print.

Dowd, Nancy and Michelle Jacobs, eds. *Feminist Legal Theory: An Anti-Essentialist Reader*. New York: New York University Press, 2003. Print.

Driscoll, Catherine. *Girls: Feminine Adolescence in Popular Culture and Cultural Theory*. New York: Columbia University Press, 2002. Print.

Eaves, D., R. P. Ogloff, and R. Roesch, eds. *Mental Disorders and the Criminal Code: Legal Background and Contemporary Perspectives*. Burnaby, BC: Mental Health, Law and Policy Institute, 2000. Print.

Edwards, Phillip, ed. *Hamlet, Prince of Denmark*. New Cambridge Shakespeare. Cambridge: Cambridge University Press, 1985. Print.

Emirbayer, M. and A. Mische. "What is Agency?" *American Journal of Sociology* 103 (1998): 962-1023. Print.

Evans Braziel, Jana and Kathleen LeBesco. *Bodies Out of Bounds: Fat Bodies and Transgression*. Berkeley: University of California Press, 2001. Print.

Ewick, Patricia, and Susan Silbey. *The Common Place of Law Stories from Everyday Life*. Chicago: University of Chicago Press, 1998. Print.

Faith, K. and Yasmin Jiwani. "The Social Construction of 'Dangerous' Girls and Women." *Marginality and Condemnation: An Introduction to Critical Criminology*. Ed. Bernard Schissel, and Carolyn Brooks. Blackpoint, NS: Fernwood Publishing, 2002. at 83-10. Print.

Fairclough, Norman. *Language and Power*. New York: Longman, 1989. Print.

Fairclough, Norman. *Discourse Analysis*. Cambridge, UK: Polity Press, 1990. Print.

Fairclough, Norman. *Critical Discourse Analysis: The Critical Study of Language*. Harlow, UK: Longman, 1995. Print.

Fairclough, Norman. *Discourse and Social Change*. Cambridge, UK: Polity Press, 1992. Print.

Farrell, Amy Erdman. *Fatshame: Stigma and the Fat Body in American Culture*. New York: New York University Press, 2011. Print.

Feld, Barry. "Violent Girls or Relabeled Status Offenders? An Alternative Interpretation of the Data." *Crime and Delinquency* 55 (2) (2009): 241-265. Print.

Ferguson, Robert. *An Anatomy of American Punishment*. Boston: Harvard University Press, 2014. Print.

Ferrari, Jacqueline. "Federal Female Incarceration in Canada: What Happened to Empowerment?" Master's Thesis, Queens University, 2011. Web. Accessed June 1, 2015.

Fine, Michelle. "Sexuality, Schooling and Adolescent Females: The Missing Discourse of Desire." *Harvard Educational Review* 58(1) (1988). Print.

Foucault, Michel. *Abnormal: Lectures at the College de France, 1974-75*. Trans. by Burchell, Graham. Picador: New York, 1999. Print.

Foucault, Michel. "Governmentality." *The Foucault Effect: Studies in Governmentality*. Ed. Graham Burchell, Colin Gordon and Peter Miller. Trans. Rosi Braidotti and revised by Colin Gordon. Chicago: University of Chicago Press, 1991. 87-104. Print.

Foucault, Michel. *I, Pierre Riverre, Having Slaughtered My Mother, My Sister and My Brother: A Case of Parricide in the 19th Century*. Trans. Jellinek, Frank. Lincoln: University of Nebraska Press, 1975. Print.

Foucault, Michel. "Lectures at Vermont University in October 1982." *Technologies of the Self*. Boston: University of Massachusetts Press, 1988. Print.

Foucault, Michel. *Madness and Civilization: A History of Insanity in the Age of Reason*. Web. Accessed June 1, 2015.

Foucault, Michel "Sécurité, territoire, population." *Cours au Collège de France, 1977-1978*. Paris: Gallimard Seuil, 2004. Print.

Foucault, Michel. *Society Must Be Defended: Lectures at the Collège de France, 1975-1976*. New York: St. Martin's Press, 1997. Print.

Foucault, Michel. *The History of Sexuality. Volume 1*. Trans. Robert Hurley. New York: Vintage Books, 1990.

Foucault, Michel. "Truth, Power, Self: An Interview with Michel Foucault (25 October 1982)." *Technologies of the Self: A Seminar with Michel Foucault*. L. H. Martin, et al. London: Tavistock. Print, 1988. 9-15. Print.

Frankenburg, Ruth. *White Women: Race Matters*. New York: Routledge, 2004. Print.

Giddens, Anthony. *Modernity and the Self-Identity: Self and Society in the Late Modern Age*. Stanford: Stanford University Press, 1991. Print.

Gelsthorpe, Lorraine. "Folk Devils and Moral Panics: A Feminist Perspective," Book review of *Folk Devils and Moral Panics: The Creation of the Mods and Rockers* (third edition)" by Stanley Cohen. *Crime, Media, Culture* 1 (2006): 112. Print.

Genette, Gerard. *Narrative Discourse*. Trans. by Jane E. Lewin. Ithaca: Cornell University Press, 1980. Print

Gerlach, Neil, Sheryl Hamilton, Rebecca Sullivan, and Priscilla Walton. *Becoming Biosubjects: Bodies. Systems.Technologies.* Canada: University of Toronto Press, 2011. Print.

Gilbert, Sandra and Susan Gubar. *The Madwoman in the Attic.* New York and London: Yale University Press, 1979. Print.

Gilman, Charlotte Perkins. "The Yellow Wall-Paper." *Great Short Stories by American Women*. Ed. Candace Ward. New York: Dover, 1996. 73-88. Print.

Godfrey, Rebecca. *Under the Bridge*. Toronto: Harper Collins, 2005. Print.

Gonick, Marnina, Emma Renold, Jessica Ringrose, and Lisa Weems. "Rethinking Agency and Resistance: What Comes After Girl Power." *Girlhood Studies* 2(2) (Winter 2009): 1-9. Print.

Goode, Erich and Nachmann Ben-Yahuda. *Moral Panics; The Social Construction of Deviance*. Oxford, UK: Blackwell Publishing, 2009. Print.

Gordon, Harvey, "Suicide in Secure Psychiatric Facilities." *Advances in Psychiatric Treatment* 8 (2002): 408-417. Print.

Graham, Burchell, Colin Gordon and Peter Miller. *The Foucault Effect: Studies in Governmentality*. Chicago: University of Chicago Press, 1991. Print.

Grassian, Stuart and Nancy Friedman. "Effects of Sensory Deprivation in Psychiatric Seclusion and Solitary Confinement." *International Journal of Law and Psychiatry* 8(1) (1986): 49-65.

Graycar, Regina and Morgan, Jenny. *The Hidden Gender of Law*. Sydney, Australia: The Federation Press, 1990. Print.

Hall, Stuart et al. "Policing the Crisis: Mugging, the State and Law and Order." *Dimensions of Criminal Law*. Ed. Toni Picard and Phil Goldman. Toronto: Emond Montgomery, 1992. Print.

Hall, Stuart. "The Work of Representation." *Representation: Cultural Representations and Signifying Practices*. London: Sage, 1997. 1-74. Print.

Hall, Stuart, D. Morley, and K.-H. Chen. *Stuart Hall: Critical Dialogues in Cultural Studies*. London: Routledge, 1996. Print.

Hamilton, Sheryl. *Impersonations: Troubling the Person in Law and Culture*. Toronto: University of Toronto Press, 2009. Print.

Hannah-Moffat, Kelly "Gaining Insight, Changing Attitudes and Managing 'Risk': Parole Release Decisions for Women Convicted of Violent Crimes." *Punishment and Society* 13(2) (2011): 149-175. Print.

Hannah-Moffat, Kelly. "Gendering Risk at What Cost: Negotiations of Gender and Risk in Canadian Women's Prisons." 14 *Feminism and Psychology* 14(2) (2004): 243-24. Print.

Hannah-Moffat, Kelly. "Losing Ground: Gendered Knowledges, Parole, Risk, and Responsibility." *Social Politics*, 11(3) (2004): 363-385. Print.

Hannah-Moffat, Kelly. "Pandora's Box: Risk/Need and Gender-responsive Corrections." *Criminology and Public Policy* 5(1) (2006): 183-192. Print.

Hannah-Moffat, Kelly and M. Shaw, eds. *An Ideal Prison? Critical Essays on Women's Imprisonment in Canada*. Blackpoint, NS: Fernwood Publishing, 2000. Print.

Haraway, Donna "A Cyborg Manifesto Science, Technology, and Socialist-Feminism in the Late Twentieth Century," in *Simians, Cyborgs and Women: The Reinvention of Nature*. New York; Routledge, 1991. Print.

Harris, Anita *All About the Girl: Culture, Power, and Identity*, New York: Routledge, 2004. Print.

Heimer, Karen, "Gender, Interaction, and Delinquency: Testing a Theory of Differential Social Control." *Social Psychology Quarterly* 59(1) (1996): 39-61. Web.

Herzog, Todd. "Crime Stories: Criminal, Society and the Modernist Case History." *Representations* 80 (2002): 34-61. Print.

hooks, bell. *Yearning: Race, Gender, and Cultural Politics*. Boston: South End Press, 1990. Print.

Hunt, Alan and Gary Wickham. *Foucault and the Law: Towards a Sociology of Law as Governance*. London: Pluto Press, 1994. Print.

Irigaray, Luce. *The Sex Which is Not One*. New York: Cornell University Press, 1985.

James, Allison, Chris Jenks, and Alan Prout. *Theorizing Childhood*. Williston, VT: Teachers College Press, 2006. Print.

Jiwani, Yasmin, 'Erasing Race: The Story of Reena Virk." *Reena Virk: Critical Perspectives on a Canadian Murder*. Ed. Mythili Ravija and Sheila Batacharya. Toronto: Canadian Scholars' Press, 2010. 82-122. Print.

Jiwani, Yasmin. *Discourses of Denial: Mediations of Race, Gender and Violence*. Vancouver: University of British Columbia Press, 2006. Print.

Johnson, Rebecca. *Taxing Choices: The Intersection of Class, Gender, Parenthood and the Law*. Vancouver: University of British Columbia Press, 2002. Print.

Josselson, R. and A. Lieblich, eds. *Interpreting Experience. The Narrative Study of Lives*. Vol. 3. London: Sage, 1995. 153-173. Print.

Karaian, Lara. "Lolita Speaks: Sexting, Teenage Girls and the Law" *Crime Media Culture* 8(1) (2012): 57-73. Print.

Kehily, Mary Jane, "Understanding Childhood: An Introduction to Some Key Themes and Issues" *An Introduction to Childhood Studies*. London: McGraw-Hill, 2004. 1-16. Print.

Kelly, Christoper and Eve Grace, eds. *Rousseau on Women, Love and Family*. Lebanon, NH: Dartmouth College Press, 2009. Print.

Kilty, J. M. "Resisting Confined Identities: Women's Strategies of Coping In Prison."Unpublished Doctoral Dissertation. Simon Fraser University, Burnaby, BC, 2008. Print.

Kilty, Jennifer M., "Examining the "Psy-Carceral Complex" in the Death of Ashley Smith." *Criminalizing Women*. Ed. Gillian Balfour and Elizabeth Comack. Blackpoint, NS: Fernwood Press, 2014. 236-254. Print.

Koffman, O. and R. Gill. "The Revolution Will Be Led by a 12-Year-Old Girl': Girl Power and Global Biopolitics." *Feminist Review* 105(1) (2013): 83-102. Print.

Kristeva, Julia. *Powers of Horror: An Essay on Abjection*. Trans. Leon S. Roudiez. New York: Columbia University Press, 1982. Print.

Kurcinka, Mary Sheedy. *Raising Your Spirited Child: A Guide for Parents Whose Child is More Intense, Perceptive, Sensitive, Persistent, Energetic*. New York: Harper Collins, 1991.

Lacey, Nicola. "Unspeakable Subjects: Impossible Rights: Sexuality, Integrity and Criminal Law." *Unspeakable Subjects*. Oxford: Hart, 1998. 98-125. Print.

Larsson, Steig. *The Girl with the Dragon Tattoo*. UK: MacLehose Press, 2008. Print.

Lefanu, Sarah. *In the Chinks of the World Machine*. London: The Women's Press, 1988. Print.

Lessing, Doris. *The Golden Notebook*. London: Grafton Books, 1972. Print.

Leverenz, David. "The Woman in Hamlet: An Interpersonal View." *Signs* 4(2) (1978): 291-308. Print.

Levi, Primo. *Survival In Auschwitz: The Nazi Assault on Humanity*. New York: Simon and Schuster, 1996. Print.

Levit, Nancy and Robert Verchick. *Feminist Legal Theory: A Primer*. New York: New York University Press 2006. Print.

Little, Nicole and Hoskins, Marie. "It's an Acceptable Identity:" Constructing 'Girl' at the Intersections of Health, Media and Meaning-making." *Child and Youth Services* 26(2) (2004): 75-93. Print.

Lucas, Gavin. *An Archaeology of Colonial Identity: Power and Material Culture in the Dwars Valley, South Africa*. USA: Springer, 2006. Print.

MacDonald, Noni, et al. "The Crime of Mental Illness." *Canadian Medical Association Journal* 182(13) (September 21, 2010). Web. Accessed September 25, 2015.

Madriz, Esther. *Nothing Bad Happens to Good Girls* Berkeley: University of California, 1997. Print.

Malloch, Margaret and McIvor, Gill. *Women, Punishment and Social Justice*. New York: Routledge, 2013. Print.

Mann, Ruth, ed. *Juvenile Crime and Delinquency: A Turn of the Century Reader* .Canada: Canadian Scholars' Press, 2000. Print.

Maurer, Donna and Sobal, Jeffrey. *Interpreting Weight: The Social Management of Fatness and Thinness*. New York: Walter De Gruyter, 1999. Print.

Mbembe, Achille. "Necropolitics." 1 *Public Culture* 1(15) (2003): 11- 40. Print.

McGill, Jena. "An Institutional Suicide Machine: Discrimination Against Federally Sentenced Aboriginal Women in Canada"

(2008) *Race/ Ethnicity: Global Contexts* 2:1. Web. Accessed June 1, 2015.

McMahon, Maeve. "Assisting Female Offenders: Art or Science?" *Assessment to Assistance: Programs for Women in Community Corrections.* Ed. Maeve McMahon. Lanham, MD: The American Correctional Association, 2000. 279-328. Print.

McRobbie, Angela. *The Aftermath of Feminism: Gender, Culture and Social Change* London: Sage, 2009. Print.

McRobbie, Angela and Thornton, Sarah, "Rethinking 'Moral Panic' for Multi-Mediated Social Worlds." *British Journal of Sociology* 46(4) (1995): 559-574. Print.

Messerschmidt, James. *Masculinities and Crime: Critique and Re-conceptualization of Theory.* New York: Rowan and Littlefield Publishers, 1993. Print.

Mills, Sara. *Discourse.* Toronto: Routledge, 1997. Print.

Moran, Leslie J. "Legal Studies after the Cultural Turn: A Case Study of Judicial Research." *Social Research after the Cultural Turn.* Ed. S. Roseneil and S. Frosh. Basingstoke: Palgrave Macmillan, 2012. 124-143. Print.

Morrow, Marina, et al. *Women's Health in Canada: Critical Perspectives on Theory and Policy.* Toronto: University of Toronto Press, 2007. Print.

Mundhane, Renu. "Cruel, Inhuman and Degrading? Canada's Treatment of Federally-Sentenced Women with Mental Health Issues." Lecture, University of Toronto International Human Rights Program, May 2012.

Munro, Vanessa. "Legal Feminism and Foucault: A Critique of the Expulsion of Law." *Journal of Law and Society* 28(4) (2001): 546–567. Print.

Myers, Tamara. *Caught: Montreal's Modern Girls and the Law, 1869-1945.* Toronto: University of Toronto Press, 2006. Print.

Myers, Tamara. "Women and Kids in the Court: Feminist History and Anthony Platt's The Child Savers." *The Child Savers: The Invention of Delinquency.* Ed. Anthony Platt. Brunswick, NJ: Rutgers, 2009. Print.

Naffine, Ngaire. *Female Crime: The Construction of Women in Criminology.* Winchester, Mass: Allen and Unwin, 1987. Print.

Naffine, Ngaire. "In Praise of Legal Feminism" *Legal Studies* 22

(2002): 71-101. Print.

Naffine, Ngaire. *Law's Meaning of Life: Philosophy, Religion and the Legal Person.* Oxford: Hart Publishing, 2009. Print.

Naffine, Ngaire. "Sexing the Subject (of Law)." *Public and Private: Feminist Legal Debates.* Oxford: Oxford University Press, 1995. 18-32. Print.

Nedelesky, Jennifer. "Embodied Diversity and the Challenges to Law." *McGill Law Journal* 42(1) (1997): 91-115. Print.

Newburn, Tim and Elizabeth Stanko, eds. *Just Boys Doing Business? Men, Masculinities and Crime.* New York: Routledge, 1994. Print.

Nowinski, Joseph. *The Identity Trap: Saving Teens From Themselves* New York: Amacon, 2007.Print.

Nunn, Kenneth B. "The Child as Other: Race and Differential Treatment in the Juvenile Justice System." *Faculty Publications.* Paper 108. 2002. Web. Accessed June 1, 2015.

Ong, Aihwa. 2006. *Neoliberalism as Exception: Mutations in Citizenship and Sovereignty.* Durham, NC: Duke University Press

Ong, Aihwa. "Boundary Crossings: Neoliberalism as a Mobile Technology." 2006. Web. Accessed September 25, 2015.

O'Reilly, Andrea. *Feminist Mothering* Albany: SUNY Press, 2008. Print.

Pate, Kim. "Women, Punishment and Social Justice: Why You Should Care." *Women, Punishment and Social Justice.* Ed. Margaret Malloch and Gill McIvor. New York: Routledge, 2013. 197-202. Print.

Pearson, Patricia. *When She Was Bad: Violent Women and the Myth of Innocence.* Toronto: Random House, 1997. Print.

Phillips, N. and C. Hardy. *Discourse Analysis. Investigating Processes of Social Construction.* Thousand Oaks, CA: Sage Publications, 2002. Print.

Pipher, Mary. *Reviving Ophelia.* New York: Random House, 1994. Print.

Platt,Anthony. *The Child Savers: The Invention of Delinquency* New Brunswick, NJ: Rutger's University Press, 2009. Print.

Plugge, E. "Female Prisoners More Obese Than General Female Population." *Eurekalert* (19 April 2012). Web. Accessed June 1, 2015.

Porter, Roy. *Madmen: A Social History of Madhouses, Mad-Doctors and Lunatics*. [1987]. Stroud: Tempus, 2006. Print.

Proctor, Gillian. "Disordered Boundaries? A Critique of Borderline Personality Disorder." psychminded.co.uk. 2007. Web. Accessed June 1, 2015.

Ragin, Charles and Howard Becker. *What is a Case?* London: Cambridge University Press, 1992. Print.

Ravija, Mithili and Batacharya, Sheila. *Reena Virk: Critical Perspectives on a Canadian Murder*. Toronto: Canadian Scholars' Press, 2010. Print.

Razack, Sherene. "It Happened More Than Once: Freezing Deaths in Saskatchewan." *Canadian Journal of Women and the Law* 26(1) (2014): 51-80. Print.

Razack, Sherene. *Race, Space, Law: Unmapping a White Settler Society*. Toronto: Between the Lines, 2002. Print.

Razack, Sherene. "Timely Deaths: Medicalizing the Deaths of Aboriginal People in Police Custody." *Law, Culture and the Humanities* 9(2) (2013): 352-374.

Razack, Sherene; Malinda Smith and Sunera Thobani, eds. *States of Race: Critical Race Feminism for the 21st Century*. Toronto: Between the Lines, 2010. Print.

Razack, Sherene. 2008. *Casting Out: The Eviction of Muslims from Western Law and Politics*. Toronto: University of Toronto Press. Print.

Réaume, Denise, "What's Distinctive about Feminist Analysis of Law? A Conceptual Analysis of Women's Exclusion from Law." *Legal Theory* 2 (1996): 265-299. Print.

Reitsma-Street, Marge. "Justice for Canadian Girls: a 1990s Update." *Canadian Journal of Criminology and Criminal Justice* 41(3) (1999): 335-64. Print.

Renke, Wayne. "Case Comment: Lisa Neve, Dangerous Offender." Case Comment. *Alberta Law Review* 33 (1995): 650. Print.

Reissman, Catherine. *Narrative Analysis*. London: Sage, 1993. Print.

Reynolds, Simon and Press, Jay. *The Sex Revolts: Gender, Rebellion and Rock n Roll*. London: Serpent's Tail, 1996. Print.

Rigakos, George S. "Risk Society and Actuarial Criminology: Prospects for a Critical Discourse." *Canadian Journal of Crim-*

inology 41(2) (1999): 137-150.

Ring, Jessica. "Incorrigible While Incarcerated: Critically Analyzing Mainstream Canadian News Depictions of Ashley Smith." *Canadian Graduate Journal of Criminology and Sociology* 3(1) (2014): 34-53. Print.

Ring, Jessica. "Incorrigible While Incarcerated: Topic Modeling Mainstream Canadian News Depictions of Ashley Smith." Master's Thesis, Carleton University, Ottawa, 2013. Web. Accessed June 1, 2015.

Ringrose, Jessica. "A New Universal Mean Girl: Examining the Discursive Construction and Social Regulation of a New Feminine Pathology" *Feminism and Psychology* 16 (2006): 405-424. Print.

Riviere, Joan. "Womanliness as Masquerade." *Journal of Psychoanalysis* 10 (1929): 303-313. Print.

Rorty, Richard. *Philosophy and the Mirror of Nature*. Princeton: Princeton University Press, 1979. Print.

Rosenfeld, S. "Triple Jeopardy? Mental Health and the Intersection of Gender, Race, and Class." *Social Science and Medicine*, 74(11) (2012): 1791-1801. Print.

Rosenfield, S. "Sex Roles and Societal Reactions to Mental Illness: The Labeling of 'Deviant' Deviance." *Journal of Health and Social Behavior* 23(1) (1982): 18-24. Print.

Roth, Veronica. *Divergent*. New York: Harper Collins, 2011. Print.

Said, Edward. *Orientalism*. London: Vintage, 1984. Print.

Sandler, Sarah. *Ophelia Speaks: Adolescent Girls Write About Their Search for Self*. New York: Harper Perennial, 1999. Print.

Sangster, Joan. *Girl Trouble: Female Delinquency in English Canada*. Toronto: Between the Lines, 2002. Print.

Sarat, Austin. *Imagining Legality: Where Law Meets Popular Culture*. Tuscaloosa: The University of Alabama Press, 2011. Print.

Sarat, Austin. "'The Law Is All Over': Power, Resistance, and the Legal Consciousness of the Welfare Poor." *Yale Journal of Law and the Humanities* 2 (1990): 343-79. Print.

Schissel, Bernard. *Blaming Children: Youth Crime, Moral Panics and the Politics of Hate*. Blackpoint, NS: Fernwood Publishing, 1997. Print.

Sawicki, Jana. *Disciplining Foucault: Feminism, Power and the Body*. New York: Routledge, 1991. Print.

Service, John. "Under Warrant: A Review of the Implementation of the Correctional Service of Canada's 'Mental Health Strategy.'" 2010. Web. Accessed June 1, 2015.

Shapiro, Michael. *Reading the Postmodern Polity: Political Theory as Textual Practice*. Minneapolis: 1992. Print.

Sharpe, Andrew. *Foucault's Monsters and the Challenge of Law*. Abingdon: Routledge , 2010. Print.

Shaw, Clare. *Women at the Margins: Me, Borderline Personality Disorder and Women at the Margins' Annual Review of Critical Psychology*.

Shields, Carol and Marjorie Anderson, eds. *Dropped Threads: What We Aren't Told*. Toronto: Random House Canada, 2001. Print.

Shotwell, Alexis. "Open Normativities: Gender, Disability and Collective Cultural Change." *Signs* 37(4) (2012): 989-1016. Print.

Showalter, Elaine. "Representing Ophelia: Women, Madness and the Responsibilities of Feminist Criticism." *Shakespeare and the Question of Theory*. Ed. Patricia Parker and Geoffrey Hartman. London: Routledge, 1985. 77-94. Print.

Smart, Carol. *Women, Crime and Criminology: A Feminist Critique*. London: Keegan, 1976. Print.

Smart, Carole and Barry Smart. *Women, Sexuality and Social Control*. New York: Routledge, 1978. Print.

Spivak, Gayatri Chakravorty. *The Post-Colonial Critic: Interviews, Strategies, Dialogues*. Ed. Sarah Harasym. New York: Routledge, 1990. 472-477. Print.

Spivak, Gayatri. "Can the Subaltern Speak." *Marxism and the Interpretation of Culture*. Ed. C. Nelson and L. Grossbergs. Basingstoke: Macmillan Education, 1988. 271-313. Print.

Steenbergen, Candis and Claudia Mitchell, eds. *Girlhood: Redefining the Limits*. Toronto: Black Rose Books, 2006. Print.

Strange, Carolyn and Tina Loo. *Making Good: Law and Moral Regulation in Canada, 1867-1939*. Toronto: University of Toronto Press, 1997. Print.

Thobani, Sunera. *Exalted Subjects: Studies in the Making of Race and Nation in Canada*. Toronto: University of Toronto Press, 2007. Print.

Tolman, Deborah. "Female Adolescents, Sexual Empowerment and Desire: A Missing Discourse of Gender Inequity." *Sex Roles*

66 (2012): 746-757. Print.

Totten, Mark. "Girlfriend Abuse as a Form of Masculinity Construction Among Violent, Marginal Male Youth." *Men and Masculinities* 6(1) (2003): 70-92. Print.

Thornborrow, Joanna. *Power Talk: Language and Interaction in Institutional Discourse.* London: Harlow, 2002. Print.

Trigg, R. "Wittgenstein and Social Science." Ed. A. P. Griffiths. *Wittgenstein Centenary Essays Royal Institute of Philosophy Supplement*,Vol. 28. Cambridge: Cambridge University Press, 1991. Print.

Ugelvik, Thomas. *Power and Resistance in Prison: Doing Time, Doing Freedom.* New York: Palgrave MacMillan, 2014. Print.

Ussher, Jane. *Women's Madness: Misogyny or Mental Illness?* Amherst: University of Massachusetts Press, 1991. Print.

Vaillancourt, T., S. Hymel, and P. McDougall. "Bullying is Power: Implications for School-based Intervention Strategies." *Bullying, Victimization, and Peer Harassment: A Handbook of Prevention and Intervention.* Ed. J. E. Zins, M. J. Elias, and C. A. Maher. New York: Haworth Press, 2007. 317–337. Print.

Valverde, Mariana. *The Age of Light, Soap, and Water: Moral Reform in English Canada, 1885-1925.* Toronto: McClelland and Stewart, 1991. Print.

Van Dijk, Teun. "Discourse Semantics and Ideology." *Discourse and Society* 6(2) (1995): 243-289. Print.

Van Leeuwen, T. and C. Jewitt. *Handbook of Visual Analysis.* London: Sage Publications, 2001. Print.

von Schonfeld, Carl-Ernst, et al. "Prevalence of Psychiatric Disorders, Psychopathology, and the Need for Treatment in Female and Male Prisoners." 77(7) (July 2006): 830-41. Print.

Walkerdine, Valerie. *Growing up Girl: Psychosocial Explorations of Gender and Class.* London: Palgrave, 2001. Print.

Walters, William. *Governmentality: Critical Encounters.* London: Routledge, 2011. Print.

Wodak Ruth. "The Discourse-Historical Approach." *Methods of Critical Discourse Analysis.* Ed. R. Wodak and M. Meyer. London: Sage, 2001, 63-91. Print.

Worrall, Ann. "Governing Bad Girls: Changing Constructions of Female Juvenile Delinquency." *Feminist Perspectives on Child*

Law. Ed. Jo Bridgeman and Daniel Monk. London: Routledge, 2000. 151-169. Print.

Worrall, Anne. *Girls' Violence: Myths and Realities*. New York: SUNY Press, 2004. Print.

Wasylenki, D. "The Paradigm Shift from Institution to Community." *Psychiatry in Canada: 50 Years*. Ed. Q. Rae-Grant. Ottawa: Canadian Psychiatric Association, 2001. Print.

Whitford, Margaret, ed. *The Irigaray Reader*. Cambridge: Basil Blackwell, 1991. Print.

Wichum, Ricky. "Security as Dispositif: Michel Foucault in the Field of Security." *Foucault Studies* 15 (2013): 164-71. Print.

Winston, Anthony P. "Recent Developments in Borderline Personality Disorder." *Advances in Psychiatric Treatment* 6 (2000): 211-217. Print.

Wirth-Cauchon, Janet. *Women and Borderline Personality Disorder: Symptoms and Stories*. Brunswick, NJ: Rutgers University Press, 2003. Print.

Zlotnick, C. et al. "Gender Differences in Comorbid Disorders Among Offenders in Prison Substance Abuse Treatment Programs." *Behavioural Sciences and the Law* 26(4) (2008): 403-12.

PRIMARY SOURCES

Formal Legal Instruments
(Legislation and International Agreements)

Canadian Charter of Rights and Freedoms Enacted as Schedule B to the Canada Act 1982, 1982, c. 11 (U.K.)

Canadian Human Rights Act. 1976-77, c. 33.

Coroner's Act RSO 1990 c. C-37

Corrections and Conditional Release Act SC 1992 C. 20.

Bill C-30 The Protecting Children From Online Predators Act, Parliament of Canada 41st Parliament, 2012

Family Services Act SNB 1980, c F-2.2, s. 1

Juvenile Delinquents Act RSC 1908 c J-3

Ontario Mental Health Act RSO 1990 c. M.7

Youth Criminal Justice Act SC 2002 c.1, s. 2.

United Nations Convention on the Rights of the Child – UN General

Assembly Resolution 44/25 20 November 1989.

Caselaw

Canada (Attorney General) v. Bedford 2013 SCC 72
Canada (Correctional Service) v. Carlisle, 2012 ONSC 6080 (CanLII)
Smith (Re), 2013 CanLII 92762 (ON OCCO) *Inquest Touching the Death of Ashley Smith: Verdict and Recommendations* (19 December 2013)
R. v. Canadian Broadcasting Corporation, 2010 ONCA 726 (CanLII)
R. v. Ellard, 2009 SCC 27 (CanLII).
R. v. Todorovic 2009 Carswell,Ont 4353 (SCJ)
R. v. Steinke, 2008 ABQB
R. v. JR 2010 ABQB 38 CanLII
Winko v, British Columbia (Forensic Psychiatric Institute), [1999] 2 SCR 625, 1999 CanLII 694 (SCC)
Smith v. Porter (Judicial Review), 2011 ONSC 2844 (CanLII)

Government Documents and Official Reports

Arbour, L. "Report of the Commission of Inquiry into certain events at the Prison for Women in Kingston" *Public Works and Government Services Canada* 1996. Web. Accessed June 1, 2015.
Blanchette, Kelley and Lawrence Motiuk. " Maximum-security Female and Male Federal Offenders: A Comparison." *CSC Research Branch* 1997. Web. Accessed June 1, 2015.
Canadian Association of Elizabeth Fry Societies' (CAEFS). 2005 Submission to the United Nations. Web. Accessed June 1, 2015.
Canadian Mental Health Association (CMHA). "Fast Facts About Mental Illness" Web. Accessed June 1, 2015.
Carlson, Kathryn Blaze. "Ashley Smith inquiry spurs federal pilot project, draws criticism" *The Globe and Mail* (1 May 2014) Web. Accessed June 1, 2015.
Corrections Canada . "Response to the Coroner's Inquest Touching the Death of Ashley Smith." December 2014. Web. Accessed June 1, 2015.
Corrections Canada. "Progress Report on the August 14, 2009, Correctional Service of Canada (CSC) Response to the Office

of the Correctional Investigator's Deaths in Custody Study, the Correctional Investigator's Report: A Preventable Death and the CSC National Board of Investigation into the Death of an Offender at Grand Valley Institution for Women." 18 December 2009. (Rec. 1 OCI, Rec. 1 CSC) Web. Accessed June 1, 2015.

Corrections Canada – Updated Response to the Report of the Corrections Investigator in the Ashley Smith Case (March 25, 2010) Web. Accessed June 1, 2015.

Correctional Service of Canada. *Quick Facts: Mental Health Strategy.* 2009. Ottawa. Web. Accessed June 1, 2015.

June 2013 Report of the Correctional Investigator as Tabled in the House of Commons. Web. Accessed June 1, 2015.

Canada. Royal Commission on Aboriginal Peoples. Report of the Royal Commission on Aboriginal Peoples, Volume 1: *Looking Forward, Looking Back.* Chapter 10, "Residential Schools." Ottawa: Supply and Services Canada, 1996. Web. Accessed June 1, 2015.

Corrections Canada. Key Indicators 2012-2013. Web. Accessed June 1, 2015.

Factum of the Respondents (Appellants) in *Smith v. Porter.* 2011. Web. Accessed June 1, 2015.

Government of Canada. House of Commons Hansard November 2, 2012. Web. Accessed June 1, 2015.

Luciani, F., L. L. Motiuk, and M. Nafekh. "An Operational Review of the Custody Rating Scale: Reliability, Validity, and Practical Utility." 199). Research Report #R-47. Ottawa: Correctional Service Canada.

Wesley, Mandy. "Marginalized: The Aboriginal Women's Experience in Federal Corrections" *Corrections Canada.* 2012. Web. Accessed June 1, 2015.

Nunn, G. Merlin. "Spiralling Out of Control: Lessons Learned From A Boy in Trouble." Report of the Nunn Commission December 2006. Web. Accessed June 1, 2015.

Public Safety Canada. "2012 Corrections and Conditional Release Statistical Overview." *Public Safety Canada.* Web. Accessed June 1, 2015.

Report of Dr. Paul Beaudry – Review of Forced Injections Administered to Ashley Smith. April 2010. Web. Accessed June 1, 2015.

Richard, Bernard. "The Ashley Smith Report." New Brunswick Ombudsman and Child and Youth Advocate. 2008. Web. Accessed June 1, 2015.

Savoie, J. "Youth self-reported delinquency, Toronto, 2006." *Juristat* 27(6) (2007).Statistics Canada Catalogue no.85-002-X. Ottawa. Web. Accessed December 10, 2010.

Gabor, Thomas. "Deaths in Custody: Final Report Submitted to the Correctional Investigator." February 2007. Web. Accessed June 1, 2015.

Mental Health Commission of Canada. "Turning the Key: Assessing Housing and Related Supports for Persons with Mental Illness." Web. Accessed June 1, 2015.

SACC/Union of Canadian Corrections Officers' "A Rush to Judgment: Report on the Death in Custody of Ashley Smith, an Inmate at Grand Valley Institution for Women." October 2008. Web. Accessed June 1, 2015.

Sapers, Howard. "A Legacy of Missed Opportunities: The Case of Ashley Smith." Office of the Correctional Investigator, 2011. Web. Accessed June 1, 2015.

Sapers, Howard. "Backgrounder: Chronic Self Injury among Federally Sentenced Women." Web. Accessed June 1, 2015.

Sapers, Howard. "Correctional Investigator's Report: A Preventable Death and the CSC National Board of Investigation into the Death of an Offender at Grand Valley Institution For Women" 2008. Web. Accessed June 1, 2015.

Sapers, Howard. Correctional Investigator. *Final Report on Ashley Smith Case*. 2010. Web. Accessed September 26, 2015.

Sapers, Howard. "Risky Business: An Investigation of the Treatment and Management of Chronic Self-Injury Among Federally Sentenced Women." Office of the Correctional Investigator, September 2013. Web. Accessed June 1, 2015.

Sapers, Howard. Correctional Investigator. "Three Year Review of Federal Inmate Suicides." September 10, 2014. Web. Accessed June 1, 2015.

Statistics Canada. "Health State Descriptions for Canadians: Section D – Eating Disorders." Web. Accessed June 1, 2015. Statistics Canada. "National Household Survey 2011." Aboriginal Peoples and Language." Catalogue no. 99-011-X2011003. Web.

Accessed June 1, 2015.

Statistics Canada: "Study: Living arrangements of Children in Canada, 1901 to 2011." *The Daily* (29 April 2014). Web. Accessed June 1, 2015.

Statistics Canada. "The Canadian Population in 2011: Age and Sex." *2011 Census* Web. Accessed June 1, 2015.

Media

Blatchford, Christie. "Ashley Smith – and jurors – blocked from answers about mystery of who her real family was." *National Post,* 21 February 2013. Web. Accessed June 1, 2015.

Blatchford, Christie. "Ashley Smith's mental disorder led to hellish encounters between teenager and staff." *The National Post,* 9 May 2013 Web. Accessed June 1, 2015.

Blatchford, Christie. "Bold Ashley Smith jurors seek shake up of Correctional Services and wake up of Canadian public" *The National Post,* 19 December 2013. Web. Accessed June 1, 2015.

Blatchford, Christie. "Christie Blatchford: Ashley Smith's personality disorder chaotic but 'not permanent,' psychiatrist testifies." *The National Post,* 2 May 2013. Web. Accessed June 1, 2015.

Blatchford, Christie. "Impact of Ashley Smith's Identity Issues Is and Remains a Giant Black Box." *The National Post,* 25 March 2013. Web. Accessed June 1, 2015.

Blatchford, Christie. "Prison system forced to pick up the pieces with the mentally ill." *The National Post,* 6 May 2013. Web. Accessed June 1, 2015.

Canada East News Service. "Ashley Smith was destroyed by prison system: mother." 5 February 2012. Web. Accessed June 1, 2015.

Canadian Press. "Ashley Smith inquest: secretive prisons need monitoring." 26 November 2013. Web. Accessed June 1, 2015.

Canadian Press "Ashley Smith's See-Canada-Tour." Infographic, 2013. Web. Web. Accessed September 26, 2015.

Canadian Press. "Few treatment options for mentally ill female prisoners: Ashley Smith inquest hears." *The Globe and Mail,* 8 April 2013. Web. Accessed June 1, 2015.

Canadian Press. "Final submissions continue in the Ashley Smith case." 26 November 2013. Web. Accessed June 1, 2015.

Canadian Press. "Fourth prison employee charged in connection with death of NB woman." 1 November 2007. Web. Accessed June 1, 2015.

Canadian Press. "Prison employee charged in connection with death of N.B. inmate." 19 November 2007. Web. Accessed June 1, 2015.

Canadian Press. "Psychologist: Ashley Smith mother won't discuss girl's parentage." 15 April 2013. Web. Accessed June 1, 2015.

Canadian Press and Allison Jones. "Ashley Smith could have been treated with more time: psychologist." 4 March 2013. Web. Accessed June 1, 2015.

Carlson, Kathyn Blaze. "Mother 'elated' as Ashley Smith's jail death is ruled a homicide" *The Globe and Mail* (19 December 2013). Web. Accessed June 1, 2015.

Carlson, Kathryn Blaze. "Ashley Smith inquiry spurs federal pilot project, draws criticism." *The Globe and Mail,* 1 May 2014. Web. Accessed June 1, 2015.

CBC. "Alone Inside." *CBC Ideas* Documentary on Solitary Confinement (2013). Web. Accessed June 1, 2015.

CBC. "Ashley Smith jurors watch video showing her death." *CBC News,* 22 January 2013. Web. Accessed June 1, 2015.

CBC. "Behind the Wall." *The Fifth Estate,* 2010. Web. Accessed June 1, 2015.

CBC. "Changes needed in correctional system: prisoners' rights activist." *CBC News Online* 16 November 2007. Web. Accessed June 1, 2015.

CBC. "Edward Snowshoe spent 162 days in segregation before suicide." *CBC News,* 11 July 2014. Web. Accessed June 1, 2015.

CBC. "Liberals call for Ashley Smith prison-death public inquiry." *CBC News,* 8 November 2012. Web. Accessed June 1, 2015.

CBC. "New Brunswick guards accused of negligence back in court in March." *CBC News,* 6 February 2008.

CBC. "New Brunswick ombudsman investigates death in ontario prison." *CBC News,* 29 October 2007. Web. Accessed September 26, 2015.

CBC. "New Brunswick ombudsman report on teen's death in Ontario prison." *CBC News,* 9 June 2008. Web. Accessed September 26, 2015.

CBC. "Ont. prison workers fired over N.B. inmate's death." *CBC News*, 17 January 2008. Web. Accessed June 1, 2015.

CBC. "Sense of panic surrounded Ashley Smith: Grand Valley psychologist testifies at inquest." *CBC News*, 18 June 2013. Web. Accessed June 1, 2015.

CBC. "State of Incarceration." *CBC Doc Zone* 9 October 2014. Web. Accessed June 1, 2015.

CBC. "The Ashley Smith case – mental health in Canadian prisons" *The Current,* 12 November 2012. Web. Accessed June 1, 2015.

CBC. Timeline: The Life and Death of Ashley Smith." *The Fifth Estate.* Web. Accessed June 1, 2015.

CBC."Videos show inhumane treatment of teen Ashley Smith." *CBC News*, 31 October 2012. Web. Accessed June 1, 2015.

CBC. "Warden didn't know of guards' confusion about entering cell." September 30, 2013. Web. Accessed June 1, 2015.

Chittley, Jordan. "Ashley Smith a child at heart failed by system." *CTV.ca,* 19 December 2013. Web. Accessed June 1, 2015.

Correctional Services Union "Press Release " (20 December 2013) Web. Accessed June 1, 2015.

CTV. "Harper horrified by Smith surveillence tapes" *CTV News,*12 November 2012. Web.

CTV. "I'll Duct Tape Your Face: RCMP Pilot Defends Actions at Ashley Smith Inquest." *CTV News,* April 18, 2013. Web. Accessed June 1, 2015.

Cunningham, Mary. "Many are to blame." *The Record,* 14 January 2014. Web. Accessed June 1, 2015.

DiManno, Rosie. "DiManno: Saving Ashley Smith a regular occurrence for guards, who faced discipline for helping." *Toronto Star,* 24 January 2013. Web. Accessed June 1, 2015.

DiManno, Rosie."Troubled teen beaten down by system." *Toronto Star,* 9 March 2009: A2. Print.

Hamilton Spectator. "Ashley Smith youth jail file lists punishments and appeals for help." 26 January 2013. Web. Accessed June 1, 2015.

Jimenez, Maria. "The last days of Stephanie Rengel." *Toronto Life,* December 2009. Web. Accessed June 1, 2015.

Jones, Allison and the Canadian Press. "Ashley Smith could have been treated with more time: psychologist" *Canadian Press,* 4

March 2013. Web. Accessed June 1, 2015.

Link, Rob. " Chained and bound: Ashley Smith was kept shackled in prison: new information reveals." *St. John Telegraph-Journal,* 24 November 2007. Web. Accessed June 1, 2015.

Lurie, Steve. "Re: Ashley Smith's Cry for Help Must be Heeded." 19 December 2014. Web. Accessed June 1, 2015.

Makin, Kirk. "Ashley Smith's death was an accident, not suicide." *The Globe and Mail,* 29 October 2010. Web. Accessed June 1, 2015.

Mandel, Michelle. "Ashley Smith mother tells inquest of daughter's two sides." *Toronto Sun,* 20 February 2013. Web. Accessed June 1, 2015.

MSN. "Isolation for Dejected Teen Called Illegal." *MSN News,* 15 October 2013. Web. Accessed June 1, 2015.

MSN. "Teen Ashley Smith inquest begins today." *MSN News,* 14 January 2013. Web. Accessed June 1, 2015.

Mulholland, Angela. "After death deemed homicide, Ashley Smith family calls for new criminal investigation." *CTV News,* 19 December 2013). Web. Accessed June 1, 2015.

Murray, Stuart and Dave Holmes. "A New Form of Homicide in Canada's Prisons: The Case of Ashley Smith." 10 March 2014. Web. Accessed June 1, 2015.

Perkel, Colin. "Ashley Smith looked hopeless and dejected, inquest hears." *Toronto Star,* 15 October 2013. Web. Accessed June 1, 2015.

Perkel, Colin. "Ashley Smith's mother speaks to inquest: most of her life she was smiling and happy." *Canadian Press,* 20 February 2013. Web. Accessed June 1, 2015.

Perkel, Colin. "Ashley Smith's mother talks about happy childhood, troubled teens." *Canadian Press,* 20 February 2013. Web. Accessed June 1, 2015.

Perkel, Colin. "Don't bother with costly recommendations, prison official tells Ashley Smith inquest jurors." *The Globe and Mail,* 16 October 2013. Web. Accessed June 1, 2015.

Perkel, Colin. "'I'll duct tape your face,' Ashley Smith was warned in troubling video shown to inquest." *Canadian Press,* 31 October 2012. Web. Accessed June 1, 2015.

Perkel, Colin. "My skin is all loose: Ashley Smith Told mother in final visit." *The Globe and Mail*, 21 February 2013. Web. Accessed June 1, 2015.

Perkel, Colin. "Prison psychiatrist testifies Ashley Smith a 'large tyrannical child'." *Canadian Press*, 25 March 2013. Web. Accessed September 26, 2015.

Perkel, Colin. "We now ask you to speak for Ashley." *Canadian Press*, 2 December 2013. Web. Accessed June 1, 2015.

Quan, Douglas. "Understanding the Ashley Smith Inquest: Before and After the Homicide Verdict" Postmedia Breaking News (19 December 2013). Web. Accessed June 1, 2015.

Runciman, Bob. "Quit Stalling on Mental Health Treatment" Press Release (14 December 2012) Web. Accessed June 1, 2015.

Sapers, Howard. "Ashley Smith: Verdict a chance to rethink how prisoners with mental illness are dealt with." *The Toronto Star*, 19 December 2013. Web. Accessed June 1, 2015.

Seglins, Dave. "Ashley Smith family settles $11 million suit." *CBC News*, 4 May 2011. Web. Accessed June 1, 2015.

Simpson, Sandy. "Lessons from the Ashley Smith Inquest." *Toronto Star*, 26 January 2013. Web. Accessed June 1, 2015.

St. Thomas Times-Journal. "St. Thomas Hospital Couldn't Help Smith: Inquest: Federally-Operated Treatment Centres for Mentally Ill Women Inmates Recommended." 21 December 2013. Web. Accessed June 1, 2015.

Stone, Laura. "CSC spent over $5 million on Ashley Smith inquest." *Global News*, 22 January 2014. Web. Accessed June 1, 2015.

Stone, Laura. "Family of dead inmate suing Corrections Canada for $10 million." *Global News,* 4 July 2013. Web. Accessed June 1, 2015.

Stone, Laura. "'Nobody's listening': Almost a year later, feds yet to respond to Ashley Smith inquest." *Global News*, 10 December 2014. Web. Accessed September 26, 2015.

Stone, Laura. "Tories won't say when they'll respond to Ashley Smith inquest recommendations." *Global News*, 3 September 2014. Web. Accessed June 1, 2015.

Story, Brett and Craig Desson. "Solitary confinement a growing issue in Canada, U.S. Prisons." *CBC News*, 8 December 2013. Web. Accessed June 1, 2015.

Taber, Jane. "Ashley Smith is finally 'at peace,' mother says after homicide ruling." *The Globe and Mail*, 19 December 2013. Web. Accessed June 1, 2015.

Than, Hate. "Officials tailored use of force reports." *The Globe and Mail*, 10 March 2009. Web. Accessed June 1, 2015.

Toronto Star. "Ashley Smith's casual conversation with guards." 19 December 2013. Video. Web. Accessed June 1, 2015.

Toronto Sun. "Ashley Smith mother tells of daughter's two sides." 20 February 2013. Web. Accessed June 1, 2015.

Vincent, Donovan. " Ashley Smith inquest: Coralee Smith Says adult jail changed her daughter." *Toronto Star*, 20 February 2013. Web. Accessed June 1, 2015.

Vincent, Donovan. "Ashley Smith inquest: teen talked about suicide, psychologist testifies." *The Toronto Star*, 24 June 2013. Web. Accessed June 1, 2015.

Vincent, Donovan. "Ashley Smith inquest: what should we do about other self-harming female inmates?" *The Toronto Star*, 19 December 2013. Web. Accessed June 1, 2015.

Vincent, Donovan. "Ashley Smith not psychotic, psychologist testifies at inquest." *Toronto Star*, 4 March 2013. Web. Accessed June 1, 2015.

Vincent, Donovan. "Questions resurface about Ashley Smith's birth mother." *Toronto Star*, 15 April 2013. Web. Accessed June 1, 2015.

Vincent, Donovan. "Solitary confinement harmful to inmates: lawyers argue." *The Toronto Star*, 12 April 2013. Web. Accessed June 1, 2015.

Vincent and Zlomistic. "Ashley Smith death a homicide: jury rules" *The Toronto Star*, 19 December 2013. Web. Accessed June 1, 2015.

Vincent and Zlomistic. "Excerpt: The life and death of Ashley Smith." *The Toronto Star*, 15 December 2013. Web. Accessed June 1, 2015.

Zlomislic, Diana. "UN urges Canada to ban solitary confinement for mentally ill prisoners." *Toronto Star*, 2 June 2012. Web. Accessed June 1, 2015.

Photo: Matthew Bromwich

Rebecca Jaremko Bromwich received her Ph.D. in 2015 from the Carleton University Department of Law and Legal Studies, and was the first ever graduate of that program. She was awarded a Carleton Senate Medal as well as the 2015 CLSA Graduate Student Essay Prize for her graduate work. This book is adapted from her Ph.D. thesis. Rebecca has an LL.M. and LL.B., received from Queen's University in 2002 and 2001 respectively, and also holds a Graduate Certificate in Women's Studies from the University of Cincinnati. She has been an Ontario lawyer since 2003. In fall 2015, she accepted a faculty appointment and now teaches full time in Carleton's Department of Law and Legal Studies. She has also been a columnist for the *Lawyers Weekly* and has authored and co-authored several legal textbooks for students and legal system practitioners, including lawyers, paralegals and police. Rebecca is married with four children.